TO ANDRÉ TCHELISTCHEFF

FOR HIS ENDURING INSPIRATION OVER THE YEARS
AS HE HAS LED US, THROUGH SCIENCE AND IMAGINATION,
TO THE REVELATION OF THE POETRY IN WINE

THE Los Angeles Times BOOK OF
CALIFORNIA WINES

TEXT AND PHOTOGRAPHS BY ROBERT LAWRENCE BALZER

EDITED BY DARLENE GEIS

HARRY N. ABRAMS, INC.
PUBLISHERS · NEW YORK

Other books by Robert Lawrence Balzer
    California's Best Wines
    Beyond Conflict
    The Pleasures of Wine
    Adventures in Wine
    Robert Lawrence Balzer's Book of Wines & Spirits
    This Uncommon Heritage
    Discovering Italian Wines

Ulrich Ruchti: Designer
Ruth Eisenstein: Associate Editor
Carol Robson: Maps
Photograph Credits: Allen A. Arthur 42; California Historical Society
Library 80; Lindy Lindquist for Parducci 114

Library of Congress Cataloging in Publication Data

Balzer, Robert Lawrence.
    The Los Angeles times book of California wines.
    Rev. ed. of: Wines of California. 1978.
    1. Wine and wine making—California. I. Geis, Darlene.
II. Balzer, Robert Lawrence. Wines of California.
III. Los Angeles times. IV. Title.
TP557.B28 1984 641.2′22′09794 84-11067
ISBN 0-8109-1287-2

Published in 1984 by Harry N. Abrams, Incorporated, New York. All
rights reserved. This is a revised and updated edition of Abrams' *Wines
of California*, text and photographs by Robert Lawrence Balzer,
originally published in 1978. No part of the contents of this book may
be reproduced without the written permission of the publishers

Printed and bound in Japan

CONTENTS

VINEYARDS AND WINERIES: BAY AREA AND CENTRAL COAST COUNTIES

VINEYARDS AND WINERIES: SOUTH CENTRAL COAST COUNTIES

VINEYARDS AND WINERIES: CENTRAL VALLEY AND SOUTHERN CALIFORNIA

ACKNOWLEDGMENTS

In this book I should like to record my continuing gratitude to the growing list of winemaker-friends of my home state. *The Los Angeles Times Book of California Wines,* which includes an expanded roster of California's dynamic wine industry, gives me an opportunity, too, to pay tribute to the young winemakers, from whom I keep learning. The articulate spokesman for the industry, John de Luca, president of the Wine Institute, earns special plaudits for his diplomatic and effective leadership through an unimaginable number of narrows. We all heed and observe the unpretentious moves of Ernest and Julio Gallo as they pursue their goals of fine winemaking. I am grateful that their doors remain open to me as a journalist.

With pride in their accomplishments I list the following young winemakers whose wisdom in field and cellar has brought international distinction to California winemaking: Leo McCloskey of Felton-Empire, Richard Arrowood of Chateau St. Jean, Doug Meador of Ventana, Steve MacRostie of Hacienda Wine Cellars, Jill Davis of Buena Vista, Zelma Long of Simi, Dawnine Dyer of Domaine Chandon, Alison Green of Firestone, Ken Brown of Zaca Mesa, Tom Ferrell of Franciscan, Gil Nickel of Far Niente, Greg Boeger of Placerville, Rob Davis of Jordan, Hank Wetzel of Alexander Valley Vineyards, Robert Pecota of Calistoga, Fred Brander of Santa Ynez, Patrick Campbell and Sam Sebastiani of Sonoma, Eric, Carolyn, and Phil Wente of Livermore, Carolyn and Michael Martini of St. Helena, and Richard Sanford of Buellton.

For almost a quarter of a century, I have been privileged to write for the *Los Angeles Times,* a newspaper that has consistently kept its readers informed about the California wine industry. I should like to thank Dr. Franklin Murphy and Robert Erburu of The Times Mirror Company for the breadth of their lively interest in our common vinous heritage. Here also is a salute to my editor emeritus of *Home* magazine, Carolyn Murray, and her successor in that important creative post, Wallace Guenther.

From the beginning I have enjoyed a happy working relationship with my chief editor, Darlene Geis, who has guided and encouraged me in the task of making the winery selections which these covers enfold. In the long process, I believe this New Yorker has wholly succumbed to my championing of California wines. So one may say that this book, just in the editing, has made one enthusiastic convert.

To my copy editor, Ruth Eisenstein, a very special thanks for her talent and skill in turning some rough phrasing into silky syntax for which I shall get credit but will always know it was her good eye and mind that brought it about.

The friendships that have "sprung from wine," to use John Gay's words, have been too many to list fully. But among the friends in wine to whom I owe particular thanks are: Florence and Sam Aaron, Burgess Meredith, Drs. Jean and Wallace Tourtellotte, Jean Leon, Price Hicks, Hernando Courtright of the Beverly Wilshire Hotel, Richard Swig of the Fairmont Hotels, Stan Bromley of the Four Seasons Clift Hotel, Patricia Delaney of *Time* magazine, Carolyn and Leonce Picot, Dr. William and Marcia Bond, Ella Brennan, Paul Kovi and Tom Margittai, Piero Selvaggio, Tony May, Emilio Baglioni, Miklos Dora, Augustine Paege, Alvin Malnick, Patrick Terrail, Alexis Lichine, Tony Vallone, Lois Dwan, Rita Leinwand, Glenn Ford, Polly Ober, David and Christina Crawford Koontz, and Jackie Olden...and this is an abbreviated list!

My two closest friends in wine, after decades of working together, are André Tchelistcheff, to whom this book is dedicated, and James Andrew Willett, whose inspiration and assistance made its completion possible.

ROBERT LAWRENCE BALZER
SANTA ANA, CALIFORNIA
JUNE 1, 1984

FOREWORD

This is Robert Balzer's very personal testimony to wine, or, as he writes, "a prolonged personal essay on the pleasures of wine." From his long experience with California wines, he certainly has a right to his opinions. Furthermore, he personally enjoys wines, and these opinions on the quality of specific wines are worth our careful consideration.

The chapter on grape varieties introduces a much-needed perspective as to the basis of California wine quality. The influence of climate on wine quality is clearly outlined. The influence of soil is repeatedly emphasized.

On individual wineries, we find a historical discussion of the genesis of the winery and in some cases something about the ideals of the winemakers. In other cases, there are discussions of specific wines. Since Balzer is a wine connoisseur, we should listen to his recommendations.

Thank you, Robert Balzer, for telling us again about the important wines of the world, particularly those of California.

MAYNARD A. AMERINE

INTRODUCTION

Given my seven generations of ancestors born in California and the heritage from my mother, who was born in Piemonte in Italy, it is not surprising that I have come to love the wines of California. Even so, it was the magic of Bob Balzer that stimulated those genes. I am one of the legions of Bob's students. It took only a few lessons for him to generate in me a special feeling about wines in general and California wines in particular.

Although my business responsibilities usually keep me far away from the world of wine, I have the good fortune to own a vineyard in the Alexander Valley in Sonoma County, and I am writing this on one of my all-too-infrequent visits there. Like all the California wine country, it has been lyricized by Bob in the countless words he has written and uttered in his quest to bring the joy of wine to an ever increasing army of true believers. If you doubt that reality measures up to the wonders he describes, take time to see for yourself. Listen carefully to the Pied Piper of Wine. He won't lead you astray. In a world filled with worry he will show you the way to many special moments.

RANCHO MIGUEL
ALEXANDER VALLEY
MAY 28, 1984

ROBERT F. ERBURU
President and
Chief Executive Officer
The Times Mirror Company

WHAT IS WINE?

"Wine itself is but Water sublim'd, being nothing else but that Moysture and Sap, which is caus'd either by Rain or other kind of Irrigations about the Roots of the Vine, and drawn up to the Branches and Berries by the virtual attractive Heat of the Sun; the Bowels of the Earth serving as limbec to that end."
—James Howell

When Galileo wrote "Wine is light held together by water," his meaning was clear to those who had worked the vineyards in the sun, gathered the grapes, and attended the transformation of the fresh juice into living wine. Realism is served by André Simon: "Wine is the naturally fermented juice of fresh, ripe grapes." But the late grand seigneur of all true wine-lovers was not content to leave it there. He continued: "Wine is, indeed, a living thing, brash in its youth, full-blossoming in its maturity, but subject, if not used in time, to senility, decay and death. It is gregarious, appearing at its best in the company of food, and as a constituent of food; and in the society of moderate men and women, priming their wit, assisting at their worship, and serving as a medicine for some of their ills."

Almost two thousand years earlier, the Roman naturalist and author Pliny the Elder had documented the people's regard for wine in the imperial city: "It has become quite a common proverb that in wine there is truth" (*in vino veritas*). Petronius Arbiter, his contemporary and a consummate bon vivant, concentrated his definition into three words: "Wine is life."

Holding up a glass of wine so that its jeweled brilliance can be seen, its fragrance noted, and then allowing its warmth to flow over the taste buds, today's connoisseur might declare cryptically: "Wine *is*!" This would recall the silent sermon of Siddhartha Gautama, the Buddha, to his disciples when, in a deliberately calm gesture, he held up a single lotus flower. Truth was apparent, needing no description, analysis, or discussion.

Throughout recorded history, in every age, appreciation of wine has been verbalized by the articulate taster. Aeschylus commented on the liquid's reach toward man's affections: "Bronze is the mirror of form; wine, of the heart." While there is poetry in such phrases extolling wine, they neither describe it nor reply to the universal question, "Which wine is best?" My answer for years has been the one offered by Pliny the Elder: "The best kind of wine is that which is most pleasant to him who drinks it." Those who find this an irritating cop-out must go further into the catechism involving the spectrum of taste, and ask whether mind or body dictates the preferences of a prejudiced palate.

In one swallow of wine some three hundred known chemical compounds may exist simultaneously in "a chemical symphony," to quote Professor Emeritus Maynard A. Amerine of the University of California's Department of Viticulture and Enology at Davis. But to appreciate this balance, this harmony, with every conceivable shade and variation, requires experience as well as sensory alertness. A learning curve is involved. It follows a natural progression from the early preference for sweetness, which is the springboard of the Pepsi generation, to those pop wines of obvious fruit taste, to more subtle flavors. The innocent charms of a simple Liebfraumilch, a light and lovely white

Antonio Perelli-Minetti, founder of the family-owned winery, tasting the dark red wine from one of his experimental grapes. Photograph taken in 1975

German Rhine wine with its edge of sweetness, or of a California Chenin Blanc, have obvious appeal for the neophyte, whereas red wines, with their astringency and lack of sweetness, are often a quick turn-off. The unfamiliar needs repetition to become welcome.

The recognition of quality arises through comparison, in which the index of memory serves the winelover as his most reliable ally. It is the winetaster's greatest asset. Immediately upon tasting an older red wine with age-enhanced bouquet, you may find it better than another red wine of a similar kind. How better? Is the difference in the grape? The soil? The method of vinification? Most probably it is in all three. Memory of other wines will hold the clues and give the answers.

In its complexity, wine is the most thought-provoking beverage known to man. Sometimes the sight of a great painting, an architectural monument, a sunset sky, the sound of a great voice, or the concentrated wonder of poetry expressing the common experience in an uncommon insight, seems almost to open your eyes to a deeper vision, with a glimpse of Truth. It happens with wine, great wine, when in moments of experiencing its complex perfection with all your senses you attain a flash of understanding. Great wines and ordinary wines differ in their component structure only by micro-minimal degrees. The source of these differences —be it the soil, the vine, or the winemaker's skills—is the fascinating enigma of what we may call "winespell," challenging us to a discriminating appreciation.

During the international congress of wine producers held in 1976 in San Francisco, I had the good fortune of being the luncheon companion of a well-known German vintner who had come there as a delegate. He had visited the wineries of the North Coast counties and tasted many of the wines of current challenge to the world market, and we fell into a discussion of the relative merits of California wines and those of Germany.

"I've enjoyed California red wines very much," he told me, "but the white wines have a much too aggressive bouquet, a pronounced nose and definite taste of the grape variety. For us, as an example, the Gewürztraminer of Alsace is too strong, too assertive; it jumps out of the glass. It is completely lacking in subtlety. I found that to be the case with many of the California white wines."

Had he, I asked, tasted the Wente Bros. 1975 Johannisberg Riesling from Monterey County, an opulent young wine of the most extraordinary fruitiness, its bouquet and flowery freshness almost room-filling? Alas, he had not tasted this outstanding California wine produced from the grape so preeminent in his homeland. But it is safe to assume that since it would "jump out of the glass" he would not have found it to his liking. As the revered California winemaker Louis M. Martini observed many, many years ago, "We like that best to which we are accustomed."

The freshness and opulence—the fruitiness—of the Wente Johan-

Fourth-generation Wentes, Eric and Philip, in front of the stainless-steel tanks where the grape harvest is stored

nisberg Riesling, as of many of the young California white wines, is due to the new methods of vinification, perhaps dreamed of ten years ago but realized only with today's technological developments. Long, slow, cool, temperature-controlled fermentation, in stainless steel, of clean, morning-fresh grape juice cleared of extraneous matter by a variable-speed centrifuge enables the winemaker to achieve better results than ever before. Such technological changes and advances are not peculiar to California; they are also the pride of leading wineries in Germany, France, Spain, Australia—in fact, wherever established winemaking can afford the capital investment required. These impeccable and ultramodern systems of vinification are enhancing the richness of current vintages at Château Latour and Château Haut-Brion in Bordeaux. Where vintners cannot afford the millions of dollars required to effect such changes, they have

17

perforce to hold fast to yesterday's methods, rationalizing their adherence as "traditionalism."

We are in a period not only of changing, improving systems of vinification but of taste transition as well. While this is a book primarily about California wines—their history and their growing significance to the winelover—its scope will include other winelands. Only a few weeks have intervened between my visits to vineyards in Bordeaux pridefully growing Cabernet Sauvignon and Merlot grapes and hillside slopes in California where wines are being made from these same species of *Vitis vinifera*. New vineyards at home and abroad seek the finest budding stock, to upgrade the quality of fruit that is to come to the press.

Things were different when Robert Louis Stevenson wrote the chapter "Napa Wine" in his *Silverado Squatters*. Most California wine buffs are familiar with his vignettes of the California wine scene of 1880. "From those paragraphs," Brother Timothy, winemaker of The Christian Brothers of Napa, told me one winetasting afternoon, "we know Stevenson's stance, and the winelover's views of his day. He raved about Golden Chasselas. We know all about the Golden Chasselas in the Napa Valley today. There's none growing at Schramsberg, where Stevenson discovered it, nor in any of the best vineyards today, because it just doesn't make a wine we think is good any more! Johannisberg Riesling can beat it all hollow."

In the post-Repeal renaissance of California wines, the route to finer wines led directly to the grape, to a new emphasis on varietal individuality. While there was some emphasis placed on the importance of region, the consumer was led to believe that the varietal name was synonymous with

A fruity, rich, vintage Chardonnay is the Golden State's pride and treasure

The post-Repeal renaissance of California wines has resulted in many more thousands of acres planted in vineyards

18

superior wine quality. It dominated winelovers' approach to California wines to such a degree that by the early 1970s ambitious French vintners were exporting Bordeaux and Burgundy wines to the United States with varietal titles! We had come full circle in the roundelay of imitative labeling. It was no longer Burgundy that arrived in America from La Bourgogne but "Pinot Noir," and good claret from Bordeaux came here as "Cabernet Sauvignon." The trend even went so far that Spanish wineries which had never seen a Zinfandel grape on the vine were sending us "Zinfandel" in addition to "Pinot Noir" and "Cabernet Sauvignon," named after grapes that were equally rare, if not nonexistent, in the vinelands of Old Castile.

We are now, happily, beyond this varietal madness. We are moving toward the next plateau: each regional winery in California is beginning to develop its own style within each single varietal category. Style derives from the third element in our triptych of soil, vine, and the winemaker's skill. As Brother Timothy points out, "We, as artists, are stamping our wines with our own style. The wines of one winemaker will always have the style of that winemaker, like an artist's signature. Even in wineries of adjacent acreage, each wine from the same varieties of grapes will be different in style."

It has been my good fortune to spend the major part of a lifetime among the wines and vines and winemakers of California. I came under the winespell only months after I was out of Stanford. Over these forty-odd years I have come to know the dreams and goals of hundreds of winemakers, not only in the states of California, Washington, and Oregon, but in Mexico, France, Germany, Spain, Italy, Sicily, Portugal, and Australia. They are everywhere men of intense dedication. Their wines, like the leaves and snowflakes of nature's divine and inexhaustible variety, are never the same, and it is a blessing. Why and how they are so different, one from another, though from similar vines, is partially answered between the covers of this book. What is wine? Which is the best wine? Curiosity may lead you to many answers, culled from the wisdom of the ages, all affirming that wine is one of man's more noble concepts, as eternal as the seasons, beginning anew with every vintage. For primary answers, we move on to the vineyards and their fruit, enjoying along the way the words of James Howell, seventeenth-century winelover and court historian to Charles II of England, who, from his many days in the vineyards of France, formulated the definition that stands as epigraph to this chapter.

THE VINES AND WINES OF CALIFORNIA

"... the wine
Must taste of its own grapes."
—Elizabeth Barrett Browning

One of the first plants to flourish in the rich mud left by the subsiding waters of the Deluge quickly became the blessing of Noah and his family and myriads of his descendants. The vine, throughout the Scriptures, rivals the olive and the fig tree for dominance. Wherever it was found among the peoples of antiquity, its origins were assigned to a divinity in appreciation of its fruit and the miraculous beverage derived therefrom—everywhere a signal of health, joy, and celebration. The Dionysus of the Greeks became the chubby Bacchus of the Romans, still today a familiar fellow with his endearing image.

Most of the world's wines evolve from one of the oldest species of the grape, *Vitis vinifera,* which followed the spread of civilization from its cradle in the rich, warm Mediterranean basin of Asia Minor. Of the genus *Vitis*—from which the Latin word evolved in Spain to *vid*, in France to *vigne*, to bring us the English *vine*—there are literally hundreds of species, vinifera being almost alone the noble parent of noble wines. America has its own indigenous *Vitis labrusca, Vitis riparia*, and *Vitis rupestris* of Eastern and Middle Western origins, from whose berries are made significant amounts of wine, enthusiasm for which is seldom shared far afield. But to these native American vines, the whole world of winelovers owes a debt of gratitude. In the last century, when the treasured vineyards of Europe were in withered ruin from the devastating scourge of the root louse *Phylloxera vastatrix* (2 1/2 million acres of vines in France alone had been destroyed), in an eleventh-hour experiment it was found that native American species such as *Vitis riparia* and *Vitis rupestris* were phylloxera-resistant. American vinestocks were imported and planted, and the noble species Cabernet Sauvignon, Pinot Noir, and Chardonnay were grafted onto them. The foreign vinestocks flourished and bore these vinifera grapes, thought to have been lost forever. Today the vines of almost every vineyard in Europe grow on American rootstocks.

A less well-known part of the story subtracts somewhat from the flag-waving glory of our to-the-rescue act: the pest was brought to Europe from America, quite innocently, on cuttings imported to England about 1860 by a botanist curious to experiment with these native American grapevines, who shared his cuttings with a fellow botanist in France. The blight spread through Europe's vinelands like fire in a dry wheatfield. French wine income dropped from over 545 million francs to 8 million francs by 1889. Mass emigrations of vineyard and winery workers began. Bordelais victims of the phylloxera disaster crossed the Pyrenees into Spain (reestablishing themselves in the Rioja district, and bringing with them winemaking techniques which continue there to this day, and which account for much of the claret style of that fine Spanish red wine). Other émigrés from France found their way to California. But so did the phylloxera, just as those new lands, in Robert Louis Stevenson's words, "already weary of producing gold, began to green with vineyards."

The bounty of California's orchards and vineyards: a still life of fruits and wines

In a remarkable instance of retribution, cuttings of *Vitis vinifera*, imported to California in the hope of making the Golden State the new wine capital of the world, brought the root louse back to America. Its toll was substantial but not as ruinous as it had been in Europe, for now the cure—resistant rootstocks—was known. Soon many California vineyards were growing the fine vinifera varieties on American rootstocks. While many regions today, with advanced systems of soil fumigation in preparation for planting, are growing the noble viniferas Chardonnay, Cabernet Sauvignon, Pinot Noir, Johannisberg Riesling, and others, on their own roots the prudent vinegrower puts down resistant American rootstock, waits the extra year, and then field-buds his choice of vinifera stock. I would defy anyone to detect a difference between the wine from grafted vines and wine from vines growing on vinifera roots.

Each grape has its own intrinsic taste, its own flower, its own scent; indeed it must move us to a state of wonder as we realize these countless subtleties of nature that differentiate the varieties. The mere mention of Concord, Muscat, or Tokay brings instantly to mind a unique and individually different taste. These are but three well-known table grapes. There are thousands of different wine grapes: every wineland has its own champion stock and esteemed varieties.

In the Zind-Humbrecht cellars of Winzenheim in Alsace, I recently tasted a 1975 vintage Tokay d'Alsace, sometimes known as Pinot Gris, which "jumped out of the glass" with its own perfume almost as positively as that Alsatian wonder wine called the spicy Traminer, or Gewürztraminer. The latter is the only accepted wine in Alsace today; old Traminer vineyards are being replaced with improved vinestock, which assures the vintner that the wine will be *gewürz*. Under the *Appellation d'Origine Contrôlée d'Alsace* only Gewürztraminer vines may now be planted. In California vineyards both Traminer and Gewürztraminer vines are growing, but one can rest assured that the better native examples of this exotic table wine are coming from Gewürztraminer vines.

But, it will be asked, why is there so much difference between Alsatian and Californian Gewürztraminer? The obvious difference is in the degree of sweetness elected by many of California's winemakers (Louis M. Martini is one exception), supporting their belief that this edge of residual grape sugar, aside from making the wine more widely popular, balances its natural acidity.

Taste analysis of a straightforward wine like Gewürztraminer is relatively simple. But we move into a profound complexity when we investigate the true taste of the Burgundian Pinot Noir. Here, we are inquiring not into the taste of the noble grape alone but, by extension, into the taste of rich red Burgundy.

The world's concept of generic Burgundy has been formed by centuries of advocates. Arguments concerning the true taste of Burgundy are

Part of Moët-Hennessy's $12-million-dollar investment in Napa Valley—the gleaming steel tanks that hold the Domaine Chandon *cuvée*

24

not new. The first came in 1395 with an edict by Philip the Bold, ruler of the Duchy of Burgundy, banishing the heavier-yielding Gamay grape forever from the already hallowed regions of Chambertin, Musigny, La Romanée, Clos de Vougeot, and Beaune. Resident monks in the area, noting the more generous harvest from the Gamay, were inclined to expand its planting, since revenues exceeded those from the shy-bearing Pinot Noir. The fate of Gamay was sealed forever by Philip's pronouncement against not only the greedy monks but the grape itself, which he declared to be "très mauvais et très desloyaux." It found a new home in Beaujolais, to the subsequent joy of Parisians and the worldwide fans of this jolly refresher. Pinot Noir continued its history of noble production in the Côte d'Or as the exclusive vine of the great growths of red Burgundy.

With this preamble, it is possible to understand the gravity of any question that dares to challenge such exalted traditions. Yet Robert Mondavi, one of California's preeminent winemakers, passionately devoted to the task of extracting the fullest potential from every wine-grape species, believes his experiments yield revealing answers to our question about Pinot Noir.

With every vintage, he and his staff make countless small batches of wines, harvested from specific areas, sampling various methods of crush, fermentation, cooperage (French oak versus Yugoslavian or American, new wood versus old), yeasts, temperatures, blendings with free-run juice and press wine . . . all toward a better, finished wine of greater finesse and flavor. Every morning, at the winery, during the bedlam of harvest and winemaking, of incoming grapes and bubbling casks, Robert and his sons, with their crew of technicians, set up for tasting a circle of glasses filled with embryonic wines when they are but hours out of the vineyard. To the layman, these are an unappetizing assembly of opaque liquids in varying dull shades suggesting anything but the jewel-bright vintages they will become. But to the knowing, the potentials are revealed in clues from scent, body, and even taste, as raw and unfinished as the wines are.

Through such dedicated experiment, Robert Mondavi's belief about the proper fermentation of Pinot Noir, progressed from 1970 (the year that produced his 1970 Pinot Noir, which took first place in the *Los Angeles Times Home Magazine* tasting) to the still greater enlightenment with his 1972 Pinot Noir as a breakthrough. Break through what? Mondavi does not believe that the accepted *typical* taste of top-ranking Burgundies either realizes the fullest potential of Pinot Noir or is even its healthiest manifestation. Connoisseurs are generally united in admiring the bouquet, the penetrating scent, of fine Burgundies, which have a pungency not present in the softer fragrance of fine clarets. Some call it smoky, some call it medicinal, and someone I know who adores great Bordeaux wines, and

Veteran winemaker Myron Nightingale of Beringer/Los Hermanos plays host to a visiting wine class

dislikes Burgundy, declares it "mousy." Heresy, of course, to thousands upon thousands of Burgundy lovers all over the world who are accustomed to that pungency as a hallmark of the finest Burgundies.

Robert Mondavi believes this scent is a result of the autolysis (breakdown of cell tissues) involved in prolonged malo-lactic fermentation. The odorous materials which are the products of this autolysis, in his opinion, are responsible for the characteristic Burgundy bouquet, present in his prize-winning 1970 wine, which triumphed in the Los Angeles tasting over '70 Chambertin-Clos de Bèze, '70 Clos Vougeot, and '70 Nuits-Saint-Georges, Clos de la Maréchale. In his 1972 wine from the same grapes Mondavi deliberately curtailed the fermentation and thus the odor. He regards this Pinot Noir as a step toward better Burgundy-style wine. It is rich, with an unobstructed bouquet from the grape, touched with the incense of oak, but lacking the overriding (autolysis) scent that connoisseurs have long sought and accepted as an attribute of Burgundian wine character.

There are confirming results from Burgundian wines produced from Pinot Noir in the Côte de Beaune at the villages of Monthélie and Savigny-les-Beaune—lovely, endearing, and straightforward wines of pure Pinot Noir, but atypical in their lack of that penetrating wood-smoke adjunct of more famed, more expensive Burgundies. The celebrated Beaulieu Vineyard 1968 Beaumont Pinot Noir and generic 1968 Burgundy were equally atypical in this respect, as was the outstanding Louis M. Martini 1968 Pinot Noir Special Selection.

After two thousand years of winemaking, and despite the intensive technological advances of recent decades, areas of uncertainty still abound. Only within recent years have we understood the function of malo-lactic fermentation in reducing total acidity and realized its importance. Once prayed for as an unpredictable development that would or would not come in its own time, it can now be induced, and at the appropriate time. In this fermentation, a wine's total acidity (the combined acids that give wines the tart sprightliness without which they are dull and insipid), when it is too high in malic acid, can be reduced by half, and the malic acid converted to lactic acid by bacterial action. Lowering of the total acidity in Pinot Noir assures a more palatable taste. Robert Mondavi's method involves a malo-lactic fermentation that is simultaneous with the yeast fermentation and of relatively shorter duration than is traditional in France. The wine is thus not in contact with the odorous cells resulting from post-fermentation activity. Experiments in the whole area of yeasts, including all their multiple strains, are part of the enological development in California, possibly accounting for some of the mysterious differences in the emergent wines of the Golden State.

In the field of viticulture there are few persons more honored than

Robert Mondavi holding a freshly cut cluster of Cabernet Sauvignon grapes; in the background, his distinctive Mission-style winery

Professor Harold P. Olmo of the University of California at Davis, a lifelong and talented plant geneticist. In his monograph on Chardonnay he veers away from science to describe the indescribable: "In matured wines of the highest quality there is often an exquisite aroma of ripe apples or of ripe peaches, but who can document it?" Others have suggested that fine examples of this splendid white wine of Burgundy and California often evoke nostalgic memories of warm dry grasses, or ripe pears. None of these are the same... *nor are the wines*. Is that any more curious than the familiar description of Château Mouton-Rothschild as being reminiscent of black currants? Or the fragrance of wood violets that haunts superb vintages of Haut-Brion?

Academicians tend to put down such verbal flights that go beyond laboratory analysis, but after years and years of pursuing the elusive tastes and bouquets of wines, and attempting to capture them in terms that make for easy communication, I believe this is the best route to follow—free, not reining in the imagination and not losing in the toils of science the poetic mystery that fascinates the true winelover.

We can leave speculation there. It does provide some answers in the tug-of-war of taste preferences when the riddle of differences between California and European wines is posed. But even in the comparison of French wines, district with district, vineyard with adjacent vineyard, we see differences revealed. Is it soil alone that makes La Tâche differ from Richebourg, from Echézeaux... all produced from Pinot Noir? Why Mouton's black currant against Haut-Brion's violet?

It is not necessary to have the answers to all the questions in order to enjoy wine, but with the knowledge that some of the answers bring comes awareness that deepens appreciation. Enology, viticulture, botany, and plant physiology are only partial routes to knowing wine and understanding its nature. It is not as a botanist, or a viticulturist, or an enologist, or a chemist—for I am none of these—but as a devoted winelover of forty years' standing that I write. And this is not a textbook but a prolonged personal essay on the pleasures of wine, and of California wines in particular.

"It is a myth," enologist Richard Peterson of The Monterey Vineyard told me, "that wine is made in wineries. It is really made in vineyards!" This is a tribute to the vineyardist who raises the grape, as opposed to the winemaker who develops the wine. Since the vineyard contributes so importantly to the quality of wine, let us take a look in the next chapter at the terrain and climate where the vine is most likely to thrive in California.

CALIFORNIA'S FIVE WINE REGIONS

"But before we plough an unfamiliar patch,
It is well to be informed about the winds,
About the variations in the sky,
The native traits and habits of the place,
What each locale permits, and what denies.
One place is good for crops, one happier
With grapes. . . ."

—Virgil

On the return of Augustus from Asia, in 29 B.C., Virgil read him the four books of the *Georgics*. In this work, which the emperor had commissioned, the poet's intention was to describe in verse the close relation of man and nature, with full appreciation of the seasons' round of labor, the importance of soil and weather, and the particular joys of cultivating the vine and the olive. Two thousand harvests later, with the riddles of sun and soil only partially solved, for all our theories and experiments, we still stand in awe and wonder before the vagaries of nature.

The vine thrives in most well-drained soils, even producing some of its most illustrious wines from relatively infertile, rocky terrain where nothing else will grow. Above and below the equator, two loosely defined isothermal belts demark the vine-growing potentials of the Northern and Southern hemispheres. The northern belt includes the broad east–west reach from Washington, Oregon, California, Arkansas, Iowa, Ohio, Michigan, and New York across the ocean to the Mediterranean Basin and extending eastward into China and Japan, with wide variations north to south, from Germany to North Africa, from Russia to Iran. Below the equator, in the Southern Hemisphere, are the enormously productive vineyard regions of Chile and Argentina, the tip of South Africa, and the burgeoning vineyards of Australia.

In our time, we have seen deserts transformed to veritable paradise gardens through the miracle of modern irrigation, drawing upon faraway sources of water. Where natural rainfall is inadequate, as in Monterey County, California's new wonderland for the grape, overhead sprinklers not only provide controlled moisture but, by means of efficient new drip systems, deliver the amount of water essential to each vine with conservation-oriented economy.

The old adage "Bacchus loves the hillsides" implies, among other advantages of site, the blessings of natural rainfall. Irrigation of the flatlands can be abused, of course, when the grower's objectives place quantity above quality. But with today's enlightened understanding of viticulture, man-made "rain" from overhead sprinklers is generally used judiciously not only to provide the necessary moisture for vine roots but to serve as a frost-protection system. When the temperature falls below freezing, clouds of spray over a vineyard can raise the temperature of the area, the water being warmer than the air. In more extreme cold, water from the overhead sprinklers will freeze, coating the vines with ice. The freezing action of the water gives off heat, and the ice-coated vines, looking like crystal sculptures, are saved.

Old hands say that the weather in June (in the Northern Hemisphere) determines the quantity of a vintage and that the subsequent weather of the summer, until harvest, determines the quality. Rainfall during blooming can cause a poor "berry set." When it is time for the berries to set, in late spring, other unfavorable conditions as well are cause for anixety.

Michael Stone, one of the founders of Sterling Vineyards, demonstrates the duplex pruning that makes possible mechanical harvesting

A system of drip lines radiating from a tank of water irrigates the vines in the high, dry Chalone Vineyards

Strong winds, temperatures that are excessively high (over 95° F.) or too low create "shatter": some of the tiny jade-green flowers with their delicate pistils fail to develop into berries, and fall off. Following the berry-set days, the vineyardist can test for shatter by cupping the cluster loosely in his hand and gently drawing his open fingers over the baby berries; shatter is present if more than a few fall off. Rainfall in the ripening period, when followed by extended high humidity, brings on leaf mildew and bunch-rot.

But weather is only one of the factors to be considered in determining the natural endowments of a wine region. Virgil was aware of the importance of soil composition, making specific recommendations about the location of plantings. The *Georgics* were serious in their intent, touching upon the vine, the olive orchard, herds and flocks, and even bees, as they related to the basic wealth and industry of ancient Rome. It was a similar concern that prompted the California State Legislature, in an act signed by Governor Perkins on April 15, 1880, to direct the Regents of the University of California to "provide for special instruction to be given in the Agricultural Department of the University in the Arts and Sciences pertaining to Viticulture and the theory and practice of fermentation, distillation and rectification . . . also, to direct the professor . . . or his assistants, to make examinations and reports upon the different sections of the state adapted to viticulture. . . ."

Count Agoston Haraszthy, an energetic, dynamic immigrant from Hungary, with prophetic visions of viticulture and winemaking in California, introduced a program of state-sponsored studies, beginning with his own authorized tour of European vineyard and winemaking regions in 1861. In Europe he purchased 100,000 vines of about 1,300 varieties. "It may take us a hundred years to find out where these vines should be planted," he wrote, adding, "To the people of this State they will in time be worth many millions." Haraszthy's seemingly extravagant prophecy was to prove to be an understatement. Agriculture is California's number one industry today, with revenues of eight billion dollars. And winegrowing, a uniquely aesthetic branch of farming, is the third-largest segment of the industry.

Recent comparative tastings of European and California wines by acknowledged experts support Haraszthy's boast, made in his 1862 report: "California can produce as noble and generous a wine as any in Europe; more in quantity to the acre, and without repeated failures through frosts, summer rains, hailstorms, or other causes." While it is generally true that "every year in California is a vintage year," in the sense that the relatively uniform climate allows grapes to ripen to acceptable sugar levels, variations in California vintages do exist. However, chaptalization—the addition of sugar to the must (fermenting grape juice) to ensure adequate alcoholic content of the wine—which is common practice in France and other European countries, is both unnecessary and illegal in California.

The importance of climate for winemaking is not limited to its effect on grape-sugar content; acid levels as well as grape-sugar content depend upon benign weather conditions. The right vine in the wrong location produces wines irrevocably out of balance. Where red-wine grapes are concerned, the wrong climate can even cause problems with coloring.

Why do wines vary so enormously in taste? Why is the Pinot Noir grape of Alsace suitable for making only an indifferent rosé, when the same vine in Burgundy, under equally optimum weather conditions, produces the liquid ruby that has elicited encomiums from popes, emperors, and poets? California's ubiquitous Zinfandel thrives as a money-crop vine in every region of the state but produces great and exciting wines of rare longevity and finesse only when it has the temperate warmth of Napa and Sonoma hillsides, the Sierra foothills of Amador County, or the blessings of similar exposure in comparable microclimates.

The concept of the microclimate (a word that crept into the wine buff's vocabulary only about a decade ago) becomes a handy explanation to account for some very fine wines now coming out of hitherto unsung southern California vineyards. By weather-station measure, the microclimate of Temecula, on a high plateau 23 miles inland from the Pacific Ocean, less than an hour's drive north of San Diego, is comparable to some northern California winegrowing regions more famed for quality.

The temperature-summation scale used to classify California's winegrowing regions is arrived at by totaling the number of degree-days above 50° F. during the days of the growing season. On the basis of this scale, the state is divisible into five regions:

REGION I   Very cool: 2,500 degree-days or fewer—Napa, Santa Cruz (Rhine in Germany, Champagne in France)

REGION II   Cool: 2,501 to 3,000 degree-days—Middle Napa, Sonoma, Monterey (Bordeaux in France)

REGION III Moderately cool: 3,001 to 3,500 degree-days—North Napa, Livermore (Tuscany in Italy)

REGION IV   Warm: 3,501 to 4,000 degree-days—Ukiah, Lodi (Sicily, Central Spain)

REGION V   Very warm: 4,001 degree-days or more—San Joaquin Valley (Jerez de la Frontera in Spain)

It may be noted that the famous Napa Valley, considered by many to have one climate, is listed under three regions. Near the northern tip of San Francisco Bay, from the Carneros region below Napa all the way up to Yountville, it is very cool. In the central region around St. Helena, Oakville, and Rutherford is the heartland similar to Bordeaux and Burgundy. Where the valley narrows at its northern tip, below Mount St. Helena near Calistoga, it can get quite warm, but just move up the hillsides and you have the microclimates of Stony Hill and Schramsberg, with their blessings of southeastern exposure and the coolness of the Champagne French region.

Present and succeeding generations of California winelovers owe an eternal debt of gratitude to the University of California and its staff, including Professor Amerine, for their prodigious studies of vine, soil, and climate undertaken at UC–Davis over forty years ago. From the comfortable vantage point of the present, all seems right with the world as today's wine pilgrim surveys the healthy green rows of vines ribbing the hills and valleys of each California wine district. But forty years ago, some of those areas were cattle-grazing land with no recognized potential for grapes, and even in yesterday's prime areas, like the Napa Valley, many vulgar, heavy-bearing varieties were grown. They made poor wines, debasing the post-Repeal California vintages to such a degree that their reputation suffered a serious setback when compared with European wines. The prejudices formed then against California wines are only now being slowly overcome in the mind of the European-oriented winelover.

"Golden Chasselas makes the greatest white wine ever produced in the Napa Valley," one winegrower in that area boasted in the mid-thirties. "Alicante Bouschet is *absolutely* a *great* variety!" To the men who owned and praised vineyards of those grapes, young Amerine's findings to the contrary were revolutionary. Rip them out? Ridiculous! Plant low-yielding Cabernet Sauvignon, Pinot Noir, or that difficult Pinot Chardonnay instead? Ridiculous!

Amerine's fieldwork continued during the years from 1935 to 1938 with Chairman A. J. Winkler of the UC–Davis Department of Viticulture and Enology. I first met Maynard Amerine in 1937 in the courtyard of the Davis experimental winery laboratories as he was unloading lugs of grapes from a pickup truck, grapes gathered from a remote vineyard at the proper harvesting moment a few hours earlier. He had little time to talk. I moved along with him and the grapes, back and forth from the truck to the labs as darkness came on. When I left, he drove off into the night to another vineyard, and another, and another, all over the state, spending sleepless weeks to harvest varieties that would provide the field knowledge resulting in today's golden age of wines in California . . . with the right vines in the right places.

CALIFORNIA WINE GRAPES: AN AMPELOGRAPHY

The beginning of vine-planting is like the beginning of mining for the precious metals: the wine-grower also "prospects." One corner of land after another is tried with one grape after another. This is a failure; that is better; a third best. So, bit by bit, they grope about for their Clos Vougeot and Lafite. Those lodes and pockets of earth, more precious than the precious ores, that yield inimitable fragrance and soft fire; those virtuous Bonanzas, where the soil has sublimated under sun and stars to something finer, and the wine is bottled poetry. . . .

—Robert Louis Stevenson

The following ampelography includes all the *Vitis vinifera* species flourishing in California's 363,491 acres of wine grapes (as of 1982). It lists, in alphabetical order, the great and the small, the famous and the little-known varieties, first the grapes destined for the production of white wine, then those destined for red.

CALIFORNIA WHITE-WINE GRAPES

Burger

Early vineyardists set out moderate-sized plots of this heavy-bearing variety to fulfill their ambitions for quantity. Known in Germany and Alsace as the Elbling, this is not the grape a vineyardist shows to visiting nabobs. Alone, it produces a commonplace wine, usually low in acidity. Its principal virtue is as an extender for the cheaper versions of generic California wines such as Chablis and Sauterne. Total planting: 1,966 acres.

Chardonnay

Professor Olmo solved the perplexing problem of the proper name for the elegant grape of the elegant white Burgundy wines Meursault and Montrachet and of Pouilly-Fuissé, Chablis, and Champagne. In his monograph "Chardonnay," published by the Wine Advisory Board in 1971, he states: "The Chardonnay should be recognized as a distinct and well-marked variety and not a white-fruited form of the Pinot Noir. It appears desirable to end the confusion by omitting any reference to Pinot in the name." Commercially launched in California as Pinot Chardonnay, the wine remains incorrectly designated on many labels and wine lists. Many wineries perpetuate the error for commercial reasons. Others, of a more purist bent, have switched to "Chardonnay," with little loss of trade acceptance.

By premium vinification in California in recent years, wines made from the Chardonnay have challenged and surpassed some of the French wines of legendary fame produced from the same grape. It was not until 1962 that a sudden flurry of widespread cultivation of Pinot Chardonnay (as it was then known in California) took place. Land devoted to that vine, according to statistical reports, increased from fewer than 150 acres in 1962 to 22,076 in 1982. This agricultural focus upon Chardonnay was probably triggered by the representative of the *Guide Michelin*, who, in a *Life* magazine article in 1962, declared that the Wente Bros. Livermore Pinot Chardonnay was the finest wine produced in America, on a par with some of the finest white Burgundies of France.

The Wente wine was in sudden demand all across the nation. Winemakers from San Diego to Mendocino wanted to buy, sell, plant, and make Pinot Chardonnay. By the boom year of 1973, choice harvests of

Young Chardonnay berries from Beaulieu's vineyards in the cool Carneros region pioneered by André Tchelistcheff

Chardonnay in Napa and Sonoma counties were bringing $1,000 per ton. By 1977, over 2 1/2 million cases of 100 percent Chardonnay wine were produced, a staggering amount. It is a sobering truth, however, that all the vines of this elegant species do not produce equally elegant wines. The wines vary not only with the region in which the vines grow but with subtleties of both harvesting and vinification.

In very cool regions such as Chablis and Champagne in France and California's North Coast counties, Chardonnay produces a high-acid, crisp wine, ideal with oysters and shellfish. In slightly warmer areas, as in the Burgundian Côte d'Or and the warmer but well-drained and sun-favored hillside vineyards of northern California counties, the microclimate difference and soil variations enable the completely ripe grapes to achieve that full-bodied richness of which Le Montrachet is the classic ideal.

It was just such a California wine, Château Montelena 1973 Chardonnay, that made history in a Paris tasting in May 1976 in a first-place triumph over a lovely Meursault-Charmes 1973 and Puligny-Montrachet Les Pucelles. Many members of the judging panel of French experts believed the California wines to which they were giving high scores were French wines!

Chardonnay vines planted in regions of California's interior valleys, in relatively less extensive acreage than in the favored coastal counties, may, if the necessary irrigation is provided, produce a heavier yield per ton, giving table wines of unremarkable character, though they are drinkable and even pleasing. But these wines lack the famed finesse of the grape variety at its best.

Chardonnay is not an easy vine to grow. An early bloomer, it is vulnerable to spring frosts. The translucent, easily ruptured skin makes it easy prey to flocks of migratory birds, and for such delicate grapes hand harvesting is mandatory. Short cluster stems make even hand harvesting a demanding task.

While sun is vital for ripening, Chardonnay berries are particularly subject to sun-scald damage when exposed, even in the cooler coastal regions. The consequent browning impairs wine quality. Innovative trellising and pruning methods are now being used to provide ample foliage for shading the delicate fruit. The moment of harvest is of the utmost importance, for, according to Professor Olmo, "There is very little in the way of distinct flavor, in either the grape or the new wine, until the fruit is almost overripe. Even experienced tasters cannot detect any mark of varietal distinctiveness in the usual wines of high acidity. However, it is exactly this delicacy and cleanness of taste that makes the variety an excellent base for champagne and a delight to the connoisseur." It is the moment of picking—whether the grapes are just ripe or very ripe—that marks the difference between the Chardonnays of Chablis and Champagne

Winemaker Walter Schug of Joseph Phelps Vineyards keeps careful watch over his temperature-controlled fermenters, in which white wines develop slowly

and the mellow Montrachet. Happily for American consumers, Chardonnay vines in the California sun are currently producing vintages of distinction costing half or even less than half as much as their European counterparts.

Chenin Blanc

This popular grape (also known as Pineau de la Loire, though it does not belong to the Pinot family) is the predominant variety in nearly all the wines of the Loire Valley—Vouvray, Saumur, Anjou, and the Côteaux du Layon—to which the ancient province has given its name.

The Chenin Blanc story in California really began in 1955, when the Charles Krug Winery won a gold medal at the Sacramento State Fair for a pale golden wine which Peter and Robert Mondavi had rechristened "Chenin Blanc." Before this, the good wine had limped along under the designation "White Pinot," one of the misleading names for the French grape. The gold medal, the new name, and, more important than anything else, prolonged cool-fermentation techniques, allowing residual sugar in the finished wine, combined to make a wine that appealed to public taste. Demand quickly outran supply. An abundant-yielding vine, producing an average of 9 to 12 tons per acre in California, Chenin Blanc repeated the Chardonnay story. When spotlighted by public favor, the limited plantings were expanded throughout the state, and today Chenin Blanc is the second most extensively planted white-wine variety in California. From the 19,826 acres in bearing in 1977, a whole sea of 100 percent varietal Chenin Blanc—8,913,000 cases—would be possible with but a 4-tons-per-acre yield! However, much of the wine goes into generic blending, and it is favored by many sparkling-wine producers as a gentle addition to their basic *cuvées*, or blends.

There are many additional reasons, beyond its high productivity, for the popularity of the vine with growers. The sturdy grapes ripen mid-season, in compact clusters that are easily harvested and are capable of being transported from the vineyard to the crushers with minimum damage.

Cool fermentation in stainless steel preserves the wine's most distinctive asset—its clean, ingratiating, thirst-quenching fruitiness. This good balance of natural grape sugar and fruit acidity allows the winemaker a challenging latitude in style. Since the grape thrives in nearly every one of the state's viticultural regions—in both cool coastal counties and warm interior valleys—subtle differences beyond sweet or dry finish can inspire the winemaker and afford varied taste experiences to the winelover.

The grapevine is essentially a pump, drawing moisture from the soil for the ultimate development of the fruit. Grapes are roughly 80 percent water. Obviously the "pump" is not drawing distilled water from the ground. A good proportion of the grape's composition, beyond wetness,

Walter Schug examining young vines

42

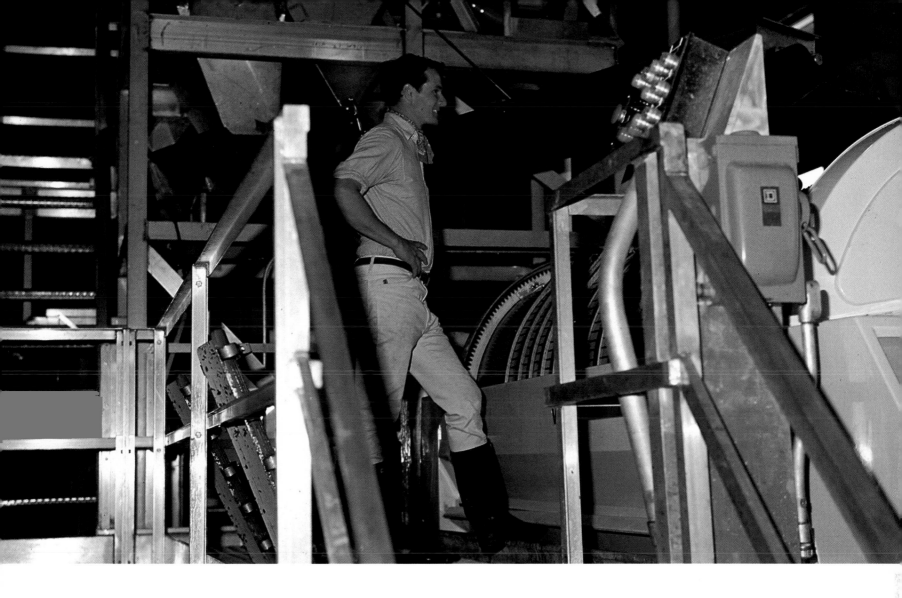

Brooks Firestone of the new Firestone
Vineyard supervising the Willmes press

is probably a concentrate of the mineral elements of the earth that supports the vine-root system. It is my belief that this is what we notice when there is too much earthiness in a wine's taste—what the French term *goût de terroir,* usually in derogation. But in this native complex of primordial elements there are the distinguishing differences that make some minute portions of the planet's surface more precious than others—worth, in centuries past, a veritable king's ransom. All because the grapevine found them good.

Some California vintners elect to produce a Chenin Blanc that is wholly dry. Beyond the sweet-edged market leaders, broad differences in taste exist. One vintner may prefer to age his wine entirely in stainless steel, preserving its freshness and fruitiness, never letting the wine touch wood. Another may keep his wine in wood for a few months. Still others may combine the two techniques. Differences in oak and in the many other sizes and kinds of aging containers also contribute nuances of taste, bringing individuality—its own intrinsic finesse of flavor—like a signature, to each vintaging of this grape.

Emerald Riesling

One of the most popular of the vinifera hybrids developed by Professor Olmo at UC–Davis, the Emerald Riesling, is a cross of the White Riesling of Germany's Rhineland with Muscadelle, one of the many variants of Muscat, a white-wine grape of Bordeaux, where it contributes to the richness of Sauternes. The resulting vine, introduced in 1946, is suitable for planting in California's warmer regions. Invariably the Emerald Riesling produces a wine of freshness and high acidity. With its floral fragrance (happily subdued) from the Muscadelle, it suggests to many the well-balanced charm of Moselle wines of good vintage. Of the present plantings totaling 3,365 acres, more than half grow in Kern and Fresno counties in the San Joaquin Valley, with commercial quantities in Monterey County.

Flora

Only 370 acres of this vinifera hybrid, developed in the course of the grape-breeding studies conducted by Professor Olmo at UC–Davis, currently exist. Produced by crossing Gewürztraminer, the highly aromatic Alsatian grape, with Sémillon, the dominant vine of French Sauternes, the sturdy moderate-yielding vine was introduced in 1958. Intended for the cooler regions of the coastal counties, Flora has appeared in a varietal wine in Napa and Sonoma counties. Its most distinguished and prominent use, taking full advantage of its distinctive bouquet, came in its contribution to the *cuvée* for the Schramsberg Crémant Demi Sec dessert champagne.

Folle Blanche

Formerly the leading grape of the Cognac regions of Charente, the Folle Blanche is easily the best variety for brandy, which is distilled from its pale, light wine of high acidity. A scant 281 acres are being propagated in the moderately cool coastal regions of California. The tightly packed grape clusters are susceptible to bunch-rot and mold in wet seasons, and this limits its popularity among growers; it is sometimes produced as a varietal wine, appealing for its tart, fresh, clean taste. When chilled it is as crisp and refreshing as iceberg lettuce, whose taste it suggests. Because of this almost neutral taste and its high acidity, it is recommended frequently for blending in *cuvées* of champagne and other sparkling wines; it adds the zest and zing necessary in effervescent wines.

Franken Riesling (See Sylvaner)

French Colombard

In France this vigorously productive white-wine grape is sometimes called the Colombar. It arrived in the 1870s in California from France, where it

Giumarra grows a French Colombard in the
San Joaquin Valley that makes a fresh,
fruity white wine

was valued in the Cognac regions for the high acidity which is desirable
in wines for brandy distillation. For a long time grape growers called it
"West's White Prolific," but following Repeal, Professor Winkler correctly identified it as the white-wine grape of Charente, and ever since, in
California, it has been known as French Colombard. It flourishes in both
coastal and interior regions, with present plantings in excess of 71,055
acres. It is a good ripener and will yield 8 to 12 tons per acre.

The amazing versatility of this very popular varietal, which produces
a wine of tart, crisp acidity and floral bouquet, has made it a mainstay in
California Chablis. But as a distinctive varietal, often made with more
than a trace of residual sugar, French Colombard gains fans for its apple
taste, unique, ingratiating, and appetizing.

45

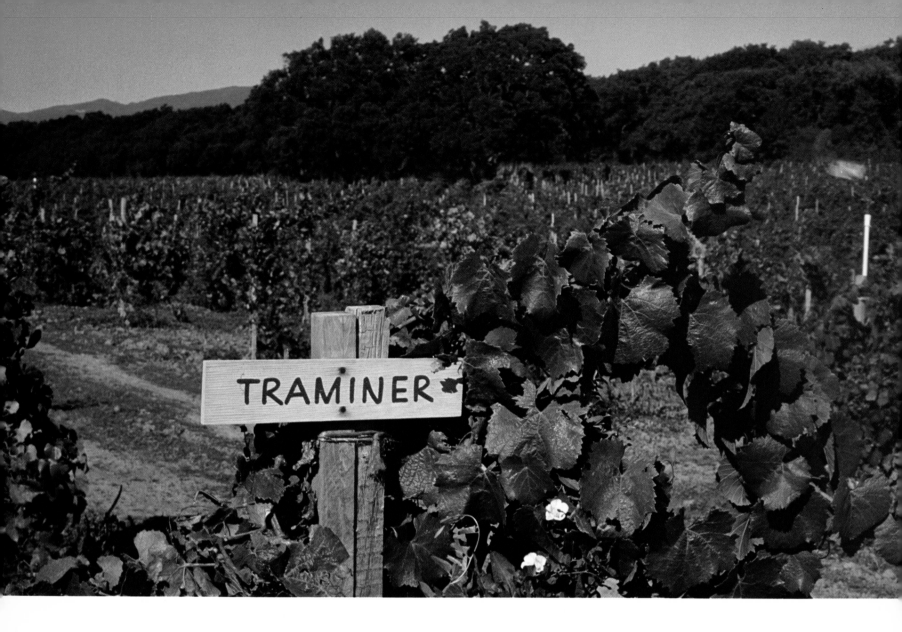

Gewürztraminer

One of the oldest identifiable vinifera varieties in the wine world, the Traminer supposedly enchanted Roman soldiers marching across the Alps two thousand years ago when they encountered it in the village of Tramin (since 1919 known as Termeno) in the Italian Tyrol. Cuttings of the vine traveled north with the Roman legions, were planted along the Danube, and ultimately arrived in Alsace and Germany under the name of Traminer, which it still bears.

Throughout the vine's planting evolution, Alsatian growers propagated those clones of the pinkish grape which had the most outstanding spicy character. From the mother vine, the Traminer, came the dominant vine we know today as the Gewürztraminer, *gewürz* being the German word for "spicy." Under Alsatian *Appellation Controlée* it is now the only strain designated for planting in that wine country. Both Traminer and Gewürztraminer vines exist in California vineyards, but a similar trend

Traminer grapes at Sebastiani Vineyards in Sonoma make their slightly sweet, spicy Gewürztraminer toward the more distinctive variety has trebled the planting in the cooler regions to the present 4,591 acres. Shy-bearing, an early ripener, yielding 4 to 6 tons per acre in irrigated plantings, the Gewürztraminer produces tough-skinned grapes which can be delivered intact to the fermenters.

With cool-fermentation techniques, the grape's very assertive characteristics are preserved. In Alsace the wine is almost always fermented totally dry, but in California some winemakers have found that vinification with an edge of sweetness from residual grape sugar wins favor. The wine requires little or no aging upon release from the winery. It is at its best when its fruitiness and spicy grape taste are fresh and young.

Golden Chasselas

This is one of the most beautiful grapes to behold on the vine, with luxuriantly long, conical clusters of yellow-gold berries to inspire an artist's eye. It is prized in California's San Joaquin Valley vineyards as a sherry grape, but for table wine it is inconsequential, producing wines that are dull, flat, readily oxidized, and almost wholly lacking in acidity. In Switzerland, where the Chasselas is known as the Fendant, it is the leading variety for the pleasant white wines of Vaud, Vallais, and Neuchâtel.

Green Hungarian

The appeal of Green Hungarian, like that of Golden Chasselas, is not inherent in the character of the grape itself, which is neutral to the point of being almost flavorless. But there is no denying the attraction of the name. Like Zsa Zsa Gabor, it has dollar-earning romantic appeal. Lee Stewart, who launched Souverain Vineyards in the Napa Valley in the early forties, was the first to introduce Green Hungarian as a varietal wine. With the renaissance of the Buena Vista Winery in Sonoma, it was only natural that its new owner, Frank Bartholomew, taking full advantage of the Hungarian background of dashing Count Agoston Haraszthy, the founder, would offer Buena Vista Green Hungarian. Poured well-chilled from its tall, slender green bottle, it attracted an immediate following. Other winemakers, seeking to improve upon the wine's rather colorless character, gave it generous additions of Chenin Blanc and/or French Colombard. The M. Lamont Vineyard at the foot of Bear Mountain on the Tehachapi slopes near Bakersfield is producing a Green Hungarian with a very distinctive taste, obviously resulting from the special qualities of that region's soil.

Grey Riesling

This grape, called Chauché Gris in its native France, came to California in the last century. By 1884 it was already known in the Napa Valley as

(*overleaf*) Almadén owns nearly 4,000 acres of vineyard at Paicines in San Benito County, where much of its Johannisberg Riesling is grown

Modern glass-lined tanks for storing wines at Weibel's historic Mission San Jose winery, founded in 1869 by Senator Leland Stanford

Grey Riesling, even though it had been brought from the Poitiers district, northeast of Bordeaux. Propagated in San Jose nurseries along with the Chauché Noir, it came into favor in the Livermore Valley because it thrived in that warmer climate. Dubbed "grey" because the reddish-tan berries are covered with a dusty bloom as they ripen, the grape acquired the "Riesling" moniker, one can only assume, because the wine was thought to resemble the crisp, clean, popular Rhine wine.

As Grey Riesling the wine has had a success that is nothing short of phenomenal. That it is not even a kissing cousin of any Rhenish grape matters not a whit to those who enjoy its charms. The wine looks like a Riesling in its tall, slender bottle.

An early ripener, harvested in the hot weather of the vintage season, the fruit must be brought in when it is at the peak of its most desirable sugar–acid ratio. With cool-fermentation techniques, often with no wood at all in its aging, it comes to market flowery and generous in mouth-filling refreshment. Although the wine has been criticized for its lack of character, its many adherents find its mildness pleasing.

Malvasia Bianca

This grape with its heady fragrance, luxurious body, and rich history has only 1,204 acres in bearing in California. Of Greek origin, cuttings established on the island of Madeira in the fifteenth century produced the famed Malmsey wine in which, as reported in Shakespeare's chronicle of King Richard III, the Duke of Clarence was drowned. Malmsey Madeira, laced with brandy, and syrup-sweet, has its own traditions connected with George Washington and Thomas Jefferson. But today in California the muscat-flavored varietal is used to produce a white table wine, sweet-finished and appropriate to serve with dessert, though it cannot rival a great French Sauternes.

Muscat

Cheap California Muscatel, the skid-row tipple, all but annihilated any acceptance for Muscat wines among connoisseurs. It remained for the late Louis M. Martini to make Muscat appealing with his still scarce Moscato Amabile, delicately sparkling and carrying an ineffable freshness of the lovely grape into light, light wine.

The present vogue for other Californian versions of *moscato*, and even the growing popularity of Asti Spumante, attest to the potential of Muscat varietals when used by talented winemakers. Bone-dry Muscat can be exciting and fully satisfying. Muscadelle de Bordelais is classically, but sparingly, blended into French Sauternes. But no matter whether it be the revered Moscato di Canelli of Asti, the Muscat of Alexandria, or Muscat de Frontignan, the perfume is inescapable. How the grape is used is the secret of making captivating wines. If it is harvested too late, the acidity is gone and a flat, dull wine results.

Souverain of Alexander Valley makes a dessert wine, Moscato Bianco, from the muscat grape

Palomino

In California the Chasselas has sometimes been mistakenly thought to be the same as the Palomino, the leading grape variety in Spain for fine sherry.

Pinot Blanc

In the family of *Vitis vinifera* there is magic to the name Pinot, associated as it is with Romanée-Conti, Le Musigny, Corton, Beaune, and Pommard, made from Pinot Noir. Cross-breeding and selective vine propagation through the centuries have produced different strains with distinctions that often confound and mystify even professional viticulturists who attempt to identify the vine varieties. Pinot Blanc is a proper member of the Pinot family, of which the illustrious Chardonnay is but a cousin. Both are most frequently used in champagne *cuvées*. In California, Pinot Blanc is an often overlooked and underrated varietal white wine. It should not be confused with "White Pinot," which is most often produced from Chenin Blanc.

A shy-bearing vine whose grapes grow in very small, compact clusters, Pinot Blanc thrives in the cooler regions of Monterey, San Benito, Alameda, and Napa counties. Its wine is invariably completely dry; sometimes aged with a slight touch of oak, it is ready to be enjoyed in its first year after the vintage. As produced by premium wineries, it is usually a 100 percent varietal wine. Though its presence is difficult to detect, some Pinot Blanc is employed in the better generic versions of California Chablis.

Pinot Chardonnay (A misnomer. See Chardonnay)

Riesling (See White Riesling)

Sauvignon Blanc

In the hierarchy of wine grapes, Sauvignon Blanc is outranked only by Chardonnay and the White Riesling of the Rhineland. Its ability to last long on the palate gives distinction to the white wine of Graves and contributes body to Sauternes. It is prized in the upper Loire Valley as the dominant variety in Pouilly-Fumé. There it is called Blanc-Fumé because the ripe grapes are a smoky grayish color (*fumé* being the French word for "smoked"), and the name has been adopted by California winemakers in recent years for their varietal interpretation of this grape of many styles.

The earthy, almost wet-sand taste of Sauvignon Blanc serves the winemakers of California as well as of France in producing wines of individual style and taste. A Livermore Valley Sauvignon Blanc is apt to be paper-dry, while one celebrated Napa Valley "château" edition is frankly sweet, styled after Sauternes. Other North Coast county wine-

The fog blanket that sometimes rolls in from the Pacific through the "Rainbow Gap" to the Callaway Vineyards in Temecula, just north of San Diego, keeps the grapes cool and allows them to ripen slowly makers have found preference in the market by calling their Sauvignon Blanc wine Fumé Blanc or Blanc Fumé. Alas, the labels do not indicate the degree of dryness, which can range from zero residual sweetness to the detectable level of more than 1 percent. Proprietary designations such as Sauvignon Fleur or Blanc de Sauvignon tell you only that the breed is there, but you may be sure that wine from this grape has more than ordinary distinction.

Sauvignon Vert

A low-acid grape, of very pronounced flavor, Sauvignon Vert is used mainly in blending generic white wines; however, California wineries produce a varietal Sauvignon Vert. Used in a varietal, the grape has modest virtues of crisp dryness, the result of early harvesting, and a slightly Muscat flavor brought out by cool fermentation. Sauvignon Vert is usually low in acid.

Sémillon

The late Frank Schoonmaker, who sponsored varietal labeling for California's premium wines, is responsible for the nationwide fame that this excellent grape attained after Prohibition. It is dominant in the blend that constitutes French Sauternes: Sémillon, Sauvignon Blanc, and Muscadelle de Bordelais. "Dry Semillon" from the Livermore Valley was one of the country's most popular wines. There are, of course, those who prefer Sweet Semillon, and still others who enjoy the very sweet Chateau Semillon golden wines.

As *the* Sauternes grape, Sémillon's illustrious destiny may lie in Monterey County plantings, where *Botrytis cinerea,* the "noble rot" of French Sauternes, is a relatively common phenomenon. The benign mold not only draws out moisture, concentrating the grape sugar, but by its presence on the shriveled, fuzzy clusters adds a complexity of taste that enriches the wine. When he was employed as the winemaster of Cresta Blanca in the early sixties, enologist Myron Nightingale produced California's first French-styled sauterne (California sauterne is spelled without the final *s*) by induced humidity and hand-implanted spores of botrytis mold. Several vintages of this "Premier Semillon" were produced, noble experiments that were far ahead of their time. Despite its excellence, the wine offered no serious competition to Château d'Yquem. Today, when we look more and more to California for all kinds of wines, including sweet sauterne, Monterey County may provide an exceptional product for this popular demand.

St.-Émilion (See Ugni Blanc)

Sylvaner

For reasons no one understands, Sylvaner as a wine name has little public appeal. The grape has wider planting than the White Riesling in Germany, where it produces a soft, earthy wine, which when young is fruity and charming. Because it is cultivated widely in Franconia, the Sylvaner is sometimes called the Franken there. In California the Sylvaner appears under other names, too: wines labeled Riesling or Monterey Riesling or Grüner Sylvaner are all made from this grape. Each is likely to have more than 51 percent of Sylvaner, and some may have 100 percent of the varietal. The wines are fairly dry, soft, round, and modestly priced.

Traminer (See Gewürztraminer)

Ugni Blanc

For many years, Wente Bros. in the Livermore Valley produced a varietal Ugni Blanc wine that enjoyed acceptance by a small, enthusiastic group of customers—the only ones who could pronounce the name. But even those who asked for "Ugly Blank" could sometimes be understood, and then the wine would come, chilled, delectable, crisp, tart, and fragrant. Ugni Blanc was not a real winner until the Wentes blended it with Chenin Blanc and renamed it Blanc de Blancs. What's in a name? Nearly everything, where a wine's popularity is concerned. Brookside winery, of Guasti, California, produces a varietal wine from this grape and calls it by the name it enjoys in the French Cognac region—St.-Émilion. Sold in Burgundy bottles, it is a puzzler to the traditionalist who orders from a wine card expecting a red Bordeaux-type wine, only to be presented with a white wine in a Burgundy bottle.

In Italy, this high-yielding vine is called Trebbiano and is one of the grapes used in Soave, which many consider the best white wine of that country. You can stop looking for Ugni Blanc, but don't be surprised someday to find a California Trebbiano that is competing for the Soave market. There are more than 1,500 acres growing in the Golden State, most of it in Central Valley vineyards. It is used for ordinary California Chablis, Sauterne, or Dry Sauterne. Ugni Blanc's lack of acidity is perhaps its greatest defect.

White Riesling (Johannisberg Riesling)

The correct name of this noble grape is Weiss Riesling but it is more commonly known in California as Johannisberg Riesling, in honor of the famous Schloss Johannisberg—and for obvious commercial reasons. It is the outstanding vinifera not only of the Rhineland but also of the Mosel, where it makes the great Bernkasteler Doktor and Wehlener Sonnenuhr. The Riesling of Alsace, Austria, Chile, and Australia is the same

Almadén Vineyards, one of the oldest and largest, must irrigate some of its 15,000 far-flung acres

At the Firestone Vineyard, late-harvested Johannisberg Riesling grapes show evidence of the prized *Botrytis cinerea*, or "noble rot"

species, but the famous Schloss Johannisberg of the Rheingau is the name that holds public favor, even when the wine is made thousands of miles away.

Native to the coldest wineland of Europe, the White Riesling's adaptation to the warmer plots of California has been productive of wines with character and finesse. But they are seldom even close in taste or nature to the fine wines of the Rhine or the Mosel. The grapes develop differently in the warmer environment, often having a higher sugar content, which means greater alcoholic strength and less delicacy.

White Riesling in California is produced in varying styles by different winemakers within one growing area. A flowery bouquet may be the aim of one winemaster, while another balances the grape freshness with the modifying fragrance and flavor that comes from aging in new oak. Vintage becomes important with some producers, whose wines may vary from year to year. Late-harvested versions will benefit from cellar aging, the higher sugar and alcoholic content acting as a preservative, but the wholly dry or even ever so slightly sweet versions are never better than within months of their release from the winery.

In recent years—with the recognition of botrytis in vineyards along the Russian River in Sonoma County, in isolated locations in the Napa Valley, in Monterey County, and in the region of Temecula in southern California—it was realized that, if late-harvested, Johannisberg Riesling can make wines that approach the *Auslese* and even the *Beerenauslese* richness of German wines. These botrytised wines have the splendor of yellow-gold liqueurs whose color and body promise extraordinary taste. Such great wines are uncommon in Germany, and equally rare in California, but all are treasures the true winelover may enjoy. Comparison is incidental, of minor significance.

CALIFORNIA RED-WINE GRAPES

Aleatico

An exotic member of the Muscat family, this grape, which thrives in the warm vineyard regions, is used to produce a very aromatic, soft and spicy table wine of pleasing pink color, and also a deeper-colored red dessert wine. Of Italian origin, Aleatico is the source of the Tuscan *vino santo*, but its greatest claim to fame is its reputation as the finest wine produced on the island of Elba. In California Aleatico table wine is produced by fewer than half a dozen wineries; a scant 90 acres are in bearing.

Alicante Bouschet

One of the very few wine grapes in the world with blood-red juice, Alicante Bouschet zoomed into popularity during Prohibition as a juice grape for home winemakers. Heavy-skinned, with high sugar content,

Angelo Papagni gives Alicante Bouschet oak aging worthy of Pinot Noir and Cabernet

Alicante's blood-red juice gives it some value as a color agent

John Moramarco, viticulturalist at Callaway Vineyard, exhibits their Cabernet Sauvignon grapes, which he cluster-thins to a two-ton-per-acre yield of richly concentrated berries

generous-bearing, and easy to harvest, it afforded California vineyardists an appealing money crop during the dry era. Later, when, following Repeal, fine winemaking transformed the standards of the California wine industry, the vulgar virtues of Alicante ceased to be advantages. But Alicante Bouschet remains the leading grape for thousands of home winemakers, and during the harvest season 175,000 tons are shipped from the San Joaquin Valley to Eastern states and Canada. Not only do the grapes ship well, but the home winemaker is assured of a wine of good (though not long-lasting) color, quick maturing, and soon ready to drink. The grape, though misprized by other winemakers (except as a color agent for California port wine), is a variety no longer touted among the ranks of the state's growers of fine wines, whose attention is focused upon the more noble varieties.

Barbera

The Barbera grape produces a big, full-bodied wine in its home region of Piedmont. Though some 17,346 acres are in bearing in California vineyards at present, much of the wine is used in Burgundy and Chianti blends. Some California vintners of Italian background give premium status to the vine, and their wines are favored by consumers seeking deep-flavored, deep-colored wines to accompany highly seasoned Italian foods. Barbera is cultivated in all the state's wine regions, and in each region the wine reflects the particular climate and soil and the style of the individual winemaker. Some wines will be wood-aged to a rich softness, while others, with accent on the berry-like bouquet, will be young wines best consumed early.

Cabernet Sauvignon

Cabernet Sauvignon ranks easily as the world's most highly prized red-wine grape. It is responsible for the great clarets of Bordeaux and the best red wines of California. The velvet-soft and deeply fragrant ruby-red wine from this vigorous *Vitis vinifera* species offers every winemaker the challenge that will test his creative skill and enhance his name. Synonymous with superior red wine, the name Cabernet Sauvignon and its appeal to the world of wine consumers accounted for much of the wine boom in California, extending the planting from 1,966 acres in 1965 to the present 22,042 bearing acres—an increase that can only be called phenomenal.

In the famed French château vineyards of Bordeaux, the vine is trained low, the rows often punctuated with red roses which flower simultaneously with the vine. It is perhaps only viticultural superstition that the rosebushes are there to warn of an onset of mildew, they and the grapevines being subject to similar diseases, or to attract bees to pollinate the berries. In California the vines are often trellised, the branching canes providing a luxuriantly shady arbor frequently more than seven feet tall.

At Freemark Abbey, Johannisberg Riesling grapes are crushed in a cylindrical press

Under normal conditions a fairly good set of the blue-black small clusters can be expected, with a yield of 4 to 6 tons per acre. Monterey, Napa, Sonoma, and Santa Barbara counties are preeminent in Cabernet planting, but there is scarcely a winegrowing region in the state that has not been tempted to plant this aristocratic variety.

The grape has a tough and durable skin, which not only makes for easier harvesting but is an advantage in case of rain late in the season, since the heavy-skinned clusters can dry without danger of bunch-rot. The heavy skins are also responsible for the high percentage of tannin in the wine, a factor that increases the winemaker's options as to method of vinification.

Professor H. W. Berg of UC–Davis demonstrated that nearly all the color is extracted from the skins of the grapes in the early period when the juice is in contact with the pomace (the skins and seeds) and suggested that further contact extracts excessive amounts of tannins that only age can soften. An accelerated maturity is thus possible if the emerging wine is taken off the skins even before the full sugar/alcohol fermentation is completed. Winemakers can argue for hours this theory versus the Bordeaux tradition of leaving the wine in contact with the pomace for two weeks or longer. From such points of difference in winemaking emerge the different styles of clarets, not only in California but in France as well.

The astringency of young Cabernet wines is decreased through aging in wood. The classic French method is to age new wine in new wood, an expensive process requiring new 50-gallon oak barrels for each vintage. The choice of Limousin, Nevers, Yugoslavian, German, or American oak will affect the taste of the wine almost as much as climate, soil, and blending with other claret grapes. But the distinctive bouquet of Cabernet Sauvignon, which is enhanced with bottle age, is the attribute that gives the breed its universal appeal.

The complexity of the Cabernet Sauvignon bouquet tests the descriptive powers of its passionate adherents. There are 100 percent Cabernet Sauvignon wines that smell like roses, others that are richly herbal, and the woodsy, cedar scents from oak aging can often marry with the fruit to give a wine an indescribable complexity.

Cabernet Franc

This leading member of the Cabernet family in Saint-Émilion also produces the popular rosé wines of the Loire, but it is not cultivated in any appreciable quantity in California. Cabernet Franc has been produced as a single varietal by Spring Mountain Vineyards in the Napa Valley and Veedercrest of Emeryville. Growing in small, compact clusters, it is valued as a grape to blend with Cabernet Sauvignon.

Cabernet pomace—the skins, seeds, and stems left after the juice has been drawn off—being poured into a basket-press at Jordan Winery for added essence

The winemaker at Jordan draws from the wood a sample of '76 Cabernet Sauvignon, the first wine from the third-leaf harvest

Carignane

This grape was once so widely planted in California that Carignane was second to Zinfandel. In 1982 with 21,166 acres in bearing, it is still an important commercial red-wine grape in the state. Produced as a single varietal wine by several wineries, it belies its reputation for being ordinary through vinification methods that achieve outstanding results for the grape. For example, the normally high-yielding vine is cultivated without irrigation. Hillside grapes from North Coast counties can produce a powerful varietal wine, its robust flavor intensified by lower yield. But for the most part heavy yield remains Carignane's chief virtue, and it becomes a payload variety for almost all generic red wines of California.

Carnelian, Carmine, Centurion

The University of California has experimental vineyards at Davis where continuing research to improve the quality of California wine production is carried on. Distinguished hybrids like Emerald Riesling and Ruby Cabernet are the results of Professor Olmo's patient work, based on the belief that the outstanding virtues of two, and sometimes even more, crossed plants may combine to produce a superior vine, with the best characteristics of each, adaptable to climate and soil environments in which no one vine had before excelled. Such a vine is Carnelian, a Cabernet × Carignane × Grenache hybrid developed for the warm San Joaquin Valley, with more than 1,767 acres now in commercial planting. Newer is Carmine, another Cabernet type, which yields a distinctly more flavorful wine than one of its august parents, Cabernet Sauvignon; the progeny of Cabernet Sauvignon × Carignane were crossed with early-ripening Merlot, a first cousin to Cabernet Sauvignon. Professor A. Dinsmoor Webb, the present chairman of the UC–Davis Department of Viticulture and Enology, believes Carmine's 20-year history of development will make it a bell-ringer for California Cabernet-type production. Centurion is another hybrid just beginning to move into the spotlight after the long wait of growing cycles designed to determine its standing in the family of Cabernet hybrids. Begun, like all the cross-variety samples, as a number, it has achieved the dignity of a name.

Charbono

This currently rare varietal, imported from Italy in the last century, probably declined in popularity because of its coarse, deep-colored, rough wines, which when blended with other wines tended to overpower them. Viticulturist Charles Wetmore condemned it in 1884 in no uncertain terms: "Those who desire to produce only high-grade wines should not plant this variety."

The present story of Charbono is a full turn-around to glory. In the late 1930s, Professor Winkler studied the vines from which Inglenook

Vintaged
Mirassou
Monterey
Monterey Riesling

Produced and bottled by Mirassou Vineyard,
San Jose, California

Alcohol 12% *By Volume*

Jesuit Wines
Noviliate
CALIFORNIA
BLACK MUSCAT
ALCOHOL 15% BY VOLUME
Estate Bottled

PRODUCED AND BOTTLED BY
Noviliate Wines, Inc.
LOS GATOS, CALIFORNIA

MAYACAMAS
1973
NAPA MOUNTAIN
CABERNET SAUVIGNON
ALCOHOL 13% BY VOLUME
PRODUCED AND BOTTLED BY
Mayacamas Vineyards
NAPA, CALIFORNIA

Felton-
EMPiRE
1976
SANTA CRUZ
WHITE
RiESliNG
Produced and bottled by
Felton-Empire Vineyards
Felton, California
Alcohol 10% by volume

Vines of Nepenthe

zinfandel

a varietal california table wine
produced and bottled in limited quantity by
nepenthe cellars, portola valley, california

bottle number   of

the
ChristianBrothers®
VINTNERS SINCE 1882

SELECT NAPA VALLEY
PINOT CHARDONNAY
An elegant dry white dinner wine of rare Chardonnay grapes
Serve chilled
PRODUCED AND BOTTLED BY
THE CHRISTIAN BROTHERS • NAPA, CALIFORNIA
Alcohol 12% by volume

RAPAZZINI
CALIFORNIA
PETITE SIRAH
MADE AND BOTTLED BY RAPAZZINI BROS. GILROY, CALIFORNIA
ALCOHOL 12% BY VOLUME

1975
Chateau St. Jean
SONOMA VALLEY
Chardonnay
WILDWOOD VINEYARDS

PRODUCED AND BOTTLED BY
CHATEAU ST JEAN • KENWOOD, SONOMA VALLEY, CALIFORNIA
BONDED WINERY NO. 4710 • ALCOHOL 13.4% BY VOLUME

WINE BY WHEELER
CALIFORNIA
Zinfandel Rosé

Produced and bottled by
NICASIO VINEYARDS
SOQUEL CALIFORNIA

Don W. Wheeler
1971 Vintager

ALCOHOL BY VOLUME 12
CONTENTS 4/5 QUART

VARIETAL WINE LABELS

was producing a medal-winning Barbera and identified them not as the popular vinifera of Piedmont for which the wine was named, but positively as Charbono. Today, Inglenook draws upon fewer than 20 acres of Charbono, but winemaker Tom Ferrell tells me there are present plans to extend the planting, with added vines almost within the shade of the winery buildings at Rutherford. Keep Charbono on your list of California specialties. Taste it young. It will upholster your mouth with brash tannin. Age is really needed to bring it around to the greatness found in it by its admirers.

Gamay

Quite simply, Gamay is the grape which produces that darling of Parisian bistros called Beaujolais. Light and gay, always to be consumed young, with the delicate appeal of vine-fresh raspberries, it is the ideal candidate for generous pouring and carefree occasions when a more illustrious wine would be out of place. The grape is known in France as *Gamay noir à jus blanc* ("black Gamay with white juice"). It thrives in California, where only recently it has begun to emerge under the proper name, Gamay Noir, as a varietal wine. There are currently 4,149 acres in bearing.

The grape has extensive use for rosé wines. To make a rosé, the juice is fermented on the skins for only a few hours, until just the desired hint of color is obtained. Both red and rosé Gamay wines require little aging and are at their best the moment they reach the wineshop.

Gamay Beaujolais

Recently discovered to be a member of the Pinot Noir family, the Gamay Beaujolais is an early ripener, with small, oval, black berries growing in compact clusters. With a yield of 4 to 6 tons per acre, it adapts well to varying types of soil, thriving almost entirely in Monterey, Napa, Mendocino, San Benito, Sonoma, and Santa Barbara counties in 3,528 bearing acres.

Though Gamay Beaujolais is not the grape of carafe wine in French bistros, several California vintners vinify the grape in the style of Beaujolais *nouveau*, bottling it young for consumption while the wine is fresh and fruity. Other winemakers give the wine added aging in wood, releasing it a year, instead of weeks or months, after harvest. Essentially a light wine, its ideal service comes with barbecue dinners and picnics.

Grenache

Charles Wetmore, executive officer of California's first State Board of Viticultural Commissioners, writing in 1884, found the Grenache "so vigorous and fertile, and so well adapted to dry, warm regions, that there is danger that it may be planted too numerously." More than half of the

Gamay Beaujolais and Sauvignon Blanc from Monterey Vineyards

17,061 acres now thriving in the state are planted in the warm central San Joaquin Valley and give varietal distinction not only to Grenache rosé wines but to blended generic vin rosé. Many examples of generic vin rosé are slightly sweet, while others are quite dry, depending upon the winemaker's marketing aims. All should be consumed young, while still fresh and fruity.

The Grenache's pronounced, almost spicy, aroma contributes to the complexity of Châteauneuf-du-Pape of the Rhône, and in Spain, where it is known as the Garnacha, its reddish-purple grapes enhance the appeal of Rioja wines. The vogue for pink wines was born of the Grenache rosé produced in the Tavel district of the Rhône. When the late Frank Schoonmaker discovered Grenache flourishing in the California vineyards of Almadén in Los Gatos, it was only a matter of months before Almadén Grenache Rosé was on its way to becoming an American favorite.

Grignolino

The reputation for individuality possessed by this unique Italian grape of the Piedmont region arises from its unusual strawberry-like fragrance and the hints of orange in its light crimson color. While the most famous editions of Grignolino have been produced in the widely separated areas of Cucamonga and the Napa Valley, as a red-wine varietal or rosé table wine, blended with Pinot Noir, it gave distinction to Beringer Brothers' original proprietary blending called Barenblut. Grignolino remains one of the favorite grapes of Joe Heitz of the Napa Valley, and customers line up for their share of each release. A total of 52 acres are currently in bearing in California, principally in Santa Clara and Napa counties.

Mataró

Plantings of Mataró, which makes a rather coarse red wine, are largely confined to southern California. The grape's utilitarian role in bulk wine production in France and Spain is responsible for whatever popularity it had. It is to the credit of California winegrowers that Mataró is rapidly being replaced as a wine grape by finer varieties. Not even its very limited use in Châteauneuf-du-Pape could rescue it from its California decline.

Merlot

While the role of Merlot is subsidiary to that of Cabernet Sauvignon and Cabernet Franc in the Médoc, the grape rises to great distinction in the wines of Saint-Émilion and Pomerol—and especially the noble Château Pétrus—to which it imparts softness and roundness. With bigger berries than Cabernet, growing in loose clusters, the grape gives suppleness and flower delicacy to wines with which it is blended.

An early ripener as a grape, Merlot is an early bloomer as a wine. In years when frosts or hail wipes it out, the wines of the Haut-Médoc that

The modern winery's ranks of stainless-steel fermenting and storage tanks represent an enormous investment

usually incorporate it into their blends will have heavier, slow-maturing Cabernets. When the weather has been kind to the grape, Merlot joins the other Médoc varieties to make winsome, graceful wines of lighter mien.

First cousin to the Cabernet family, Merlot is just beginning an independent varietal career in California. It thrives in the Napa Valley, where 100 percent Merlots from Sterling Vineyards have shown that the wine can have the same soft grace and charm as endear it to the wine-growers of Saint-Émilion and Pomerol. Quicker-maturing than Cabernet wines, Merlot, as an ingredient along with Cabernet in claret blending, is coming into vogue among California winemakers. Their customers are beginning to understand that 100 percent Cabernet Sauvignon is not essential for deluxe editions of that famous varietal. Acreage of Merlot in California had a hundredfold increase from its scant 35 acres in 1966 to 2,161 in bearing sixteen years later.

Mission

Few grape varieties have as romantic a history as the Mission grape or have played a more important role in the development of a region. Long thought to be a Criolla seedling first brought to the western world by Cortez and the conquistadors, it is believed today by UC–Davis viticulturists to be a variant of the Spanish Monica. Named after the Spanish missions established by Franciscan fathers throughout California, the grape was first planted by Padre Junípero Serra in San Diego de Alcalá in 1769. From San Diego north to Sonoma, twenty-one Franciscan missions grew up along El Camino Real, each with its vineyards proving the land was receptive to *Vitis vinifera*.

The blue-black grapes, "round as a musket-ball," from abundant-yielding vines taller than a man, produced a wine reminiscent of Málaga. The Mission grapevine continued to be the only species in California until the 1830s, when Jean Louis Vignes arrived in Los Angeles from Bordeaux bringing French vine cuttings and winemaking traditions that would improve upon the product of the padres. There are still 3,218 acres of Mission vines yielding abundant crops from San Diego to Sonoma.

The Mission grape is used in California today for both port and sherry, but its finest role is in the production of a rich, sweet, golden dessert wine called Angelica, named after the city of Los Angeles.

In the Livingston vineyards of Ernest and Julio Gallo, Mission vines, with gnarled and sturdy trunks indicating an age of several decades, are planted along the bank of the Merced River, where they are prized for their contribution to Gallo's Livingston Cream Sherry.

Montonico

Only 8.4 acres of this rare vinifera, brought from Calabrian vineyards by members of the Filice family of San Martin Vineyards, are known to exist in California. Originally thought of as a sherry grape, it went almost unnoticed until, in 1973, 11,000 gallons of the 1967 vintage were found by winemaster Ed Friedrich, quietly resting in oak. Unbaked, slowly aged in wood, the wine was a facsimile of the *vino santo* made in small amounts by farmers all over Italy. The ancient grape species has a heritage that dates back at least to 720 B.C., when the Calabrian city of Sybaris was founded.

Nebbiolo

Only 386 acres of this splendid Italian red-wine grape are in bearing in California—in Fresno, Stanislaus, Tulare, and Amador counties. But it is not unlikely that its distinctive and compelling varietal flavors, which give recognizable character to the great Italian wines, Barolo, Barbaresco, and Gattinara of Piedmont, will inspire extended planting in California; at present only the Monteviña winery of Plymouth produces a varietal Nebbiolo. The vine is named for the *nebbia,* the cool morning fog that

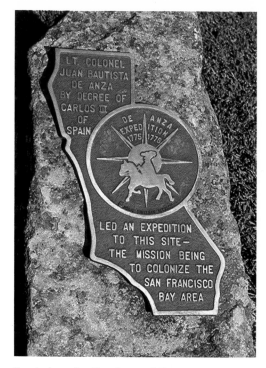

Reminders of earlier times at Mission San Jose along El Camino Real, where the Mission grape was first planted by Franciscan friars

rides softly across the rolling vineyard landscape of Piedmont during the hot pre-harvest months, allowing the grapes to mature gradually. The sturdy red wines of Nebbiolo grapes require considerable aging, but when mature they have outstanding attributes of bouquet, assertiveness, and class.

Petite Sirah

André L. Simon wrote: "The true origin of the Syrah grape is unknown." Clonal descendants of the ancient Shiraz vine from Persia allegedly thrive today in the vineyards of France, Switzerland, California, Australia, and South Africa. Whether or not the California Petite Sirah, currently enjoying tremendous popularity among winelovers with an appreciation for bold red wines, originated in Persia, its charms are not to be denied.

When the French crusader Gaspard de Sterimberg quit the Holy Land in 1225 and built himself a hermitage near Lyons, legend tells us that he not only took home to the valley of the Rhône his taste for the wines of Persia; he brought back vine cuttings as well. And here the legend accommodates the fact that the oldest vineyards in France, those that resisted Domitian's edict against the vine, A.D. 92, were in this region of Roman Gaul. The vineyard of the crusader-turned-hermit produces wine that has been called "the manliest of all French wines"—Hermitage.

The Syrah vine came to dominate the Rhône. It is the grape that gives longevity, color, and flavor to Châteauneuf-du-Pape. In color, wines of the Syrah or Petite Syrah vine will vary from dark garnet to almost transparent ruby. The bouquet is a complex that may suggest almond, cedar, or raspberry. In the mouth-filling taste there is strong tannin that may be puckery in young wines, giving way to softness as the wine ages. Intensity of color, acid, and tannin increases as the temperature of the region in which the vine is grown decreases.

California Petite Sirah thrives in 8,344 acres with plantings in the foothills of the Sierra, in the northern reaches of Mendocino County, in Napa and Sonoma, in the great San Joaquin Valley, and as far south as San Diego. Frank Schoonmaker suggested that the California Petite Sirah, while presumed to be the Syrah of the Rhône, was probably a more vulgar vinifera called Duriff, a heavy-bearing variety that also grows in the Rhône Valley and that resembles the Petit Syrah of Hermitage. This is probably a partial truth, but I believe that some true Syrah clones, descendants of the ancient Shiraz, give greatness to some California vinifications of Petite Sirah wines. André Simon, after his visit to Australia, declared the Shiraz, widely propagated there, to be "the same variety that is planted extensively in the Rhône Valley of France, where it is the basis of Hermitage wines." In Australia I tasted the wine against memories of Rhône wines, and agree.

Pinot Noir

Pinot Noir, both the grape and the wine, remains an enigma to California viticulturists and winemakers alike. More than 200 clones, or variants of the species, have been identified, but it is also known that numerous differences in the species exist in the celebrated vineyards of the French Côte d'Or. We can only speculate on how many of the differences found in the true Pinot Noir wines of California and France result from soil or vine variations.

The shy-bearing vine can be as temperamental as a spoiled child. The early-ripening grapes come to maturity during the warmest period of the harvest season and can quickly become overripe, losing their proper sugar/acid ratio. Thin-skinned, the clusters require careful handling. Although it is primarily used for red wines, the white juice of the black grapes has an elegant fruitiness that recommends it for *cuvées*, or basic blends, in champagne. In Blanc de Noirs editions, consummate skill is required to keep the pigment of the skins from "bleeding" into the wine, giving it an unwanted blush of color.

Pinot Noir in California seems to elude even the most intelligent application of enological science in the production of wines comparable in stature to those of the French Côte d'Or. In the words of wine writer Norman S. Rody, "Pinot Noir is the thorn in the side of the California wine industry."

I can cite isolated examples of superlative California Pinot Noir, but they are few and far between. California Pinot Noir, like fine French Burgundy, is affected by the soil in which the grapes grow and by the vinification methods and aging procedures. Few wineries can afford more than a year or so of bottle age before general release. That aging is the beginning of the refinement necessary to achieve a wine's full potential. It is up to you, the wine buyer, to allow your wines the time they need to reach their peak.

Pinot St. George (Red Pinot)

Though a true vinifera, it is doubtful that Pinot St. George is a member of the regal Pinot family. Grown in hillside vineyards of the Napa Valley, it produces a wine of distinctive character, which, with added age, deepens in complexity. The obvious advantages of the Pinot name have been responsible for increased planting of the variety, though at present only 472 acres are in bearing, mostly in Monterey and Napa counties.

Refosco

Transplanted to France in the last century, the Refosco grape of Italy fooled even the famed ampelographer Count Oudart, who listed it as Petit Pinot, which obviously made it a more attractive candidate for importation. Some believed that the Refosco which arrived in California

was in reality a Pinot Noir, but to settle the question for a while, one planter gave it his own name; Crabb's Black Burgundy enjoyed a lively fame as a red-wine grape in turn-of-the-century California vineyards. Today Refosco is often used in small amounts in Cabernet blends. The number of acres planted in the Napa Valley, currently 99, will probably decrease.

Royalty

This California-developed hybrid, like the Rubired, Salvador, and Alicante Bouschet, has red juice. It has long been used to give color to California port. Beyond the pigment of the skins and juice, Royalty has little interesting potential as a red-table-wine grape. It does not, despite its name, belong in the company of truly noble varieties. At best, it is a rather commonplace wine, sweet-edged and as obvious as a Valentine.

Ruby Cabernet

The distinctive flavor and bouquet of Cabernet Sauvignon and the high yield of Carignane inspired the marriage of these two viniferas at the Agricultural Experiment Station of UC–Davis in 1936. Their offspring was released for commercial planting as Ruby Cabernet in 1948, and it did indeed seem to inherit the hoped-for parental characteristics. Even when planted in warm Central Valley regions the grape produced wines of a quality to gain immediate acceptance. Public recognition of the wine's attractive bouquet, good fruit, acidity, and excellent color accounts for the steady growth of the plantings to the 13,291 acres currently in bearing. As a varietal, it has even earned some gold medals at the Los Angeles County Fair.

Souzão

In the production of fine port wine, beyond the aesthetic importance of the mellow ruby color derived from the skins of the grapes, sufficient acidity to balance sweetness is critical. Without acidity, the most beautiful, velvet-soft port would be cloying. The virtue of the Souzão grape resides in its peculiar ability to retain, in the process of ripening, a good balance of natural acidity, even as it develops a high sugar content.

Valdepeñas

The vine takes its name from the large wine-producing area of the ancient province of Spain whose rocky soil earned it the name "Valley of Stones." The wine from this vinifera is undistinguished even in its homeland, but the generous yield is the reason it is propagated for *vino corriente*, the inexpensive wine for daily or "current" consumption. More than 1,289 acres in California vineyards are planted in Valdepeñas, important for the same reason: the vine thrives and gives a bountiful yield per acre for generic blendings of inexpensive and undistinguished red table wines.

The noble Pinot Noir, autumn-ripe, is used primarily for red wines, but the white juice can also add a touch of elegance to champagne blends

Zinfandel

Zinfandel is California's own wine, unique, complex, and as varied in its character as the climate in which it grows. While it enjoys the distinction of being produced from one of the most widely planted vines in the state, no one has yet been able to establish the land of its birth with certainty.

History and legend tell us the vine was brought back from Hungary in 1862 by Count Agoston Haraszthy, but today it is totally unknown in that country. Zinfandel thrived in America long before Haraszthy made his famous grape-gathering trip to Europe. In his authoritative volume *The Wines of America*, Leon D. Adams reveals the existence of a European grape named Zinfandel "grown under glass by William Robert Prince on Long Island, N.Y., as early as 1830, 10 years before Haraszthy immigrated to the United States." In his own *Treatise on Grapes,* Prince declared that Zinfandel came from Hungary.

The most recent clue to the possible origin of Zinfandel emerged in 1967, when Dr. Austin Goheen, plant pathologist with the U.S. Department of Agriculture, visited vineyards in Puglia, in southeastern Italy, where he saw rows of vines that looked to him like California Zinfandel. Called *Primitivo di Gioia* in reference to their early ripening, the big, heavily winged bunches of compactly clustered black grapes were first gathered in August. A second crop, well-shaded by foliage, ripened much later and produced a fine, full-flavored red wine capable of great age.

Almadén makes nearly every variety and kind of wine produced in California, and many of its thousands of vineyard acres thrive with the help of sprinkler systems

The deep red Zinfandels from cooler North Coast regions of California resemble the wines of the Médoc. A lighter, fruitier version from the warmer districts suggests Beaujolais

Like other vinifera species, California Zinfandel also will set a second crop of fruit, and it matures both in the middle of the growing period and late. Dr. Goheen reported his observations to Professor Olmo, casting new light on the mystery of Zinfandel's origins.

Three different Primitivo vines that flourish in the Taranto area of Puglia are now growing in the UC–Davis experimental vineyards under the watchful eye of Professor Olmo. As a result of his study of leaf conformation, fruiting and ripening characteristics, and ultimately by wine analysis, it may eventually be determined that Zinfandel had an Italian rather than a Hungarian origin, but we will have to wait perhaps five or ten years for confirmation.

As of 1982, of the 363,491 acres of wine grapes growing in California, Zinfandel with 28,045 acres in bearing is the number one red wine grape. There are heavy plantings in the warm central and southern counties and also in the cooler North Coast counties. Since in the warmer districts grapes mature much earlier, and with the same degree of sugar have less total acid and less color, it is immediately apparent that two different types of Zinfandel, one lighter·and one heavier, will emerge by reason of vineyard location. California's highly skilled winemakers today produce not merely two types of Zinfandel but five:

1. A light, young, and fresh Zinfandel, its berry-like flavor suggesting the French Beaujolais.

2. A heavier-bodied, deeper-colored wine, capable of long cellar aging, comparable to the finest French clarets of the Médoc. Such wines are most likely to emerge from the cooler regions.

3. Late-harvest Zinfandels, with alcohol content as high as 17 percent by volume and with minimal residual sugar. These have rare aging potential and suggest the results that will be possible when viticulture and enology marry in the science of winemaking.

4. The rare Blanc de Noirs Zinfandel, white wine from black grapes. Cool, controlled crushing and fermentation preserve the grape's characteristic aroma and bouquet and give satin richness of body. Only a few examples of this wine exist.

5. Zinfandel Rosé, incomparably fresh, fragrant, usually dry, to be enjoyed young. This is a stunning surprise to winebibbers accustomed to pink wines that are innocuous and lacking in character.

TWO HUNDRED YEARS OF WINE HISTORY

"And all these tidal gatherings, growth, and decay,
Shining and darkening, are forever
Renewed; and the whole cycle impenitently
Revolves, and all the past is future. . . ."
                                        —Robinson Jeffers

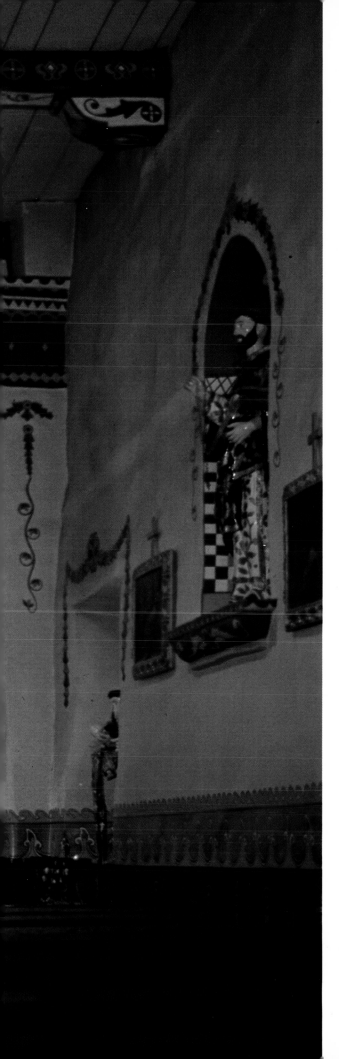

Long before the Pilgrims landed on Plymouth Rock, three small ships sailed into the harbor near what would later be the town of San Diego. They belonged to the expedition of Juan Rodríguez Cabrillo, a Portuguese navigator in the service of Spain. The year was 1542, less than a quarter of a century after the conquest of Mexico for Spain by Hernando Cortez, which brought about the capture of Montezuma in chains, followed by the plundering of one civilization by another and the cruel imposition of Spanish rule. Out of this high drama came the transposition of cultures that still marks the land. Spanish colonists were commanded to plant, every year for five years, one thousand vines for every one hundred Indians living on the land. Mexico, it was hoped, might become one enormous vineyard.

It was not fertile California in which Cabrillo planted the first flag to fly over that land, on October 10, 1542. With the ensign of Carlos V of Spain, he took possession of California near Mugu Lagoon in Ventura County, a cactus-studded, rocky, sun-drenched peninsula, hot as a furnace, according to some of the explorers.

In England, Queen Elizabeth's interest in the New World inspired a rather piratical voyage by Sir Francis Drake. On his freebooting expedition around the world in the *Golden Hind* he managed to raid every Spanish ship he encountered, but beyond raising the English flag with the Cross of St. George, and nailing a sixpence to a post on the shore of Drake's Bay, just north of San Francisco, Sir Francis failed to make "New Albion" a real threat to Spanish empire.

However, reverberations of Drake's exploits troubled the Spanish court and ultimately set in motion the expedition of Gaspar de Portolá and Padre Junípero Serra. The simultaneous planting of the Cross, the sword, and the vine at San Diego in 1769 truly begins the romantic wine history of California, with the ultimate establishment of the chain of the twenty-one missions, the presidios, and the pueblos that have become today's cities, ranches, and farming communities.

The gentle face of Padre Junípero Serra in the portrait by a contemporary artist belies the enduring strength and dynamic force that marked his leadership of the missionary expedition until his death at the Mission San Carlos Borromeo del Rio Carmelo, in January 1784.

His is a life story of overcoming the most incredible hardships, pushing against the impossible toward accomplishment, and achieving the miraculous. It was this superhuman drive in Serra that converted the dry, thorny thickets and desert land of California into gardens, orchards, vineyards, and thriving communities. At every mission vine roots went into the ground as certainly as the foundations were begun.

The wines of San Gabriel and San Fernando, San Juan Capistrano and Santa Barbara gathered such fame, life in Alta California became so like paradise, that reports to the viceroy in Mexico brought orders from

The Serra Chapel in Mission San Juan Capistrano honors the memory of Padre Junípero Serra, who brought wines and vines to California in 1769 jealous administrators to curtail even small luxuries. All the wooden *carretas* were burned to keep the good friars from riding. Shoes and stockings were forbidden. Rooms that were large and comfortable were taken from the friars and assigned to travelers.

San Juan Capistrano, the seventh of the missions founded, and permanently established in the year of our nation's birth, 1776, played a tiny but significant part in our beginnings—the mission padres donated $229 to help the cause of the American Revolution, and among their early records is a notation that a priest said a prayer "for the success at arms of Mr. George Washington, whose cause seems to be just."

At this same mission in 1818, raiding French pirates flying the revolutionary flag of Buenos Aires and allegedly seeking to achieve Argentine independence from Spain, so enjoyed the wines of San Juan Capistrano that some of them had to be dragged back to the ship and lashed to the cannons. Who could blame the poor sailors, after months at sea, for wanting to stay at this virtual palace garden? Like the swallows who return to Capistrano every March 19, those tipsy pirates must have had wishful urgings to return to this bit of Paradise on earth!

Over the years, revolution, secularization, earthquakes, plunder, and desertion reduced most of the missions to adobe ruins. Because their chapels could serve as granaries, a few were spared, among them San Juan Capistrano, sold to a private buyer for $710. With the admission of California to the Union in 1850, the Catholic Church began petitioning for a return of its properties. President Lincoln deeded Capistrano and other missions back to the Church in 1865. But restoration of the whole chain along El Camino Real had to wait for future generations to realize the profound meaning resting in the ghostly walls of those once happy oases for pilgrims and travelers in California.

It is significant that the California wine industry makes its own divisions of the two centuries from 1769 to the present, as here summarized.

The Mission Period (1769–1834) saw the establishment of the first vineyards at most of the twenty-one missions along El Camino Real from San Diego to Sonoma, the present Coast Highway 101. Established at sites one day's walking journey apart, with orchards, grain fields, and livestock (including riding horses), they became way-stops for California's first tourists. The arrival of the Russians at Fort Ross in 1812 determined the location of the last of the mission/forts at Sonoma under the command of General Mariano Vallejo as a barrier to any further inroads by the intruders. The garrison still stands, as does Vallejo's house, whose vineyards were admired by Count Haraszthy. John Chapman, the first American vineyardist in California, planted a vineyard of 4,000 Mission grapevines in Los Angeles in 1824. But the breakthrough to imported

Padre Junípero Serra in a contemporaneous portrait

Vitis vinifera came with Jean Louis Vignes, whose El Aliso Vineyard, on the site of Los Angeles's Union Station, was established in 1834, the year in which the secularization of the missions took place.

The Pioneer Period (1835–1861) fulfilled the rich promise of the Los Angeles area for vinifera wines which would exceed in quality the wines already being produced in large quantities by Mission San Gabriel and Mission San Fernando. The discovery of gold at Sutter's Mill in 1848 and the ensuing gold rush brought the forty-niners; many of them came from France, Italy, and Germany and found more enduring riches in vineyards and winemaking than in the goldfields. In 1858, bearing vineyards in Los Angeles were selling for $1,000 an acre. Poor harvests in 1859 and 1860 brought on the inevitable bust after the boom. It was at this time that Count Agoston Haraszthy, sensing the potential for California to become the leading wine region of the world, applied to the governor for sponsorship of his voyage to European wine countries. Étienne Thée arrived in the San Jose area in 1852, beginning the Almadén/Paul Masson saga, and Pierre Pellier arrived in the same area in 1854 and started the Mirassou Vineyards.

The Founders' Period (1861–1919) saw the establishment of Buena Vista in Sonoma by Count Haraszthy. A succession of winemakers—including Gustav Niebaum of Inglenook, Jacob Schram, Charles Krug,

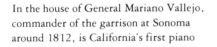

In the house of General Mariano Vallejo, commander of the garrison at Sonoma around 1812, is California's first piano

Carl Wente, James Concannon, Joseph Korbel, and Georges de Latour of Beaulieu—put down their first vines. Each of these men established a dynasty as well as a fine *Vitis vinifera* vineyard, and enjoyed growing acceptance for their wines not only in America but in the wine markets of the world. The disaster of Prohibition allowed only a small handful of wineries making wine for medicinal and sacramental purposes to continue to function. Thousands of acres of low-yield noble vinifera were uprooted or regrafted to heavy-yielding juice grapes for shipping to Eastern communities where home winemaking was being carried on. And many vineyards were turned into pastureland. For thirteen years the California wine industry was virtually nonexistent.

The Post-Repeal Period (1932–1945) found an eager and enthusiastic, if inexperienced, generation of Americans ready to buy California wines. Stocks of aged, well-made wines were tragically small; the fine vineyards had been destroyed during Prohibition. Through the assistance of the well-organized viticulture and enology classes at UC–Davis, the evolution of quality wines began its long progression from the vineyard to the cellar. Newly planted vines require three years before a commercial crop can be obtained. From this "third leaf" onward, tonnage increases. But experienced European vintners have always held that the measure of a vine's true quality cannot be determined until the tenth year, and, to its sorrow, California found this to be true. Its immature wines were at first rejected by many emerging "experts," who could, with safety, evaluate the established clarets and Burgundies of France to build their reputations.

The Prestige Period (1946–1965) brought a new generation of graduate viticulturists and enologists onto the scene in the California dynasties, and more understanding of winemaking skills into the industry itself; the technological advances that resulted from scientific breakthroughs during World War II were applied to the fields and laboratories of California wineries.

After World War II, microbiology was applied to winemaking, and the millipore filter, capable of screening out a single yeast cell, seemed an indispensable answer to wine stability. It was not until 1962 that the best California wines were recognized as the equals of their fine French counterparts. Brilliant wines were everywhere. Consumer enthusiasm grew. There was talk about the "golden age of wines" in California. Another boom was beginning.

The Corporate Investment Period (1965–1974) saw the expansion of wineries as they moved from the traditions of yesterday into the technology of today, subjecting the juice of the grape to impeccable scientific methods —a development that ran into millions of dollars of capital investment. With every journal in the land reporting the consumer boom in wine buying, and diversification being touted as the key to success for large

Charles LeFranc, partner and son-in-law of Etienne Thée, was one of the founders of Almadén

The original cellars of Agoston Haraszthy at Buena Vista, tunneled out of the rock by Chinese laborers in 1857 and still in use

TASTING ROOM

Established 1832

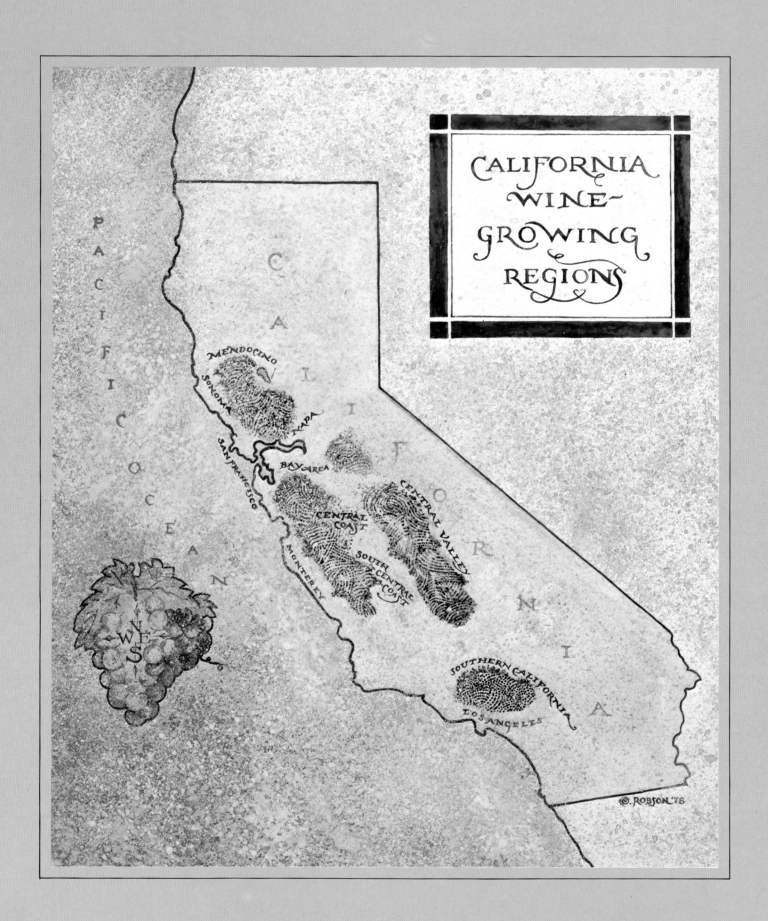

corporations, wineries one after another were acquired by giant companies, many of which had had no experience in the wine business.

Both tax shelters and get-rich-quick schemes lured land investors to new vineyard areas such as Monterey County, and farther south to Santa Maria and Santa Barbara. The golden wand of Nestlé of Switzerland transformed Beringer in the Napa Valley with a $6-million-dollar investment, dwarfing the earlier purchase of Inglenook by Petri. In turn, Petri was swallowed up by United Vintners, which bought 82 percent of its stock, as well as all of Beaulieu Vineyard. Coca-Cola Bottling of New York bought Franzia; Pepsi-Cola moved into wines with Monsieur Henri imports. Southdown of Texas acquired heavily in San Martin; Pillsbury invested in both Napa and Sonoma with its acquisition of Souverain, which was sold to North Coast Cellars in 1976. Rainier Brewery of the Pacific Northwest invested in Robert Mondavi when he split off from the family enterprise of Charles Krug Winery. In 1943 Seagram had acquired Paul Masson, and in 1967 National Distillers acquired Almadén. Schlitz embarked upon a multi-million-dollar enterprise in Sonoma County called Geyser Peak. Beatrice Foods of Chicago, a two-billion-dollar corporation, acquired the Brookside Vineyard Company. And even the illustrious Moët-Hennessey of France bought 600 acres in Napa and Sonoma to produce sparkling wine in large commercial quantities. This is but a partial listing of acquisitions and investments made during the hectic nine-year period that altered the character of the California wine industry. Telephones rang in every winery with offers to purchase at inflated prices that few could resist. But nothing lasts forever. With inflated values, a crisis was in the air.

Financial Adjustment and the Post-Boom Crisis (1974–1976) followed as the recession of the seventies loomed. A wine scandal in Bordeaux, which should have created immediate and large benefits for the California wine trade, helped a little, but two years of abundant harvests and tightened spending by the American consumer slowed the industry's growth. Speculators lured by the high prices paid for grapes—as high as $1,000 per ton for Chardonnay in 1973—faced a declining market, and by 1975 some grapes were left unpicked, with no offers. An anticipated glut of wine from large '73 and '74 harvests, and the depressed grape market of '75 threatened the outlook for 1976. Nevertheless, consumer purchases of wines increased 10 percent beyond previous record highs. The 1976 drought, which affected the vineyards of Europe and California, substantially reduced the quantity, and in some instances the quality, of the vintage. Many speculators were wiped out in marginal vineyard operations. Some untended vineyards were overgrown with weeds, others were uprooted and converted to orchards or row crops. But the market was stabilized, and the price for premium grapes returned to comfortable levels. A rapid increase in consumer consumption of white wines affected everyone in the industry, and once more the happy signal of demand brought smiles to the faces of growers and vintners.

Competition with the rising volume of imported wines (1976–1984) in a time of growing recession created a new crisis for California wines that became more pronounced as the nation began to recover its economic health. Wine imports that had accounted for a mere 5 percent of the American market in the 1950s, by 1984 had increased to 25 percent.

The competition from abroad did not deter newcomers to the field, however, and by the 1980s the number of California bonded wineries had climbed beyond five hundred. From 26,000,000 gallons of wine produced in 1934, the tide of California wines swelled to more than 375,000,000 gallons in 1983; hundreds of new labels from new wineries appeared on supermarket and wineshop shelves.

The "white wine switch" spread across the land as more and more winelovers replaced the cocktail or highball with a glass of white wine— often a California bottling. Hundreds of acres of red-wine varieties were T-budded over to popular white-wine grapes such as Chardonnay and Sauvignon Blanc.

The proliferation of general wine knowledge through a growing number of wine societies, newspaper and magazine articles, books, and even university courses in wine appreciation, will increase the per capita annual consumption in the United States beyond the present modest 2.2 gallons annually. Consumer education remains the most promising way of raising that figure. As Brian St. Pierre noted, "If you drank one glass of wine with your dinner every day, your yearly consumption would be 17 gallons."

The wine industry is subject to moments of inspiration, visionary goals and ideals, impractical aspirations like those of the artist, but it is also subject to the demands made on the farmer for endurance, strength, and the psychological stamina to face the tests imposed by the often cruel caprice of nature. There are heroes in this history, like Padre Junípero Serra, Count Agoston Haraszthy, and, in modern times, dynamic innovators like Frank Schoonmaker, Louis M. Martini, Ambassador J. D. Zellerbach, Ernest and Julio Gallo, Georges de Latour, and Herman Wente. To these moving forces must be added the scientific leaders on whose breadth of knowledge the industry depends, the teachers Maynard Amerine and André Tchelistcheff. The shadows of all these men are long upon the California wine country. To them the wineries we shall visit in later chapters make deep obeisance.

VINEYARDS AND WINERIES: NORTH COAST COUNTIES

"Let the great world spin for ever
down the ringing grooves of change."
—Alfred, Lord Tennyson

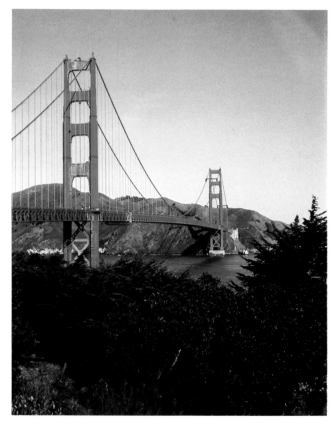

The Golden Gate Bridge crosses San Francisco Bay to the North Coast wine country

As we move into the wine country, we find yesterday, today, and tomorrow coexisting. Our inventory of wineries includes stable, entrenched establishments along with almost unknown fledgling enterprises. There can be no permanence to such a listing, nor claims to completeness. As Rodney Strong of Sonoma Vineyards said to me, "Wineries are springing up, and dying off."

Logic, as well as geography, dictates our division into these unofficial groups of counties: North Coast, Bay Area and Central Coast, South Central Coast, Central Valley and Southern California. Our odyssey begins in Sonoma County, where, by general historical agreement, the roots of the modern California wine industry were first established in 1857.

As we go from winery to winery in the California wine regions, what are the criteria of judgment? My answer always remains the same, and it bears repeating,

like a theme song. The focus must be upon the three basic elements: the soil, the vine, and the winemaker's skill.

In each wine-growing region there are different pockets of soil, and within one block of the same vines the berries will differ. Add to this that each winemaker picks at a different time, makes his wine in changing ways, for changing goals. The explanation of why and how wines differ cannot be further simplified. Change is the only constant.

SONOMA AND MENDOCINO COUNTIES

Once across the Golden Gate Bridge and heading north to the wine country, we encounter the coastal mountain barriers that hold back the cool—even cold—ocean cloud banks, and they seem almost inhospitable; the native shrubs and trees are wind-pruned, and angled landward from the constant onslaught of the Pacific wind currents. This is Marin County, a cold area, which in pre-Prohibition days had extensive vineyard acreage. On one steep, protected slope there are 11 acres of Cabernet Sauvignon—the pride of the Cuvaison winery of the Napa Valley—but otherwise,

Wines aging in European-oak barrels at Cuvaison

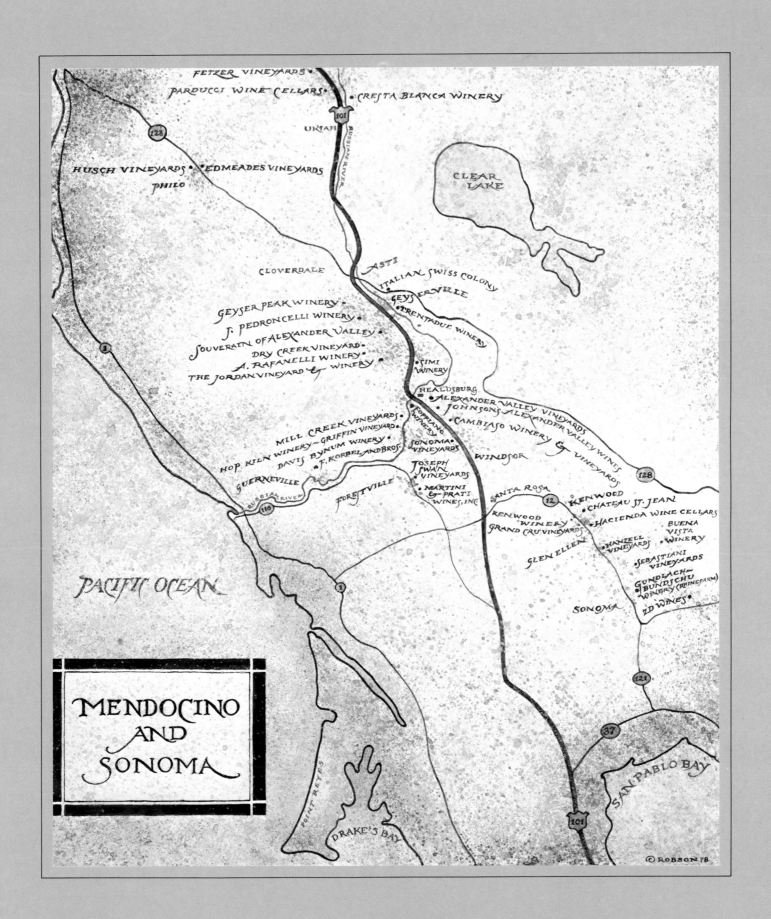

as a result of today's realization of the importance of the microclimate environment, few vines remain. Hence "Marin County" as an appellation has no real significance, and the area functions (at least insofar as wine interest goes) chiefly as a border to the broad region of Sonoma and the westward approach to Napa.

As a wine district, Sonoma County includes both the Sonoma Valley—called Valley of the Moon by the Indians and made famous by Jack London—and the winding course of the Russian River Valley. Two-thirds of California's red wines were once produced in this region, where there are areas (the Sonoma Valley) that have a climate comparable to Burgundy's and (along the Russian River) as cool as the Rhineland's. But there are also inland valleys with the same temperate climate as Bordeaux. These include the new appellation of the Alexander Valley, once pastureland and prune trees, today boasting some of the state's finest varietal vineyards. In the foothills of the Maya-camas Range, the tree-clad mountains that separate Sonoma and Napa, new vineyards with limestone, shale, and granitic rock beneath them are indicative of the renaissance of this once first-ranking wine region.

Mendocino, to the north, is having its merits appreciated with the establishment of wineries proud to place this appellation on their labels. The land is rolling and warm, favorable for fine red wines, but there is also a considerable richness to the white wines of this incomparably Californian redwood country.

ALEXANDER VALLEY VINEYARDS

8644 Highway 128, Healdsburg, California 95448

In 1842, Cyrus Alexander came to this fertile valley with two leagues of land to call his own for cattle grazing. The first vineyards in this new Alexander Valley appellation were planted by Russ Green in the 1960s at his home on Hoot Owl Creek, a branch of the Russian River. In 1963, Green persuaded his Signal Oil Company associate, Harry H. Wetzel, Jr., to acquire the Alexander homesite, and those acres were planted to vines the following year. In 1970, Green purchased the Simi Winery, contracting for the grapes until 1974.

These were the years young Harry H. (Hank) Wetzel III was attending UC–Davis and helping out during the vintages at Stony Hill and Freemark Abbey while the Wetzel winery was being completed; the first Alexander Valley Vineyards wines date from 1975. Winemaker Hank Wetzel and his father have reason to be proud. This is one of California's most beautiful properties, with a succession of wonderful wines from every vintage; the homesite is elegantly restored, as befits a fine wine estate.

SAMPLER SELECTION

Chardonnay (Alexander Valley). Estate-bottled vintage wine, with hints of ripe pears; a touch of oak in the nose. Always outstanding.

Gewürztraminer (Alexander Valley). A lovely floral bouquet. Beyond the spicy zing of this exotic varietal there is a lovely floral bouquet. A slight edge of sweetness.

Cabernet Sauvignon (Alexander Valley). Deep, dark, aristocratic wine, touched with Merlot. Each vintage is one to lay away with pride.

BUENA VISTA WINERY

27000 Ramal Road, Carneros District, Sonoma, California 95476

References to Count Agoston Haraszthy must abound in any account of the wineries and winemakers of California because this remarkable man played an important part in the formative years of the California wine industry. Some may question the authenticity of his title, but his right to the sobriquet "the father of California viticulture" is indisputable. Haraszthy planted grapevines wherever he lived in America—in Wisconsin, in San Diego, in San Francisco near Mission Dolores. But it was not until 1857, when he bought 560 acres northeast of the old Spanish garrison town of Sonoma, called it Buena Vista, and planted vinifera vines there that his influence on California wines began.

As early as 1859, anticipating a shortage of oak casks, which had to be brought from Europe on long sea voyages, he had some small casks constructed of redwood, filled them with wine, at the same time filling similar oak casks with the same wine, and set both

Built by Cyrus Alexander when he owned the valley that bears his name, the one-room schoolhouse now stands among young vineyards

redwood and oak casks aside to watch developments. It was the beginning of redwood cooperage for aging a large volume of young red wines—which still endures significantly in California.

At the Sonoma County Fair of 1860, Haraszthy anticipated the establishment of the state viticultural college of the University of California by twenty years: "How differently we should be situated," he declared, regretting the paucity of general winemaking knowledge, "if we had an Agricultural School, where a vineyard would be planted and cultivated, and wine made by competent professors. Our youths would there be taught the business in all its branches, and the older farmers, during their seasons of leisure, would learn all the various manipulations at a trifling cost."

The following year Haraszthy went on his historic mission to Europe, from which he brought back the priceless collection of vine cuttings that were to have so great an effect on California winemaking.

The lavish years at Buena Vista, with its Pompeian villa, its formal gardens, its wine cellars tunneled into the sandstone hill by Chinese coolies, were not many. By 1868 heavy taxes—and a costly fire—had led to financial troubles. Haraszthy went to Nicaragua, where, after only a year, he perished. In his fifty-seven years his accomplishments were noteworthy and of lasting significance.

Buena Vista continued its long decline—the vineyards were decimated by phylloxera, the winery cellar collapsed in the 1906 earthquake, the estate was sold and allowed to fall into decay. But the legend of Haraszthy's Buena Vista was to have an exciting revival after World War II. Frank Bartholomew, executive vice-president of the United Press, had bought the property in 1941. By 1949 he and his wife, Antonia, were happily settled in a comfortable country house on the property. In the fields, gnarled survivors of Haraszthy's Zinfandel vines still bore grapes. The collapsed cellars had been reopened and crushing equipment installed. Ambitions and hopes were directed at goals of which Haraszthy himself might have dreamed.

In 1951 the winemaker was Al Brett, with André Tchelistcheff as consultant. From the young Cabernet vines Tchelistcheff suggested making a rosé. It proved to be memorable. Buena Vista "Rosebrook" is but a memory, but it spawned a host of Cabernet Sauvignon rosé wines in California.

In 1968 The Bartholomews sold the winery to Young's Market Company of Los Angeles, retaining the Buena Vista Vineyards and their home on this pioneer ranch. The winery had to look beyond the ranch for grapes, and in 1971 acquired 600 acres of pastureland in the cool region of Carneros. Managing director Philip Gaspar appointed René Lacasia, a superbly trained enologist and viticulturist with extensive experience in South American winelands, to plant the new acreage. In 1974, as the project flourished, an additional 150 acres were purchased. While the coolness dictated the planting of Chardonnay and Pinot Noir, the rolling land offered several microclimates, one warm enough for Cabernet Sauvignon. Some old hands thought this a mistake, but that was their mistake. Burgundians would never plant the Cabernet, nor Bordelais the noble Pinot in their regions, but in this California vineyard both are producing prize-winning wines. The Buena Vista 1979 Special Selection Cabernet Sauvignon has won more prizes than any California Cabernet in the history of wine competitions.

Antonia and Frank Bartholomew take their ease at Buena Vista

Wine and roses—Buena Vista's Gewürztraminer and Zinfandel

On October 1, 1979, Buena Vista Winery was purchased by the A. Racke company of West Germany. The ultra-modern winemaking facility on Ramal Road in Carneros is headed by young Marcus Moller-Racke. Born and raised in the Rheingau, he is no stranger to the arts of grape growing and winemaking and makes no bones about his love for his new California home. André Tchelistcheff continues as the winery consultant, and the winemaker is a young Davis graduate, Jill Davis, enthralled with this important challenge, which she has already met with high style and elegance.

SAMPLER SELECTION

Gewürztraminer (Sonoma). Intensely fragrant, edged with sweetness. Seductive grace.

Green Hungarian (Sonoma). While it recalls the origins of founder Haraszthy, the name is more exciting than the wine, which is rather neutral in taste.

Cabernet Sauvignon (Sonoma Valley–Carneros). One of California's most prized clarets. A rich, deep, velvet-smooth, estate-grown wine.

Pinot Noir (Sonoma Valley–Carneros). Translucent wine of regal character and rich, lingering aftertaste.

DAVIS BYNUM WINERY

8075 Westside Road, Healdsburg, California 95448

Journalist Davis Bynum unquestionably got into winemaking through family influence: his father, Lindley Bynum, UCLA historian for the famed Bancroft Library, was among the pioneer wine judges of the Los Angeles County Fair. Davis started making wine in the East Bay suburb of Albany. He bought grapes, sold home winemaking equipment, and made such good Cabernet in his converted store that connoisseurs pushed him into serious winemaking. A facetious label—"Barefoot Bynum's Burgundy"—for his more ordinary, yet good-value, table wine spread his fame, but today, with the Albany tasting room serving merely as a salesroom, with a full-scale winery in the Russian River area eight miles downriver from Healdsburg, "we're out of the Barefoot business," he told me. The 14,000-square-foot winery of 85,000-gallon capacity, acquired in 1973, on the way to 25,000-case annual sale goals, is concentrating on Pinot Noir and Chardonnay. Son Hampton Bynum, with some UC–Davis training, is winemaker, and under the new Davis Bynum label a limited number of choice varietals are giving new stature to the name.

SAMPLER SELECTION

Pinot Chardonnay (Sonoma). From adjacent vineyards of Joseph Rochioli, Jr., and Howard Allen on the Russian River. Vintage.

Fumé Blanc (Sonoma). Russian River Sauvignon Blanc grapes give this very dry, brilliant, pale gold wine its luster and taste.

Davis Bynum, journalist-turned-winemaker

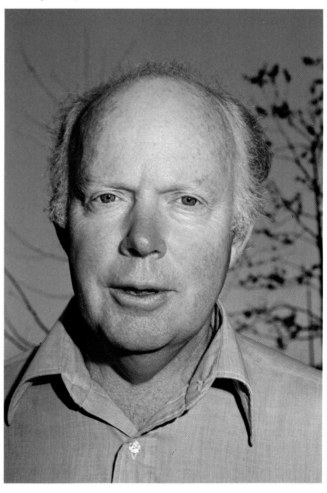

Chateau St. Jean's elegant mansion at the foot of the Sugar Loaf Ridge

Pinot Noir (Sonoma). A translucent ruby wine of aristocratic and noble bouquet, which, with added age, will have true finesse.

Camelot Mead. A Bynum honey-wine specialty, deservedly popular, with a gentle sweetness of 3 percent.

CAMBIASO WINERY & VINEYARDS

1141 Grant Avenue, Healdsburg, California 95448

Shortly after the repeal of Prohibition, in 1934, Giovanni Cambiaso, who had learned winemaking in his native Italy, established this small winery with his wife, their son, and two daughters. Though the winery, which produced generic and varietal wines for bulk sale for many years, has now been sold to non-resident conglomerate financiers, The Four Seas Investment Company, Cambiaso remains a family affair. Son Joseph makes the wine, and his sister Rita is general manager. These are sturdy regional wines, patiently attended in stainless steel until they are ready for bottling from the veteran redwood aging tanks.

SAMPLER SELECTION

Cabernet Sauvignon (Sonoma County). A pleasant claret-style wine of nonirrigated hillside grapes of modest value.

Petite Sirah (Sonoma County). A full-bodied wine from long-established vines.

CHATEAU ST. JEAN

8555 Sonoma Highway, Kenwood, California 95452

It was Lord Byron who said, "Glory, the grape, love, gold...in these are sunk the hopes of all men of every nation." In winemaking today, when one stainless-steel fermenter costs more than a tract home, a centrifuge more than a Rolls-Royce, the gold must come before the grape, with wisdom a close third. For Robert and Edward Merzoian and their brother-in-law, Ken Sheffield, their hopes have come together in the Valley of the Moon. They bought an elegant mansion surrounded by 255 acres of virgin land for vines. Named for Edward's wife, Chateau St. Jean is pronounced in the American way. Of the 255 acres, 105 are given over to Chardonnay, Johannisberg Riesling, Sauvignon Blanc, Pinot Blanc, and Pinot Noir. On the remaining 150 acres a complex of separate buildings encloses the winemaking, aging, and bottling facilities.

From the beginning, winemaker Richard Arrowood held with uncompromising courage to his belief that separate vineyards would produce wines of the most distinctive character. Nearly all Chateau St. Jean wines carry vineyard designations. The "Robert Young Vineyard" Chardonnay and late harvest Riesling wines from individual clusters of botrytised grapes have brought the winery medals and national fame.

In the autumn of 1983 two private Pullman cars, handsomely restored by the Merzoians and another railroad buff, Allan Hemphill, crisscrossed the country for the introductory tour of Chateau St. Jean deluxe *méthode champenoise* sparkling wines. From city to city the "Sonoma Valley" and "Golden Mission" carried a selection of vintage Brut and vintage Blanc de Blancs. Both wines were made with a luxurious three years on the yeasts in order to achieve classic proportions of bouquet and taste. Pete Downs heads the sparkling winemaking in a separate new winery.

Chateau St. Jean is synonymous with elegant white wines, whether dry or sweet, still or sparkling.

SAMPLER SELECTION

Chardonnay (Robert Young Vineyards). Rich in varietal character, oak-scented. "Belle Terre" is also fine.

Fumé Blanc (Robert Young Vineyards). Rich, dry Sauvignon Blanc, almost like Chardonnay in its buttery softness.

Gewürztraminer (Frank Johnson Vineyards). Abundantly fruity, yet dry enough to accompany food, with .73 percent residual sugar. Also some late-harvest bottlings.

Brut & Blanc de Blancs (Sonoma County). Sparklers of classic Chardonnay and Pinot Noir grapes, three years on the yeasts. Limited production.

CRESTA BLANCA WINERY

Ukiah, Mendocino County, California 95482

If it is confusing to find San Francisco as the

address of the winery on the label, a quick spin through the history of this well-known winery will answer the question of where the wine is made and why the label also reads "Since 1889."

The original winery was established by Charles Wetmore at Livermore in Alameda County in 1882. The vineyard was set out with cuttings from Château d'Yquem and Château Margaux, and wines from those grapes were the first California wines to be honored with a Grand Prix at the Paris Exposition of 1889. The name Cresta Blanca was derived from the sheared-off chalky cliff into which the aging tunnels of the Livermore winery were dug.

In 1940, Cresta Blanca was bought by Schenley, Inc., and in 1971 Guild Wineries acquired it with Roma Wine Co. There are generations who can remember the radio jingle that hammered out the spelling "C-R-E-S-T-A B-L-A-N-C-A. . . . *Cresta Blanca!*" almost ad nauseam. And there are wine merchants who can remember how the brand later faded almost into oblivion. It had one moment of glory, however, before the winery was closed and the operation moved to the gigantic Roma winery in Fresno. That was in 1961, when enologist Myron Nightingale produced the first French-style sauterne ever made in America.

Guild, which is the nation's largest grower-owned cooperative, with over a thousand members in every winegrowing area of the state, had an increasing inventory of remarkably fine wines produced at their Mendocino winery in Ukiah. The decision was made to set up a separate marketing and production division for Cresta Blanca with executive offices in San Francisco, and that is the address on the label.

SAMPLER SELECTION

Gewürztraminer (North Coast). A happy discovery as an aperitif wine; fragrant, light, thirst-quenching.

French Colombard (North Coast). Delightful luncheon wine. Crisp and clean, but not bitingly dry. Flowery nose.

Triple Cream Sherry. Honored with gold-medal acclaim for its rich depth and luxurious satin-smoothness.

Zinfandel (North Coast). Beyond the grape, there is a souvenir of pine and cedar forests in its fascinating bouquet.

DRY CREEK VINEYARD

3700 Lambert Bridge Road, Healdsburg, California 95448

David Stare and his burgeoning winery are further evidence that with youth, intelligence, and single-focus drive you *can* make it from scratch as a grape grower and winemaker. It's not easy, nor in any sense a get-rich-quick process. But all is in order today for this Harvard graduate, who got fed up with a civil-engineering career in West Germany, chucked it, and headed California way to become a winemaker.

With missionary zeal, young Stare obtained and promoted an appellation of origin for his vineyard area—Dry Creek Valley. If it's on the freeway signs, why not on a wine label? His first wine to come to market was a 1973 Dry Chenin Blanc which showed immediately that there was nothing imitative or compromising in his approach. It was bone-dry, crisp, clean, and fragrant, but very different from everyone else's Chenin Blanc, tending toward gentleness and grace. There is the same rugged individuality about Stare's Zinfandel of 1973, the first heavy red wine released.

SAMPLER SELECTION

Fumé Blanc (Sonoma County). Vintage wine of Sauvignon Blanc bouquet; deep, richly complex dry wine of high style.

Dry Chenin Blanc (Sonoma County). An unusual and refreshing wine eminently suited to service with shellfish, poultry.

Zinfandel (Sonoma County). A big wine that collectors can age with assurance; it will round out in balanced mellowness.

EDMEADES VINEYARDS

5500 California State Highway 128, Philo, California 95466

Winding over the rugged, tree-clad flanks of the Coast Ranges between Boonville and Mendocino's Pacific Coast, Highway 128 follows the Navarro River to the sea. Philo is here in this remote mountain-valley region, and nearby is the 40-acre vineyard of Cabernet Sauvignon, Chardonnay, and French Colombard which are bringing recognition to Anderson Valley. The wines offer a sound argument in favor of Anderson Valley's having its own appellation of origin as a cool Region I.

Dr. Donald Edmeades planted the vineyard in 1963, when winemaking was his hobby. In 1972, Paula and Daron Edmeades took up their father's quest for good wines and bonded an old farm building to be used as a winery. The erstwhile hobby is now a small and pleasant business.

SAMPLER SELECTION

Apple Wine (Anderson Valley). Produced with great pride from Baldwin, Spitzenberg, Golden Delicious apples; aged, like Chardonnay, in French-oak casks. Intriguing and refreshing.

Gewürztraminer (Anderson Valley). The unmistakable fragrance of the varietal grape is achieved with notable success.

Cabernet Sauvignon (Anderson Valley). Vintage; small lots of this popular varietal concentrate the grape's richness.

FETZER VINEYARDS

1150 Bel Arbres Road, Redwood Valley, California 95470

"Fine winemaking is ideally a family enterprise." That was Bernard Fetzer's thought when, with his wife and eleven children, he moved to California from Oregon in 1954 to accommodate the needs of his lumber business. While Mendocino County is basically lumber country—redwoods, pine, cedar—it is also making dramatic inroads into the premium-wine business.

To house his family, Bernard Fetzer bought a ranch in Redwood Valley, two hours north of the Golden Gate Bridge and two minutes north of Ukiah.

After some careful research, Fetzer decided to plant his 150 acres of vineyard land with Bordeaux varieties—Cabernet Sauvignon, Sémillon, and Sauvignon Blanc. But as the third-leaf commercial crop came on in the early sixties, even though famed major wineries bought Mendocino County grapes, "they kept it a secret, beggaring the price below Napa levels" according to Bernard Fetzer. So he sold his grapes to amateur winemakers all across the country, most of them doctors. Many won local prizes for their wines made from the Fetzer grapes and began singing his praises. It was enough to inspire him to think about building his own winery.

And so a small cluster of buildings grew, housing winemaking equipment of stainless steel geared to the vineyard's less than heroically proportioned needs. Tiers of French, Yugoslavian, and American oak in casks and barrels neatly accommodate 100,000 gallons of aging wines. John Fetzer, in his twenties, moved into the role of winemaster, with James to help and with Richard and Robert assisting as and where needed.

Long vatting on the skins of Fetzer's red wines makes further aging in bottles necessary, but just taste a Fetzer Zinfandel or Cabernet Sauvignon, Petite Sirah

The late Bernard Fetzer measuring the sugar level of his wine with a saccharometer

Bouchonnier.

41

or Carignane, and you will understand why he is a firm believer in the procedure. These are big wines, possibly requiring decanting at least an hour before serving.

SAMPLER SELECTION

Zinfandel (Ricetti Vineyard). A big, big wine that is soft and round, with the bouquet and spice of the Mendocino region.

Cabernet Sauvignon (Estate Bottled). Pure, 100 percent Cabernet Sauvignon, always vintage, deep, complex.

Carmine Carignane. From grapes high in the benchlands of the area, an uncommonly big wine from a rather common grape.

FOPPIANO WINERY

12707 Old Redwood Highway, Healdsburg, California 95448

John Foppiano arrived in the Russian River Valley from Italy in 1864. The original lure had been the goldfields, but the most lasting reward, for him, came from grapes and wine. In 1910 his eldest son, Louis, took over the winery. In those days the Foppianos sent wagonloads of cask wine to San Francisco wine merchants for customers who had their own jugs refilled. The third and fourth generations of the family are now operating this 200-acre winery. In addition to selling bulk wines to other wineries, they present a wide range of varietal wines from the Cabernet Sauvignon, Pinot Noir, Petite Sirah, Chardonnay, Sauvignon Blanc, Gamay Beaujolais, and Zinfandel vines now in bearing, an advance beyond the generic Burgundy and sauterne of yesterday.

GEYSER PEAK WINERY

22280 Geyserville Avenue, Geyserville, California 95441

Geyserville was one of the early California boomtowns developed by the gold seekers, many of whom were also attracted to this area because of the hot min-

eral baths fed by geysers, famed for their health-giving properties from the time of the Indians. August Quitzow established the first winery in this area in 1880, in the belief that the volcanic soil was ideally suited for growing wine grapes.

The history of the winery since those founding days includes a succession of changes, right up to 1984. In the wine boom days of the 1970s the winery was bought by the Jos. Schlitz Brewing Company of Milwaukee. Under this ownership, Geyser Peak's popular Summit Chablis "wine in a box" became a market leader. With the introduction of premium wines under the Geyser Peak label, the winery became the country's sixth-largest in national distribution, following Almadén, Taylor, Paul Masson, Inglenook, and Sebastiani.

In November 1982, Geyser Peak began its most decisive development when it was purchased by Henry Trione of Santa Rosa. A self-made multimillionaire, Trione has an unquenchable fervor for Sonoma County. A first-generation American of Italian descent, he gave up his job with a large winery when a promotion would have moved him and his young family to the East Coast. Choosing to remain in California, he entered the world of real estate finance in Sonoma County. This was the beginning of the Trione fortune. He became president of Wells Fargo Mortgage Company and a director of the Wells Fargo bank. Henry's sons Victor and Mark are co-owners of the winery. Vic, a Stanford graduate holds an MBA from UC–Berkeley. Mark, who holds a degree in agricultural economics from UC–Davis, is in charge of the 1,000 acres of vineyard. All three Triones are avid polo players.

When John McClelland, president of Almadén during its largest growth years, became its chief executive officer, Geyser Peak was primed to move dramatically toward its 300,000-case goal. A super-premium Trione label has been introduced, augmenting the Geyser Peak label. Winemaster Armand Bussone continues the high-quality direction of the winery. Delightful picnic grounds, free open-air concerts on summer Sunday afternoons, and public hiking paths maintained by the winery along the banks of the Russian River will keep the new Geyser Peak enviably in the forefront of prestige wineries.

Le Bouchonnier (The Corkmaker). Engraving by Robert Benard from Denis Diderot's *Great Encyclopedia*, Paris, 1762. (The Christian Brothers Collection)

Chardonnay (Alexander Valley). Under the Trione label, this buttery-rich wine, edged with oak, reflects its estate-grown origins.

Winterchill (California). A Summit "wine-in-a-box" blended of Chenin Blanc and Colombard for popular acceptance. Convenient for picnics and sports events. Modest price, fine quality.

Blanc de Noirs (Carneros). A Trione label *méthode champenoise* sparkler, 100 percent Pinot Noir, prestige sparkling wine.

GRAND CRU VINEYARDS

No. 1 Vintage Lane, Glen Ellen, California 95442

Grand cru, literally "great growth," is a Burgundian wine classification designating the best vineyard of each parish. It implies the potential of the property to produce great wine, and in the case of this small winery the name is appropriate.

A vineyard and winery were first established in 1896 on these 37 acres in the Valley of the Moon, near the historic Wolf House of Jack London. Closed down during Prohibition, Grand Cru was reactivated in the 1950s as a producer of bulk wines, but its prestigious career began in 1970, when co-founder and winemaker Robert Magnani, with a small group of enthusiastic winelovers, acquired the landmark property. Old vats were remodeled into neat aging vaults, and shining stainless-steel fermenters introduced twentieth-century technology to the old winery.

In 1981 Bettina and Walter Dreyer became sole owners of Grand Cru Vineyards, doubling its production to 50,000 cases annually, while still following winemaker Magnani's quest for distinctive style with Gewürztraminer and Chenin Blanc. Grand Cru Zinfandel from the almost century-old vines, of minimal yield, has brought the winery medals with every showing, but as new vines are planted, that Zinfandel will make only a token showing.

The difficulty with Gewürztraminer, as its champions know, is in the moment of harvest. As the berries take on their pinkish color, and the sugar content rises, they have a peak moment of perfect balance. Alsatians declare the winemaker must sleep in the vineyard to catch this instant of balanced ripeness. The reward for well-timed picking is an exotic wine with spicy nutmeg, litchi-nut zing and supporting acidity. Picked too late, the grape loses acidity and acquires bitterness. Magnani has a record of getting his Alexander Valley Gewürztraminer grapes in precisely at their peak. In fermentation, he follows the German style of leaving a slight amount of residual sugar.

Equally dedicated is the care given to Chenin Blanc and Sauvignon Blanc, both wines made with emphasis on fruitiness.

Gewürztraminer (Alexander Valley). Award-winning wine of extraordinary varietal depth and charm; sweet-edged. Always outstanding.

Dry Chenin Blanc (Clarksburg, California). Rich with hints of honeydew melon taste and aroma; splendid acid balance. A charming luncheon wine.

Cabernet Sauvignon (Alexander Valley). In the "Collector Series" a dark ruby wine of black-currant/ oak aromas. Rich, elegant.

GUNDLACH-BUNDSCHU WINERY (RHINEFARM)

2000 Denmark Street, Vineberg, California 95487

Gundlach, Bundschu, and Dresel are among the pioneer names of winemaking and wine selling in nineteenth-century California. Karl Bundschu was general manager of Inglenook forty years ago. Emil Dresel, a great friend of Agoston Haraszthy, is said to have helped the Count plant the greater portion of the famed Zinfandel and other vines at Buena Vista. He was also one of the original partners in the Gundlach-Bundschu Rhinefarm, a recently replanted 300-acre ranch in Sonoma, now managed by direct descendant James Bundschu, president of the winery. Lance Cutler is winemaker at Rhinefarm. The revered old trade name returns to the marketplace, offering wines made from grapes grown on the original land, gathering medals at every competition.

The Rhinefarm is unique in having two acres of a rather celebrated and rare clone of Johannisberg Riesling called Kleinberger. Another exclusive proprietary wine, in addition to the Kleinberger Riesling, is a slightly sweet Sylvaner christened Dresel Sonoma Riesling, honoring the pioneer vintner Emil Dresel. Vintage Zinfandel and Cabernet Sauvignon complete the roster of one of the newer Sonoma wineries.

SAMPLER SELECTION

Kleinberger (Sonoma County). The Rhinefarm's own clonal berry of Riesling makes an always pleasing, fruity wine.

Johannisberg Riesling (Sonoma County). "Late Harvest" editions carry a golden-rich sweetness, intense bouquet.

HACIENDA WINE CELLARS

1000 Vineyard Lane, Sonoma, California 95476

Midway between the entry gates and the handsome winery, a vine-clad wooden gateway displays a marker that proclaims: HERE IS WHERE IT ALL BEGAN. The vista opens onto the "Clos de Agoston" block of Chardonnay vines, the site where, in 1862, Count Agoston Haraszthy founded the Buena Vista Winery, destined to become the paternal estate of the modern California wine industry.

After Frank Bartholomew sold the Buena Vista Winery, in 1968, retaining only the vineyard ranch, the temptation to make wine from his grapes led him to convert a two-story former state convalescent home on the property into a winery. He named it Hacienda Wine Cellars, and with his talented wife, Antonia, set about giving the tile-roofed, rather plain building some colonial character. Old wooden beams from an ancient bridge, used brick, and wrought-iron gates plus— naturally—up-to-the-minute crushers, fermenters, and French-oak casks, brought the winery to handsome completion.

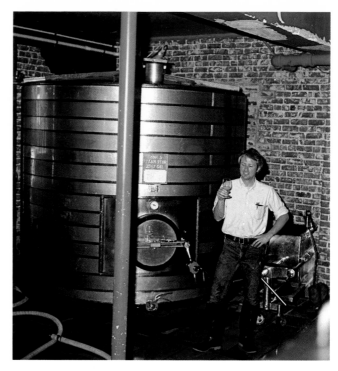

Steve MacRostie of Hacienda sampling the contents of a 2,387-gallon tank

A. Crawford Cooley joined the enterprise in 1977 and is its principal stockholder and president. UC–Davis graduate Steve MacRostie is Hacienda's skilled winemaker.

Gold medals have come to the winery for every one of their varietals. Vinestock for the translucent Pinot Noir is traced to Romanee-Conti vines.

SAMPLER SELECTION

"Claire de Lune" Chardonnay (Sonoma Valley). One of California's most elegant Chardonnays, estate-grown, aged in French oak.

Gewürztraminer (Sonoma County). Grapes come from the Sonoma and Alexander valleys, ripe-harvested for maximum richness of aroma and taste.

Pinot Noir (Sonoma Valley). Always a wine with which to prove the fine potential of the Burgundian grape in select California soil.

HANZELL VINEYARDS

18596 Lomita Avenue, Sonoma, California 95476

The late Ambassador James D. Zellerbach, founder of the paper company bearing his name, had a connoisseur's appreciation of fine Burgundies, nourished no doubt during the years between 1948 and 1950 when he served as chief administrator for the Marshall Plan in Europe. In 1947 he acquired a rolling 200-acre expanse of foothill land in the Valley of the Moon. The first Pinot Noir and Chardonnay vines were planted in 1948, but spill-water erosion indicated that they were improperly located. In 1953 the vineyard—11 acres of Pinot Noir, 5 of Chardonnay—was completely replanted in semicircular terraces, banked below the site for the winery building. If California counterparts of the ruby Romanée-Conti and golden Montrachet, the Ambassador's favorite wines, were to be produced here from the ground up, nothing short of perfection would do.

The winery project was undertaken with equally high goals, and no expense was spared. Bradford Webb, a California-trained biochemist, was employed to design the functional facilities. These were fitted into a building that externally resembled the Château Clos de Vougeot, but any similarity to a Burgundian installation ended there. Stainless-steel fermenters were designed and built to accommodate the imported crusher's capacity. In the 1950s, stainless steel was priced for custom use, and it cost nearly as much as platinum. Temperature-controlled fermenters on calibrated levels were unknown outside the UC–Davis laboratories for winemaking. The new wine, like its Burgundian models, would age in wood from the oak forests of Limousin coopered in Nuits-Saint-Georges. Preparations for the revolutionary concept were made with little awareness of their eventual effect upon the industry.

Samples of the first 1956 Chardonnay were forwarded to Zellerbach in Rome, where he was then serving as our ambassador to Italy. You can imagine his delight when local experts thought it was a white Burgundy from the Côte d'Or! The Ambassador's million-dollar project had succeeded. It was the first

ripple of a wave that was to roll over the California wine industry during the next decade, causing more changes than the shift from wood or concrete to stainless steel as the material of fermenters. It also increased the necessary capitalization for winery equipment, including French-barrel cooperage, to six- and seven-figure sums, an amount well beyond the limits of most private fortunes.

When Zellerbach died, in 1963, orders were given to dispose of all the wine in bottle and barrel. (It was bought by Joe Heitz of the Napa Valley, who cared for it meticulously.) All winemaking ceased during '63 and '64. In 1965 the estate was bought by Mary and Douglas Day, who followed Ambassador Zellerbach's lead and planted 4 more acres of Chardonnay, making a

A stainless-steel, temperature-controlled fermenter, one of the sophisticated pieces of winemaking equipment pioneered in California total of 20 planted acres. Mr. Day died in 1969, and Mrs. Day in 1973. The early 1970s were the height of the wine boom, and in 1975 a buyer of vast means looking for a very small winery on a large country estate was found in Barbara de Brye, the major stockholder in Easton United Securities, Ltd., of Calgary, Canada.

In assessing the contribution made by Ambassador Zellerbach, we find that two factors were responsible for his revolutionary impact on the winemaking industry: the stainless-steel tanks, which made possible the maximum preservation of bouquet through cool, slow fermentation in a vessel that did not impart any taste to the wine, and the touch of French Limousin oak on a white wine. These two factors wrought the subtle difference that delights American connoisseurs of California Chardonnay and makes it competitive with Burgundian white wines for the first time.

The role of wood in the aging of both red and white wines is important. With the American rush to buy European-oak cooperage, the prices for 50-gallon barrels has more than trebled in the last five years. When you see tiers of French-oak barrels in a California winery, often more than 5,000 in one room, you are looking at an investment of half a million dollars or more, excluding the contents or inventory aging costs. The arithmetic is even more staggering when you try to estimate the costs of great batteries of stainless-steel tanks. Such multi-million-dollar installations explain why large corporations and conglomerates were needed when the Zellerbach-launched revolution overtook the small family business of winemaking.

For Hanzell Chardonnay, and all those other California Chardonnay wines which have enjoyed preeminence through the touch of French wood, it would seem that success was achieved. But, alas, wood has not wrought the victory with Hanzell Pinot Noir. It is good but not great, though, like the Chardonnay, it now costs $8 per bottle.

SAMPLER SELECTION

Chardonnay (Sonoma Valley). Vintage wine, grown and bottled at the estate. On allocation at the winery.

Pinot Noir (Sonoma Valley). A marked peppery, earthy taste gives this deep ruby wine a less than ideal personality.

HOP KILN WINERY–GRIFFIN VINEYARD

6050 Westside Road, Healdsburg, California 95448

The artistic dedication of the owners of this 65-acre vineyard and winery located beside the state-landmark hop kiln, one of the most handsome of the chimneyed buildings indigenous to the region, promises fine, interesting wines. The first crush, in 1975, carried the subsidiary label "Sweetwater Springs," commemorating one of the oldest vineyard ranches of the Russian River Valley.

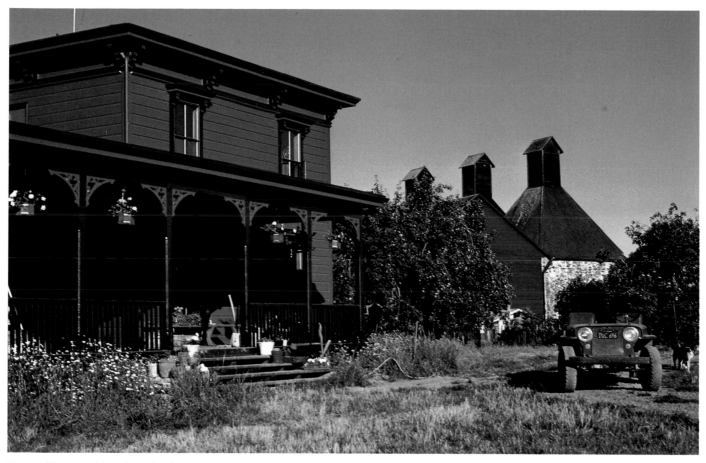

These oddly shaped buildings for drying hops (a form indigenous to Sonoma County) adjacent to Hop Kiln Winery are a state landmark

Winemaker at Hop Kiln Winery is Marty Griffin, who also serves as chairman of the Health and Social Welfare Committee of the Wine Institute of San Francisco. All wines are produced in small lots, are racked by gravity or siphon to avoid any bruising by pumping, and are unfiltered, with a view to achieving full body, complexity, and long life.

SAMPLER SELECTION

Zinfandel Primitivo. A big, dark, heavy-bodied wine with a familiar "briar" nose. Sold only at the winery.

Petite Sirah (Russian River Valley). A big, mouth-filling wine from Marty Griffin's "1880" vineyard of established vines.

HUSCH VINEYARDS

4900 Star Route, Philo, California 95466

You don't have to be a millionaire to achieve the goal of winemaking in California. Inflation was not yet as devastating as it was to become later when, in 1968, Tony and Gretchen Husch decided to abandon city life in San Francisco. They found a hillside ranch in the cool Anderson Valley, 13 miles southwest of Ukiah. There on a southerly slope they planted their first 8 acres of Chardonnay vines. As a result of loving care, the vines prospered despite the cool Region I climate. The Husches bonded a tiny winery in Philo in 1971, the first for the area. Their Chardonnay had such character that they expanded the vineyard to 25 acres and included some Pinot Noir and Gewürztraminer plantings. In 1974 they enlarged the winery to a capacity of 5,000 gallons. From their timid beginnings, with

107

only textbooks to guide them, they have now flowered into first-rate winemakers.

Husch Vineyard wines—all from grapes grown in their own vineyards—are 100 percent varietals, dry, assertive in character, and crisp with the natural acidity of the cool growing conditions.

SAMPLER SELECTION

Chardonnay (Mendocino). Vintage and estate-bottled. Expensive. Just enough French oak. Needs development time.

Pinot Noir (Mendocino). Also vintage wine, confirming the wisdom of planting this grape in this area.

Gewürztraminer (Mendocino). Vinted with a hint of sweetness, in the California style, which seems to balance the grape well. The 1983 edition was selected by President Reagan for service at the banquet tendered to his Chinese hosts during the visit of April 1984 to China.

ITALIAN SWISS COLONY

Highway 101, Asti, California 95413

The history of this commercial giant of the California wine industry began with organizational turmoil in 1881, and today the courts are wrestling with problems emanating from the company's size.

Andrea Sbarboro, a boy of thirteen, arrived in San Francisco from Italy in the middle of the last century. For twenty years he worked in his brother's grocery store, nurturing ambitious dreams in which the ownership of land would put him on the road to security and wealth. He founded five mutual loan groups, which handled receipts of $6.5 million dollars. This led to the purchase, with a group of local businessmen, of a 1,500-acre tract of pastureland. Italian and Swiss immigrants working this land contributed as little as $5 per month from their wages toward ultimate ownership. The pastureland became the vineyard still known as Asti, but the immigrants decided they would rather keep all of their wages instead of having shares in the land.

Sbarboro raised more money and by 1900 had a thriving winery operation. A 300,000-gallon stone winery built in 1887 made wines that won gold medals in competitions as far away as Genoa, Dublin, Bordeaux, and Paris. The winemaster was Pietro Rossi.

With Repeal, Rossi's twin sons, Robert and Edmund, revived Italian Swiss Colony. The present organizational troubles began after World War II, with a series of changes in ownership following the Rossis' sale of the Asti winery to National Distillers. In 1953, National sold Italian Swiss Colony to Louis Petri, who had merged his family winery with United Vintners. In 1969, Heublein acquired 82 percent of United Vintners, and also acquired prestigious Beaulieu Vineyard. The tangled skeins of Heublein's corporate holdings are made more complex by their marketing ties to Allied Growers, one of the larger cooperatives of grape growers in the Napa Valley. But more relevant to the Italian Swiss Colony empire are its enormous $16-million glass factory, bottling plant, wine and champagne cellars, and shipping facility in Madera in the San Joaquin Valley, from which emerge wines not only of the Italian Swiss Colony but of Inglenook, Lejon, Petri, Annie Green Springs—and more.

As far as the consumer is concerned, the last few years have brought some improvement to the wines under the Italian Swiss Colony label: the list of wines has been shortened and the overall image upgraded, with better generic and varietal wines. John Powers, Italian Swiss Colony's president, made an impact on the popular-price market with the release of a screwcap Cabernet Sauvignon at $1.69, which, for the price, had remarkable varietal distinction. Bob Rife, the winemaker since 1969, produced the wine largely from North Coast counties grapes, with sufficient aging to concentrate an undeniable Cabernet bouquet. Consumers accepted it as intended—for immediate consumption.

At present the Italian Swiss Colony label is in the competition among producers of volume wines which have no regional designation beyond California as an appellation of origin. But even those ordinary table wines today are an unusually good value, possessing a finish and finesse far ahead of Europe's *vins ordinaires*.

SAMPLER SELECTION

Colony French Colombard. Fresh and fruity, brilliant

Foppiano
Vineyards

RUSSIAN RIVER VALLEY
PETITE SIRAH

ALCOHOL 12% BY VOLUME
PRODUCED AND BOTTLED BY L. FOPPIANO WINE CO.
HEALDSBURG / SONOMA COUNTY / CALIFORNIA

Grand Cru' Vineyards
Brand

GARDEN CREEK RANCH
Alexander Valley

Gewürztraminer
"induced botrytis"

1975

PRODUCED & BOTTLED BY GRAND CRU VINEYARDS, INC.
GLEN ELLEN, CALIFORNIA, USA
ALCOHOL 10.0% BY VOLUME

Italian Swiss Colony.

Colony Cabernet Sauvignon is a distinctive, full bodied, dry, red wine. The robust flavor and unique character of this elegant wine go especially well with hearty meat dishes.

Cabernet Sauvignon

A California Varietal Wine

Vinted and bottled by
Italian Swiss Colony, Asti, California · Alcohol 12% by Volume

SIMI

SINCE 1876

ALEXANDER VALLEY
GEWÜRZTRAMINER
1975

Alcohol 12½% by Vol.
Produced and Bottled by SIMI Winery, Healdsburg, California., U.S.A.

KORBEL
NATURAL

CALIFORNIA

Champagne

Extremely Dry

Souverain
of Alexander Valley

PINOT NOIR
NORTH COAST

produced & bottled at the winery by Souverain, Geyserville Ca Alcohol 13% by volume

Parducci

MENDOCINO COUNTY
PINOT NOIR

PRODUCED & BOTTLED BY PARDUCCI WINE CELLARS
UKIAH, MENDOCINO COUNTY, CALIFORNIA
ALCOHOL 12% BY VOLUME

Trentadue

ESTATE   1974   BOTTLED

32

SONOMA

Merlot

PRODUCED AND BOTTLED BY
Trentadue Winery and Vineyards
GEYSERVILLE · SONOMA COUNTY · CALIF.
ALCOHOL 13.4% BY VOLUME

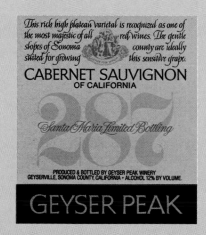

This rich high plateau varietal is recognized as one of the most majestic of all red wines. The gentle slopes of Sonoma county are ideally suited for growing this sensitive grape.

CABERNET SAUVIGNON
OF CALIFORNIA

287

Santa Maria Limited Bottling

PRODUCED & BOTTLED BY GEYSER PEAK WINERY
GEYSERVILLE, SONOMA COUNTY, CALIFORNIA · ALCOHOL 12% BY VOLUME.

GEYSER PEAK

MENDOCINO AND SONOMA WINE LABELS

straw-yellow; good acid balance and soft finish.

Colony Ruby Cabernet. Pronounced varietal bouquet and aroma from this hybrid developed for warm valleys.

Colony Cabernet Sauvignon. The best wine under the ISC label and an excellent value for daily table-wine use.

Colony Zinfandel. Fine color, good vinous bouquet. Well-blended wine, ready to drink, of zesty, balanced complexity.

JOHNSON'S ALEXANDER VALLEY WINES

8333 Highway 128, Healdsburg, California 95448

Since 1952, the Johnson family has been farming grapes and pears in the Alexander Valley on 111 acres of an old Spanish land grant. Planting of top-flight varietals—Pinot Noir, Cabernet Sauvignon, Johannisberg Riesling, Chardonnay, Gewürztraminer, and Chenin Blanc—was begun in 1967, and the small winery and tasting room emerged from a refurbished barn in 1975. Picnic and camping facilities amid the vines on the bank of the Russian River aided the winery's growing popularity. Two of the brothers—Jay, the vineyardist, and Tom, the winemaker—now have a silver medal for their Chenin Blanc, and a bronze medal for Pinot Noir, won at the Sonoma Harvest Fair, giving official recognition to their development of fine wines in the Alexander Valley. With the 1976 harvest they also produced what is probably the first and only estate-bottled Bartlett-pear wine in California; light, delicate, and sweet, it is called Alexander Valley Gold.

SAMPLER SELECTION

Pinot Noir (Alexander Valley). Vintage and estate-bottled. Chewy, oak-aged. Modestly priced. Good varietal character.

Chenin Blanc (Alexander Valley). A very fresh and fruity wine, for early enjoyment.

THE JORDAN VINEYARD & WINERY

1474 Alexander Valley Road, Healdsburg, California 95448

Founded in 1972, the Jordan Vineyard & Winery was committed to the dream of producing a truly distinctive California Cabernet Sauvignon in the manner of Bordeaux's famed claret. In November 1980, less than a decade after the first vines were planted, on his second visit to the state, prompted by his interest in wines, Dr. Valentin Berezhkov, First Secretary of the Soviet Union in Washington, D.C., and editor of Soviet scientific journals, toured the California wineries. At dinner with Jordan's owners, Sally and Tom Jordan, Dr. Berezhkov remarked, as he savored the memorable Alexander Valley Cabernet Sauvignon 1976, "Only in America could such a splendid wine estate be created in less than ten years."

Few would dispute that the Jordan Vineyard & Winery is one of California's outstanding labels. Every release, from that first 1976 wine to the 1980s, is a monument to the Jordans' dedication. André Tchelistcheff remains as consultant; Rob Davis is winemaker.

There is a lesson to be learned about the surprising age potentials of California Cabernet. Most people thought that the 1976 was a "pleasant, distinctive wine, rather light," and drank it young. Those who held it know that it developed stunning greatness.

An estate-bottled Chardonnay, from some of the Cabernet that had been T-budded in the 275 acres of vineyard, is another winner for Jordan. Rich, aromatic, buttery, it is the crown jewel of the Alexander Valley.

SAMPLER SELECTION

Cabernet Sauvignon (Alexander Valley). Softened and enriched with Merlot, touched with both American and French oak, always a wine with age potential.

Chardonnay (Alexander Valley). Estate-grown and bottled, in classic balance of fruit and oak, released only when ready for pouring; still, time will enhance it.

KENWOOD WINERY

9592 Sonoma Highway, Kenwood, California 95452

The evolution of this humble board-and-batten winery, established by the Pagani family of Italy in

1905, and acquired by six enthusiastic winelovers from San Francisco in 1970, follows penciled observations found in Jack London's "Confessions": "The stairway of Time is ever echoing with the wooden shoe going up, the polished boot descending." From gnarled old Zinfandel and Sauvignon Vert vines to bulk wine aged in redwood for local jug-wine buyers and noble varietals finished in classic oak, a transformation is under way here. The setting remains rustic. The new owners —Martin Lee, a former San Francisco policeman, and his sons Mike and Marty; Bob Kozlowski, research chemist and winemaker; and Neil Knott and John Shella—make up a crew that is taking the renamed winery into fine winemaking with positive strides.

While the emphasis is upon red wines—Pinot Noir, Zinfandel, and Cabernet Sauvignon—vintage-dated fine white wines of Chardonnay, Johannisberg Riesling, and Chenin Blanc are produced with equal finesse. Gold medals from the Sonoma Harvest Festival Fair were awarded to the 1973 Sonoma Valley Pinot Noir and 1974 Sonoma Zinfandel.

Kenwood's system of fermenting each varietal separately and later marrying the vintage casks in a blend accenting the desired style, with a minimum of fining or filtering, has come to mark their red wines as *vins de garde*, good to lay away for added bottle age.

SAMPLER SELECTION

Zinfandel (Sonoma Valley). Vintage wine of fine ruby depths, almost harsh tannins, needing time for maturity.

Petite Sirah (Sonoma Valley). Vintage wine of exceptional promise in its full body and notable bouquet and breed.

F. KORBEL AND BROS.

Guerneville, California 95446

Redwood stumps among the vineyards are reminders of the lumbering business that brought Joseph Korbel and his two brothers, Anton and Francis, from Bohemia to this bend in the Russian River in 1862. The present winery was built in 1886 with great timbers cut from the Korbels' domain and red brick fired in their own homemade kiln. A round tower with a conical roof, topped with a gargoyle holding a banner, served originally to house a distillery for brandy making. Legend has it that one of the Korbels designed it from his memory of a jail in Czechoslovakia in which he had spent some time, but today, masked with ivy, it stands only as a picturesque trademark of one of California's finest champagne houses.

Frank Schoonmaker was one of the first to recognize the superior merits of Korbel California Champagnes, and through his effective writings and Korbel's merchandising the brand was established among the more knowing American wine consumers. In 1954, Anton Korbel sold the winery to another family of winemakers, Adolph Heck of Alsace and his three sons, Adolph, Jr., Paul, and Ben. The elder Heck had been the champagne master at Cook's Imperial Champagne Cellars in St. Louis.

While Gary Heck has succeeded his father as president of Korbel, the elder Heck remains the champagne master in charge of the critical blending of cuvées. In 1982, two classic champagnes were introduced, a 100 percent Blanc de Noirs and a crisp 100 percent Chardonnay champagne, a splendid Blanc de Blancs. Korbel Brandy is no longer distilled here, but it is still aged and blended by the Heck family to their own mellow ideal.

The Korbel Champagne Cellars Garden, with its noted collection of roses and seasonal flowers, is open for daily tours summer and fall.

SAMPLER SELECTION

Korbel Natural California Champagne. Subtitled "Extremely Dry," this brilliant wine has a beguiling softness.

Korbel Brut California Champagne. The most popular wine, accounting for 60 percent of the output. Crisp, clean, dry.

Korbel Blanc de Noirs California Champagne. Dry finish with a delicate salmon-color blush from the enriching cuvée of Pinot Noir grapes.

Korbel Blanc de Blancs California Champagne. The most delicate and most limited creation; crisp, clean, 100 percent Chardonnay.

One of California's oldest wineries, Korbel first won fame for its bottle-fermented champagnes

MARTINI & PRATI WINES, INC.

2191 Laguna Road, Santa Rosa, California 95401

While most of the wine produced by Elmo Martini and Edward Prati, descendants of pioneer Sonoma wine dynasties, is sold in bulk to other wineries, a memento of earlier times remains in the Fountain Grove label, acquired when that historic winery of the last century was closed. Visitors to the tasting room can buy Fountain Grove Cabernet Sauvignon and also some quite fine Burgundy at modest prices, making the stop worthwhile.

MILL CREEK VINEYARDS
(CHARLES KRECK WINERY)

1401 Westside Road, Healdsburg, California 95448

More than ten years ago, the Kreck family planted their first vineyard of Cabernet Sauvignon in the green, tree-clad Russian River region. Next would come Merlot, Chardonnay, and Pinot Noir. Charles Kreck manages the winery operation today, with the help of his sons Bob and Bill. Wives work right alongside, keeping this an almost 100 percent family-operated winery.

All the vineyards of their Mill Creek Ranch, in cool Region II, ride alluvial slopes to the hills overlooking Dry Creek. The 6,200-square-foot winery, housing stainless-steel fermenters and French, American, and Yugoslavian oak barrels for aging, is close enough to the vines to permit crushing within minutes of harvesting. The family intends to produce only 100 percent varietal wines, using only grapes grown under their own supervision.

113

Pinot Chardonnay (Sonoma County). A rich vintage edition with well-balanced hints of oak.

Cabernet Blush (Sonoma County). The idea began as a Blanc de Noir of Cabernet, but evolved a strawberry-pink rosé.

Pinot Noir (Sonoma County). A remarkable wine, even in its less-than-mature release. Full, true varietal nose.

Cabernet Sauvignon (Sonoma County). Certain to become a wine in demand by connoisseurs for its breed and character.

Surrounding Parducci's winery are some of the 30-year-old varietal vines with which Adolph Parducci pioneered in Mendocino County

PARDUCCI WINE CELLARS

501 Parducci Road, Ukiah, California 95482

In December of 1973, the Parducci family—Adolph and his two sons, John and George—concluded an arrangement which brought in the more than seventeen hundred California schoolteachers of the Teachers Management & Investment Corporation as financial partners. The educators wisely chose to leave the responsibility of winemaking with the Parducci family, who had established the vineyard and winery at Ukiah in 1931. That decision had effects reaching far beyond capital expansion and the costly goals of introducing a small winery to the technological advances of the day. With cellarmaster Joe Monostori, Hungarian-born winemaker and experienced wine lecturer, an extensive and comprehensive three-year correspondence course in the related sciences of winemaking and wine appreciation was launched for the new teacher–partners. The course has given the winery an academic aura transcending the goals of Adolph Parducci's initial modest hopes of producing 100,000 cases of wine annually. A third Parducci generation is growing up directly in the traditions of contemporary winemaking techniques.

The distinction of Parducci varietal wines, beyond the technological nurturing from field to cellar, derives mainly from two related influences: adherence to strict appellation of origin for vineyard sources (Home Ranch, Talmage Vineyards, Largo Vineyards, and some Cabernet Sauvignon purchased from Philo in the Anderson Valley), and John Parducci's strong belief that it is the grape, not wood, that should sing a wine's tune. One has only to follow John into the winery, climb the metal stairs, and taste, from stainless-steel tanks, a Pinot Noir, a Cabernet, a Petite Sirah, or even a Carignane to know the reason for his passionate belief. The separate characteristics of each wine are sharply differentiated, and the wines will later acquire a gentle finish in wood—some redwood, but never the overriding oak. Little, if any, cellar fining or clarification is given the vintage-dated wines.

French Colombard (Mendocino County). From free-run juice. Crisp and well-balanced. Very fruity. A medal winner.

Pinot Noir (Mendocino County). Rich, elegant, true to Burgundian aroma; bouquet reminiscent of dried rose petals.

"Very well! How do you like this one?" Lithograph by Honoré Daumier from *Charivari* (The Christian Brothers Collection)

J. PEDRONCELLI WINERY

1220 Canyon Road, Geyserville, California 95441

No one can tell the Pedroncelli story better than Jim Pedroncelli: "Where we are geographically is a key part of our story. Dry Creek originates a couple of miles over these foothills. The fog in late summer follows the Russian River up and curves into Dry Creek. It runs into a headwall there, and then begins backing down and burning off. We get the fog, just a lovely amount of it, then we get blue sky and sunshine, and we get them sooner than places below, for a balance of chill and warmth and moisture that is quite all our own. We find our wines have a mini-character to them. In essence, that's why we started bottling our own wines. In the early days we sold all our wines in bulk for blending, and my dad always felt it was a shame to blend them away, they were so distinctive."

With wit and modesty his brother John completes the honest legend: "Grapes make wine more than human beings. I often wish I could take a lot of the people I meet in the tasting room out into the vineyards in September and put a grape in their mouth from this first hill, and then take them just a few miles down the road or up the road at random and give them a grape from the same variety and let them notice the difference. Sometimes I must admit this makes me feel a little useless in my role as winemaker. Jim and I frequently refer to 'non-winemaking.' Every time you put a wine through a procedure, you take something out of it. We're definitely non-procedure types. We *tend* wine more than we make it. Incidentally, we try to tend it quite elegantly; many of our oak barrels come all the way from Bordeaux."

The humble old barn of their father's day, with its vats of redwood now replaced with more elegant oak and stainless steel, continues to serve as a winery. All the wines, both red and white, have an intensity of flavor that is as welcome as the modest pricing. From their 135 acres, doubled since their father's day, and with some of the old vines replaced, there has been sufficient wine (50,000 cases per year) for most of the better wine merchants in California, with enough to allocate in 14 states across the country.

SAMPLER SELECTION

Gewürztraminer (Sonoma County). A golden-yellow wine of spicy, racy bouquet and silky softness. Not wholly dry.

Zinfandel Rosé (Sonoma County). One of the first editions in California. Dry, crisp, almost brittle.

Cabernet Sauvignon (Sonoma County). The breed is very apparent in nose and aroma. A vintage wine, to lay away. Great value.

A. RAFANELLI WINERY

4685 West Dry Creek Road, Healdsburg, California 95448

Winemaker and grape grower Americo Rafanelli, with his wife, Mary, as co-owner and chemist, has transformed an old barn building on their vineyard-ranch into a modern winery of technological efficiency. But there are hints of old-fashioned Italian style. Rafanelli punches down the cap on his fermenting Zinfandel and Pinot Noir himself, over and over, for the extraction of all the wealth of color and flavor his grapes contain. The first vintage to carry their label, as yet unreleased, is of 1975. The Rafanelli unfiltered red

wines are certain to be one more reason for a growing sentiment in favor of a regional appellation for the Dry Creek area.

SAMPLER SELECTION

Zinfandel (Sonoma County). Grown, produced, and bottled in Dry Creek. Big, unfiltered wine, of impressive complexity.

Pinot Noir (Sonoma County). Rich in body and color, of an earthiness indicating further promise in the area for the varietal.

SEBASTIANI VINEYARDS

389 Fourth Street East, Sonoma, California 95476

In 1893, among the many immigrants was a fourteen-year-old boy from Tuscany who spoke no English and had no money left after paying for his steerage-class ticket. Samuele Sebastiani went to work and eventually earned enough money to buy a run-down winery in one corner of the original Mission San Francisco Solano. Now known popularly as Sonoma Mission, it was the last of the chain founded by Padre José Altimira in 1823. With it came a 501-gallon redwood tank. Samuele Sebastiani was in the wine business.

The Sebastiani winery has a storage capacity of over 6,000,000 gallons and is still growing. The late August Sebastiani, who died in 1980, inherited his father's business acumen and was able to guide the winery through the lean years of Prohibition and afterward through the expansion that brought it into the ranks of California's largest producers.

In the 1980s, with the founder's namesake and grandson, Sam Sebastiani, in charge, the winery has made a quantum leap forward. Changes are everywhere: in the vineyards, where finer varieties have been planted; in the fermentation cellars, where technology has advanced; in the aging cellars, with their imported cooperage; and in the style of the wines, with the accent on premium quality. Research and development are the new bywords of the $5 million turnaround. While the company continues to produce its line of lower priced "Country" wines, it has added premium estate-grown wines.

The tasting room at Sebastiani

Sam Sebastiani's proudest addition comes from the Eagle Vineyard, his homesite, where he makes a Proprietor's Reserve Cabernet Sauvignon, aged in French oak, limited to 1,700 cases from each vintage. With the third generation now at the helm, the new wines are light-years ahead.

SAMPLER SELECTION

Barbera (North Coast Counties). The vintage selection is a hallmark of the winery. Big, fragrant, dark, dry.

Zinfandel (North Coast Counties). The label carries a subtitle calling attention to a "bramble" flavor, a berry-like taste.

Cabernet Sauvignon (Sonoma Valley). Berry-freshness, round elegance in taste; the epitome of Cabernet breed. Estate-grown.

SIMI WINERY

16275 Healdsburg Avenue, Healdsburg, California 95448

The Alexander Valley takes its name from Cyrus Alexander, who moved from the Rockies in 1840 to manage the great Sotoyome Land Grant rancho for Captain John Fitch of San Diego. His pay for overseeing the livestock range after four years was two leagues of land. Not only do these 9,000 acres of an obscure valley today bear his name; with a mean climate approximating that of Napa Valley's Oakville Experimental Station, which in turn is said to have a temperature range equivalent to the Médoc of Bordeaux, Alexander Valley is an official appellation of origin for fine California wines. This came about in 1973, largely as the result of Russ Green's one-man crusade.

The Simi Winery dates from 1876, when Giuseppe and Pietro Simi, who had come from Montepulciano, Italy, thirty years earlier, paced off the dimensions of a knoll just north of Healdsburg whose slope would facilitate the flow of grape juice and fermenting wine from a top-floor winery to aging and storing rooms below. After Carignane, Zinfandel, Cabernet Sauvignon, and Riesling vines were planted, the Simis began gathering local stone to raise walls for the winery building. With nostalgic pride they lettered a long sign over the canopy of their railroad shipping dock: Montepulciano Winery. But few of the locals could pronounce that mouthful of syllables. The winery became known instead by the brothers' name, and as the Simi Winery it brought fame to the Healdsburg area in pre-Prohibition days.

When Russ Green, president of Signal Oil Company, came to the area in 1958 in search of a second home, he had no winemaking intentions, and he bought an old sheep-grazing ranch in the Alexander Valley. Simi was barely existing as a winery at that time. By 1970, when Green's 50-acre ranch had been planted to vineyard, the acquisition of the winery from Giuseppe Simi's elderly daughter seemed a logical step.

From here on, the story is one of quick changes (three owners in six years), with Russ Green in the background transforming the area, the winery's reputation, and even the winery itself. André Tchelistcheff was signed on as consultant and helper to Mary Ann Graf, a UC–Davis enology graduate with experience in three wineries.

In 1974, Green sold the winery to Scottish & Newcastle Vintners of Scotland, who brought in their chairman, Michael Dixon, as president of Simi. In 1976 the winery was sold to Schieffelin & Co. of New York. Dixon remained as president and began a $5.5 million expansion and renovation program, with winemaker Zelma Long in charge of redesigning Simi's fermentation cellars. The new winemaking procedures and high style of Simi wines reflect California's current international stature as a producer of fine wines. Thus it was not surprising when, on January 6, 1981, Moët-Hennessy, one of the most prestigious wine and spirits firms of France, purchased Schieffelin (who distributed its wines in the United States), thereby acquiring Simi and making the winery's future even brighter.

Zelma Long, who had spent seven years as chief enologist for the Robert Mondavi Winery, is the co-owner of Long Vineyards. Her career in winemaking has been distinguished by the constant pursuit of excellence. With her scientific background she is often innovative, taking a holistic approach embracing all the factors that influence wine quality.

Montepulciano, birthplace of Simi's founders, is memorialized above the winery's loading platform

SAMPLER SELECTION
Chardonnay (Mendocino County). The Long technique blends barrel-fermented wine with some fermented in stainless steel; leaving the wine on the skins results in ultimate richness.

Cabernet Sauvignon (Alexander Valley). A new "trickle down" method replaces the time-honored pumping down of the pomace, bringing fuller, richer, softer wine. Elegant.

SONOMA VINEYARDS

Old Redwood Highway, Windsor, California 95492

Sonoma Vineyards is a thriving and handsome ornament of Sonoma County's renaissance as one of California's finest wine regions. The concept began modestly when Rodney Strong and his wife, Charlotte, both with Broadway credentials in theater and dance, established a winetasting facility in a 20-room Victorian house in Tiburon, where they sold the wines they bottled themselves. The business was successful, and a decade later a million-gallon winery had been built at Windsor, near the Russian River; 5,000 acres of choice varietal vineyards were in bearing; and the $10,000 annual sales had zoomed to $2 million.

"Each year we plotted recklessly the spread of our varietal vineyards, each in its own proper climate/soil environment," says Strong. Today, with the Renfield Corporation joined to Sonoma as shareholders and national distributors and with expediency dictating less expansive and distant vineyards, Sonoma has 2,000 acres remaining. Strong could write *the* book of the winemaker's travails.

"In any artistic form," Strong says, "one has a right to expect subtle differences. So we have different vines, different soils, different woods—Yugoslavian, Nevers, Limousin, and American oak—to age our wines. Plus all those doodads considered essential,

Rodney Strong at harvest time displays a cluster of his Burgundian Pinot Noir grapes

including the centrifuge. Some people have been so enamored of the centrifuge they've spun the bejesus out of the juice. I like my Chardonnay to be a nice golden wine, *some* oak, not too much, with style, not just a little dry, acid wine. Oak must be used with a great deal of discretion."

Rod's skill as a winemaker and his Pinot Noir and Chardonnay vineyards were attractive to Piper-Heidsieck of Reims, who entered into a joint venture with Renfield. A brilliant sparkler, Piper Sonoma, made its debut in September 1982. Its fullness illustrates Strong's desire "to get some *wine* back into the champagne." Piper Sonoma Brut is 80 percent Pinot Noir and 20 percent Chardonnay, the vintage Blanc de Noirs, a tour de force of the noble Pinot Noir.

The newest significant change at Sonoma Vineyards is a long overdue "Rodney Strong" label for the premium table wines, each with a vineyard designation. Once again the charismatic Strong takes center stage.

SAMPLER SELECTION

Piper Sonoma Brut (Sonoma County). A California sparkler in classic *méthode champenoise* style.

Piper Sonoma Blanc de Noirs (Sonoma County). An estate-grown wine of rich distinction, suitable for special occasions.

River West & Chalk Hill Chardonnays. Under the Rodney Strong label, two different Chardonnays, both

worthy of connoisseurs' consideration.

River East Pinot Noir. Grapes from well-drained soil on the banks of the Russian River give a noble wine of Burgundian quality.

Cabernet Sauvignon (Alexander's Crown). Volcanic soil and full sunshine ripen this hilltop estate's nonirrigated vines. A 51-acre plot produces one of California's greatest wines from the French claret grape.

SOUVERAIN OF ALEXANDER VALLEY

Independence Lane/Souverain Road, Geyserville, California 95441

When the Pillsbury Company of Minneapolis joined the corporate rush to the California wine fields in the early seventies, patience was left out of their ambitious plans. Even though numerous medals had been awarded the Souverain wines in June 1976, the landmark winery was sold to North Coast Cellars. North Coast is an association of grape growers comprising 150 vineyardists from Napa, Sonoma, and Mendocino, said to represent almost 80 percent of the growers of those areas. Under the new ownership Souverain concentrates on selecting the best grapes from the finest vineyards for each type of wine, the winery becoming a showcase for the resulting products. Following winemaker Robert Mueller's plans, particularly outstanding lots are aged and bottled separately and sold with the designation Vintage Selection; this policy was inaugurated with a 1973 Cabernet Sauvignon of extraordinary merit. The winery has a distinguished president and CEO, Augustin Huneeus, who brings 24 years of wine management experience, much of it spent with Joseph Seagram and Sons, Inc.

Souverain of Alexander Valley's building, designed by Sausalito architect John Marsh Davis, is among the outstanding examples of winery architecture. Davis drew inspiration from the few remaining old hop kilns that can still be seen off the byroads of Sonoma County.

SAMPLER SELECTION

Chardonnay (North Coast Counties). Modestly priced vintage wine of outstanding value. Oak-aged to

Souverain's winery borrows the distinctive shape of the old hop kilns still seen in Sonoma County

September 25th harvesting. The retired Western Airlines captain was using both arms for the task. A heady scent of fermentation filled the winery, but visible action had subsided in this vat. The pomace of skins and seeds, with the wine, had become a deep, dark reddish-purple gruel, thick as pudding. "I think it will be a fine wine," he said with quiet modesty, and I knew he was pleased with his wine at this stage of its extended contact with the skins. Together we tasted the '75 from the wood. Its elegance and breed told me why Tchelistcheff had suggested my visit here. California has reason to be proud of these wines.

Joseph Swan's wines are sold largely through mail orders from a roster of enophiles who have discovered the sturdy excellence of each custom-made varietal.

SAMPLER SELECTION

Chardonnay (Sonoma County). Vintage, estate-bottled wine, French-oak-aged to a well-balanced fruit-and-wood richness.

Zinfandel (Sonoma County). The Swan style is always intense, with maximum varietal bouquet from long fermentation.

Pinot Noir (Sonoma County). In the opinion of many expert winemakers, this is one of California's finest

Joseph Swan punches down the cap of pomace on top of a vat of Pinot Noir

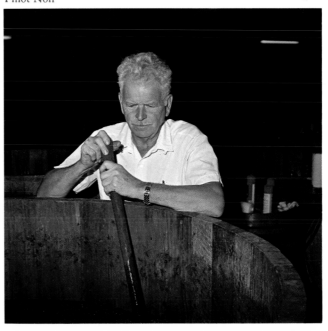

crisp, balanced elegance.

Cabernet Sauvignon (Vintage Selection). Winemaker Mueller's pride among the red wines. Full breed and character to enjoy now, or to age.

Moscato Bianco (North Coast Counties). A newcomer bound to enchant lovers of dessert wine with its delicate sweetness.

JOSEPH SWAN VINEYARDS

2916 Laguna Road, Forestville, California 95436

It was André Tchelistcheff who suggested I track down Joseph Swan because of his success with the true Burgundian Pinot Noir grape, which has defied so many winemakers in California. I found Swan in his tiny, unpretentious cement-block winery, punching down the cap of his '76 Pinot Noir that had been in its open redwood fermenter for two weeks after its

red wines. Always estate-bottled, vintage, from a true Burgundian clone of the temperamental grape variety.

TRENTADUE WINERY

19170 Redwood Highway, Geyserville, California 95441

Encroaching subdivisions in 1959 moved Leo Trentadue and his family from a Santa Clara County ranch to the Healdsburg–Geyserville area of Sonoma County. Along with Bernard Fetzer and Russ Green, he was among the first to plant fine varietal vineyards in commercial quantities in this northern area of Sonoma County. This was no doubt a part of the attraction that drew Pillsbury to the area for their Souverain venture, and Trentadue sold them 20 acres of his original 160 for the splendid winery, completed in 1973, which now stands near his own more modest facility. There is a gold medal for his Napa Gamay and genuine enthusiasm for his big, robust, and fragrant Petite Sirah. Each of his labels carries the number 32—*trentadue* being the Italian word for thirty-two.

SAMPLER SELECTION

Merlot (Sonoma). A vintage, estate-bottled wine, of full ruby color and intense flavor. Bottle-aging suggested.

Gamay (Sonoma). This is from the Napa Gamay grape of the true Beaujolais variety, of substantial vinosity here.

Petite Sirah (Sonoma). Even when young this estate-bottled vintage wine has gutsy swagger; for serving with game.

ZD WINES

20735 Burndale Road, Sonoma, California 95476

ZD stands for the names of the owners and winemakers, Gino Zepponi and Norman de Leuze. Both partners share the belief that exceptional wines can be made only from exceptional grapes given intensive care and personal attention. The tiny winery, not much bigger than its name, with a fermenting capacity of only 6,400 gallons, is fortunately near the source of the two varieties that interest the owners most—Chardonnay and Pinot Noir. Located just north of San Francisco Bay, at the southern junction of Napa and Sonoma counties, the Carneros district is cooled by early morning fog and breezes off the bay. Several Napa Valley wineries pioneered this location, originally thought to be too cool for proper ripening of grapes. But when it was realized that Burgundian varieties thrived in such a climate, Carneros began to garner praise as an area well suited to the growing of Chardonnay and Pinot Noir.

Zepponi and de Leuze frequently extend their devoted winemaking attentions to grapes from other areas: Zinfandel from the Sierra foothills, Chardonnay from Tepusquet Vineyards of Santa Maria, Cabernet Sauvignon from Paso Robles, and even a Pinot Noir from the Umpqua Valley of Oregon.

SAMPLER SELECTION

Chardonnay (Sonoma). From the Zepponi Vineyard, an intensely flavored varietal, well-balanced. Big enough to age well.

Gewürztraminer (Winery Lake Vineyard). Rich and clean, with full measure of the spicy bouquet and aroma of the grape.

Pinot Noir (Napa). From the Winery Lake Vineyard of Carneros, a dark, garnet-red, 100 percent varietal; enhanced with aging.

Zinfandel (Amador). Made in the same style as the Pinot Noir; dark, rich, full-flavored, and long-lived.

NAPA COUNTY

Napa, the proudest name among California's wine districts, refers to the county, which lies just east of Sonoma, separated from it by the Mayacamas Mountains, but more specifically to the Napa Valley, a 35-mile stretch from San Pablo Bay northwest to Mount St. Helena, where many of California's most illustrious vineyards flourish.

The Napa Valley today has more than double the vineyard acreage it had in 1919. Ten thousand acres of

Visitors are welcome at Beaulieu, known familiarly as BV, one of the oldest vineyards in Napa

vines, preponderantly the noble vinifera, were in cultivation when the Eighteenth Amendment struck like a plague. Some of the vines survived, but many were uprooted or grafted to vulgar "juice grapes" that could withstand shipment to the East for the making of home wines during Prohibition. When Repeal came, in 1933, Chardonnay was all but unknown, and even by 1965 only a scant 942 acres of Cabernet Sauvignon were in bearing.

Inexpensive jug wines carrying a Napa Valley appellation and generic name will soon become a thing of the past. Although many a famous Napa winery owes more than a little of its present prosperity to the Mountain Burgundy and Mountain Chablis blendings from Carignane, Crab's Black Burgundy, Alicante Bouschet, Burger, Sauvignon Vert, and Golden Chasselas vines, those varieties are now being replaced with fine Pinots, Rieslings, Cabernet Sauvi-

gnon, and Chardonnay. The land is too expensive for any but premium varieties today.

Harvest from the present 28,362 acres in fine grape varieties from 121 wineries remains insufficient for the demand created by the magic word Napa. The larger wineries based in Napa must reach out to other regions, other appellations, to fill the demands for their wines. Meanwhile the small winemaker, producing on the basis of his own grape supply from limited local plantings, gains enthusiastic patronage as he makes his small lots of expensive quality wines. They cannot help but be costly, but to the connoisseur they are worth their premium price.

Winemaking remains an intimate thing, despite the dominance today of impersonal stainless-steel tanks. For these fermenters are holding living wines safely and securely—and also the hopes and dreams of the most creative farmers of our land. The profile of

124

the land remains much as it was in centuries past, but the patchwork design of vineyard plots is more lush than yesterday's landscape, and the wines are ever finer.

BEAULIEU VINEYARD

1960 St. Helena Highway, Rutherford, California 94573

The prestige of California wines following Repeal depended principally on those wineries whose vineyards were maintained for the legal production of sacramental wines. Preeminent among them was Beaulieu Vineyard, established by Georges de Latour, a native of the Périgord region of France, who came to America in 1883 and, with his wife, established at Rutherford in 1900 a vineyard, winery, and gracious home. The enterprise was sold to Heublein by Fernande de Latour's daughter Hélène, the Marquise de Pins. The family has retained the founder's country house and its sunken gardens, rose arbors, vegetable and herb plots, and, most important, Cabernet Sauvignon plantings. This is the "beautiful place"—Beaulieu—for which the vineyard was named, a word so difficult for Americans to pronounce that the initials BV have become its most familiar designation.

The question is often asked, what is the difference between the regular Beaulieu Vineyard Cabernet Sauvignon and the Georges de Latour Private Reserve Cabernet Sauvignon? Both are 100 percent Cabernet wines, but the Private Reserve is produced from the grapes of the family estate on the west side of Highway 29, these well-established vines being responsible for the subtle difference (which the late founder ascribed to "Rutherford dust," a whimsical reference to variation in soil).

While a nucleus of 745 acres of Beaulieu vineyards remains, grapes are also bought from other Napa Valley vineyards. But particular credit is due to the Chardonnay and Pinot Noir plantings in the cool Carneros region pioneered by André Tchelistcheff during his tenure as enologist and winemaster, from 1937 until 1973.

Though still owned by Heublein, Beaulieu now has as chairman and general manager Legh Knowles,

Jr., with Thomas B. Selfridge its president/winemaker. In 1977 Beaulieu Vineyard '71 Champagne de Chardonnay emerged in first place in an open competition with all other leading sparkling wines of California. Even the generic Beaulieu Vineyard Napa Valley Chablis and Burgundy are accorded uncommon acceptance among winelovers everywhere.

SAMPLER SELECTION

Pinot Chardonnay (Napa Valley). Also known as Beaufort. Grapes from the Carneros region. Crisp, clean.

Chateau Beaulieu (Sauvignon Blanc). In French Sauternes style, 73 percent Sauvignon, with a touch of Muscadelle. Sweet.

Cabernet Sauvignon (Private Reserve). Aged in French oak in the Tchelistcheff-established tradition. Always outstanding.

Champagne de Chardonnay. Produced in classic *méthode champenoise* on the Beaulieu estate. Breed and high style.

BERINGER/LOS HERMANOS

2000 Main Street, St. Helena, California 94574

In 1970 the golden wand of Nestlé of Switzerland touched the Napa Valley with the $6-million purchase of the Beringer/Los Hermanos winery and vineyards. (Beringer Brothers was the original name of the winery, while Los Hermanos—"The Brothers" in Spanish—was the name of the vineyard owned by the family before Prohibition. The winery now uses Beringer for the estate wines and Los Hermanos for jug wines and less expensive labels.) The transformation, almost immediate, was beneficial and lasting. The landmark winery established by Jacob and Frederick Beringer, German immigrants from Mainz, in 1876, had been the oldest continuously operating winery in the Napa Valley, but after 1950 it was in decline, though the old limestone caves were a continuing tourist attraction.

Thanks to excellent renovation, Beringer is a model of winery design. The Beringer wine production business is controlled by the Labruyère family of France, who lease the distinguished winery facility from

Nestlé. E. Michael Moone, experienced wine merchandiser, is president, assisted by William T. Ryan, an E. & J. Gallo marketing alumnus. Myron Nightingale, Sr., though technically winemaker emeritus, remains very much in the Beringer picture. With a full schedule of roving ambassadorial assignments, he conducts tastings and seminars and takes on speaking engagements. Ed Sbragia, Beringer's winemaker, would be the first to claim continued reliance upon Nightingale's counsel during the crucial times of grape harvesting and winemaking.

From Beringer vineyards in the Napa Valley, the Carneros and Yountville regions, and Knights Valley in nearby Sonoma, and from Tepusquet Vineyards of Santa Maria, Nightingale and Sbragia have produced a succession of magnificent wines. Perhaps the most outstanding have been the Chardonnays. Both the Napa Valley Estate Chardonnay, and the barrel-fermented Chardonnay from the Gamble Ranch are worth seeking out for their engaging richness and complexity. Both have qualities recalling the finest white Burgundies of France. Beringer editions of Sauvignon Blanc, titled Fumé Blanc, golden from their time in oak, are equally exciting, with impressive depth.

For value hunters, the Los Hermanos jug decanters of Chablis, Chardonnay, Johannisberg Riesling, Chenin Blanc, Gamay Beaujolais, Zinfandel, and Burgundy are winners for everyday wine.

SAMPLER SELECTION

Chardonnay (Napa Valley) Gamble Ranch Vineyard. Rivals the finest white Burgundy of France. Aged in Limousin oak. A big wine.

Sonoma Fumé Blanc (Sonoma). Marvelous intensity and complexity, with appetizing dryness yet silky finish.

Cabernet Sauvignon (Napa Valley). Grapes from the Lemmon Ranch, its soil studded with obsidian, yield a richly varietal wine.

BURGESS CELLARS

1108 Deer Park Road, St. Helena, California 94574

In the early forties, J. Leland Stewart, an execu-tive of a national meat-packing firm, decided to seek a new life in the Napa Valley on a 60-acre tract of land that had a small vineyard, a prune orchard, and a tiny winery. He called his new enterprise Souverain Cellars.

In 1970, he sold the house, the winery, and the name to a group of investors, who in turn sold the entire estate in 1972 to Tom Burgess, a young jet pilot.

The greatly expanded winery facilities have been enhanced with stainless-steel fermenters for controlled-temperature fermentation, a centrifuge for cleaning the fresh juice of select grapes, most of which are purchased from premium vineyards in the valley. Burgess has continued Stewart's preference for the fine harvests of Jerry Draper's nearby vineyard. From the 22 acres of Burgess's vineyard come choice nonirrigated Cabernet Sauvignon and Cabernet Franc. With his winemaker, Bill Sorenson, Burgess believes that white wines emerge softer and silkier when fermented in the European manner, in white-oak casks. The Chardonnay, a beautifully balanced wine, demonstrates the validity of this thesis.

SAMPLER SELECTION

Chardonnay (Napa Valley). Linda and Tom Burgess are proud of the Yountville grapes from their own vineyard, that give complexity to this wine.

Cabernet Sauvignon (Napa Valley). A classical text-book claret of haunting richness, the "Vintage Select" edition is always worth its higher price.

CARNEROS CREEK WINERY

1285 Dealy Lane, Napa, California 94558

It is not likely that the proliferation of "boutique" wineries in the premium winegrowing regions of California will abate. Not as long as there are enthusiasts like Balfour and Anita Gibson who know that dedication and knowledge, plus choice, select grapes, are a route to fine wines, bound to win recognition. Their first wine, a 1973 Napa Valley Pinot Noir, made from a vintage blend of Carneros grapes balanced with some from the fine Trefethen Vineyards of Napa, is full-bodied, aged in French oak, unfined, and certain to age with splendid bouquet. Francis Mahoney is the wine-maker.

SAMPLER SELECTION

Cabernet Sauvignon (Shenandoah Valley). Expensive vintage wine for the collector; well worth the price.

Zinfandel (Sutter Basin). Fans of California's "big Zin" find this full-bodied wine a prize.

Petite Syrah (Napa Valley). Big and almost exotic wine needing added age to round out its complexity.

CAYMUS VINEYARDS

8700 Conn Creek Road, Rutherford, California 94573

A tub-thumping viticulturist of the eighteenth century declared, "Fine wine is made in the vineyard." There's not a grape grower alive who wouldn't agree with this sentiment. Charles Wagner, a longtime Napa Valley grape grower, finally could not resist the temptation to bond the barn near his home and vineyard into a winery. He owns 70 acres of magnificently attended vines and buys choice lots of grapes from as far away as Amador County, in the foothills of the Sierra, an area noted for exceptional Zinfandel. With his son to help him, there will surely be winemakers' wines with the Caymus label—not in great quantity, but characteristic of the vintner who knows his grapes and makes his wines without compromise. The 1974 Cabernet Sauvignon quickly claimed California connoisseurs' attention, sending them scurrying for a share of this richly endowed, heavy-bodied varietal wine, a rival of fine French clarets—a worthy *vin de garde*.

CHAPPELLET VINEYARD

1581 Sage Canyon Road, St. Helena, California 94574

A peaceful domain was what Donn and Molly Chappellet of Beverly Hills were seeking as an alternative life-style for themselves and their six children. Donn, like many other capitalist dropouts mentioned in this book, looked to the land, and in 1967 his explo-

rations of the Napa Valley were rewarded with this site—sloping, with a westerly exposure for terracing, almost entirely new to vines.

The 100 acres of vineyard were planted to four varieties: Johannisberg Riesling, Chenin Blanc, Chardonnay, and Cabernet Sauvignon. The handsome triangular winery building, designed by an artist friend and constructed by an engineer, was ready for the first harvest in 1969. Chappellet is now well on its way toward its 20,000-case yearly goal.

With the 1969 Cabernet Sauvignon, it was obvious that with this vine in this setting the winery was destined for continuing greatness, and as the vine roots go deeper into the reddish, iron-rich soil on this mountain, the wines grow in complexity.

SAMPLER SELECTION

Chardonnay (Napa Valley). Vintage, estate-bottled wine of pale, straw-yellow brilliance. Crisp, clean, elegant.

Johannisberg Riesling (Napa Valley). Like the Chenin Blanc, which is fermented dry, this is of noteworthy delicacy.

Cabernet Sauvignon (Napa Valley). Wine of singular depth and rich-textured complexity, assuring long, unfolding life.

CHATEAU CHEVALIER

3101 Spring Mountain Road, St. Helena, California 94574

Jacob Beringer planted his first vines in the 1870s on the curving knolls surrounding this great estate. It was acquired in 1884 by the Fortune Chevalier family, San Francisco wine merchants. Even before Prohibition, the difficult and steep vineyards suffered neglect, and like the fairy-tale castle of "Sleeping Beauty" the Chateau Chevalier, its grandeur all but obliterated, had to wait for its moment of awakening—until September 1969.

The prince of this engaging history was winelover Gregory Bissonette, a disenchanted stockbroker seeking a new life in the wine country. With his wife, Kathy, and their six children Greg began the odyssey of full

Chappellet's terraced vineyards on Pritchard Hill overlooking the Napa Valley

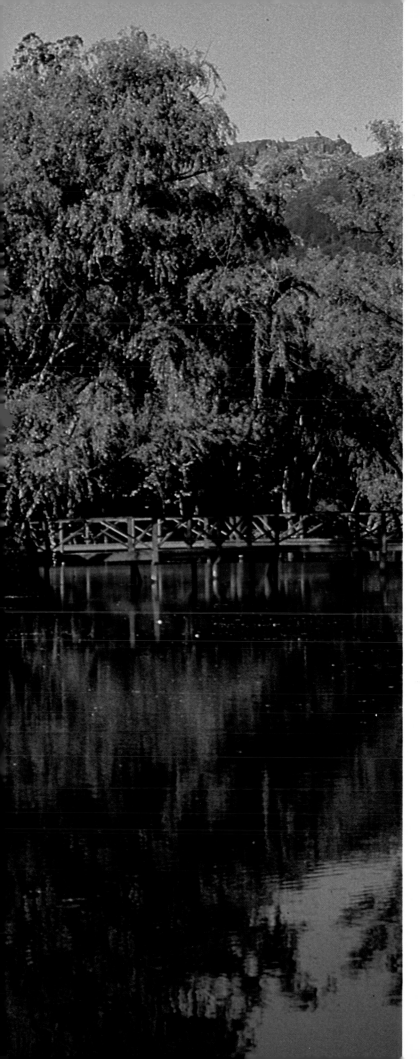

reconstruction, clearing the grand stone staircase to the gardens that lead to the mountainside vineyards. After the dense wild scrub was removed, 54 acres of new vineyards were added. Cabernet Sauvignon, Merlot, and Chardonnay dominated these 1970 and 1971 plantings, with a few acres of Pinot Noir "to play around with." In ten years Chateau Chevalier reached a goal of 10,000 cases a year of three varietals: Cabernet Sauvignon, Pinot Noir, and Chardonnay, all of which won gold medals at the Orange County Fair.

Financial sponsorship came in 1983, when Seagram's American Classics Wine Company selected Chateau Chevalier as one of its California wineries, placing it under exclusive contract. In February 1984, Greg and Kathy sold the winery to Gil Nickel of Far Niente Winery, so that they could move onto another undeveloped neighboring property to begin their own wine saga anew.

John Nickel and his brother Gil are reworking the vineyards, from which one may expect more medal-winning wines, of Chardonnay, Cabernet Sauvignon, and Pinot Noir.

CHÂTEAU MONTELENA

1429 Tubbs Lane, Calistoga, California 94515

Château Montelena burst upon the American wine scene like a skyrocket, without advance notice and with only modest distribution of its new label, when its Napa & Alexander Valleys Chardonnay scored a stunning victory over illustrious white Burgundies of France in a tasting by a French jury of experts in Paris on May 24, 1976. It was a well-earned award, underscoring modest but positive determination to produce fine wines at a historic location.

The 100-acre vineyard was established in 1882 by Senator Alfred A. Tubbs, whose travels to the château wine country of Bordeaux inspired him to establish traditions no less elegant on his own vineyard estate.

In 1968, industrialist Lee Paschich and his wife, Helen, amateur winemaking enthusiasts, bought the 142-acre property, converting an upper portion of the old winery to a country house. In May of 1972, the

Jade Lake, with its oriental bridges and red pavilions, was part of the original Château Montelena estate nearly a hundred years ago owners, well aware of the greater potentials, formed a partnership with attorney James Barrett, administrative financier Ernest Hahn, and winemakers Jerry Luper and Miljenko ("Mike") Grgich, whose qualifications included nine years with the legendary André Tchelistcheff at Beaulieu.

The wine world still remembers vividly the 1973 Chateau Montelena Chardonnay made by Mike Grgich, which took top honors in Paris in 1976. James Barrett's son, Bo, learned his skills under Grgich, and it is he who is making the present memorable wines. The winery, one hundred years old in 1982, has reached another pinnacle. Its constant "search for the great Cabernet Sauvignon" achieved its goal with the splendid centennial bottling of their estate-grown 1978.

SAMPLER SELECTION

Johannisberg Riesling (Napa & Alexander Valleys). Flowery, full-bodied wine, suggesting citrus and peaches.

Chardonnay (Napa & Alexander Valleys). Big, creamy, rich, in Meursault style, golden from judicious aging in oak.

Zinfandel (Napa Valley). Unique and zingy, the berry taste modified with oak. Dark, deep, highly enjoyable.

Cabernet Sauvignon (Napa Valley). Needing age to bring out the potential of its plentiful tannins.

THE CHRISTIAN BROTHERS

Mont La Salle, Napa, California 94558

There is a stunning contrast between the humble beginnings of The Christian Brothers as winemakers in 1882 and their position today as the largest Church-owned producer of wine in the world. The 300-year-old teaching order maintains 600 teaching centers in 80 countries, partially supported by revenues from their winemaking. The first Christian Brothers in California made their first wine at Martinez in a horse-watering trough, crushing the grapes with a wooden club; their present circular stainless-steel fermenting facility at St. Helena looks more like a "Star Trek" launching pad than a grape-receiving station. The contrast sums up an unparalleled success story.

By 1937 production at a big vine-clad brick winery at Mont La Salle stood in need of marketing assistance. Fromm and Sichel of San Francisco was chosen to market and distribute Christian Brothers wines and brandies and champagnes and has made them a household name not only in America but in forty-five countries abroad as well. Today, The Christian Brothers own and operate three major wineries in the Napa Valley, two in the San Joaquin Valley, and 2,400 acres of fine varietal vineyards, 1,400 of them in the Napa Valley.

From the beginning, Brother Timothy, the distinguished cellarmaster at Mont La Salle and a one-time chemistry teacher, has had an abiding belief in blending for the production of the finest table wines, nonvintage and ready to drink. The red wines go from the fermenting tanks into a diversified library of cooperage that includes American oak as well as the fine varieties from European forests. They are given two to five years before they enter the blending program. Further aging marries the blend in wood before bottling, and six months later it arrives in the market.

The estate-bottled wines are made entirely from grapes grown in the Mont La Salle Monastery vineyards in the Napa hills. Each bottle indicates a special *cuvée* on the neck label, giving the number of the blending lot. The wines designated as Brother Timothy Special Selections have additional aging in a variety of wood cooperage for a minimum of two years. Dessert wines and brandies come from the two wineries and vineyards in the San Joaquin Valley, in Reedley and Fresno.

SAMPLER SELECTION

Pinot Chardonnay (Napa Valley). Always an outstanding value. Buttery soft; wood has accented the grape's breed.

Napa Fumé (Napa Valley). Dry-finished Sauvignon Blanc, rich in fragrance and with an enticing, refreshing fruitiness.

Pinot Saint George (Napa Valley). Estate-bottled from the Mont La Salle vineyard. Ruby-red, dry, softens with aging.

At the Napa Valley property of The Christian Brothers, Mont La Salle, the novitiate is surrounded by flourishing vineyards

Gamay Noir (Napa Valley). Of the true grape of Beaujolais, the Napa Gamay. Dark, soft in the mouth, berry-like taste.

CLOS DU VAL WINE COMPANY

5330 Silverado Trail, Napa, California 94558

It was barely rumored that Bernard Portet, son of the winemaster of Château Lafite-Rothschild, had selected the Napa Valley for his career in winemaking before eagerness to taste his wines began to mount. Astute wine merchants vied for their quotas of the only two wines he would make, the Cabernet Sauvignon and Zinfandel. The first releases were of the 1972 vintage, and while nowhere near the peak of their potential, they satisfied the most critical that here indeed was a small winery deserving a more honorific description than "boutique," for there was nothing diminutive about the stature of the wines. The goal of 15,000 cases has already been achieved, with distribution in thirty-two states at this writing.

"Of all the wine-growing regions in the world that I had visited," Portet said, "this California region seemed the most favorable spot in which to launch a premium winery enterprise." A 120-acre site was bought just off the Silverado Trail, below the rocky pinnacles of Stag's Leap on the valley's eastern slopes. A small winery, completed in 1974, is equipped with stainless-steel fermenters, upright oak tanks for early aging, and, of course, French-oak 50-gallon barrels for the traditional Médoc finishing before bottling.

Portet has added a Chardonnay and a Pinot Noir from his acreage acquired in the cool Carneros region and, true to his Bordelais background, is making stylish wines from Sauvignon Blanc and Semillon.

SAMPLER SELECTION

Zinfandel (Napa Valley). Dark, full-bodied wine of rich balance; needs longer age in bottle for full enjoyment.

Cabernet Sauvignon (Napa Valley). Vintage; estate-bottled. In Bordelais style, rounded with Merlot.

CUVAISON

4560 Silverado Trail, Calistoga, California 94515

Set back of and above the Silverado Trail, this trim new winery among its 30 acres of Pinot Noir, Gamay, and Riesling vines is a monument to trial and error. Established by Dr. Thomas Cottrell, a physicist, and his fellow scientist Thomas Parkhill, it was christened with the French word for the fermentation of red wines on the skins—*cuvaison*. The first vintage, in 1970, was made in stainless-steel fermenters installed just in time for the arrival of the first grapes.

After producing eighteen wine varieties, none of stellar quality, Cottrell recognized the need for capital and professionalism. He invited Oakleigh B. Thorne of New York's C T Corporation System to assume ownership and control, and engaged Philip Togni as winemaster. Togni, whose brilliant, peregrinating career had included Montpellier, Chile, Bordeaux, Alsace, and finally California (Gallo, Inglenook, Mayacamas, Chalone, and Chappellet) came to Cuvaison in January of 1975. The original inventory was sold off to visitors to the handsome tasting room, and a new policy, in the French estate tradition, of making only three wines—Chardonnay, Cabernet Sauvignon, and Zinfandel—was adopted by merchandising manager Winston Wilson.

Late in 1979, Cuvaison was acquired by a Swiss family. Alexander Schmidheiny is the board chairman. Togni's longtime cellar master and assistant, John Thacher, is the full-time winemaker. Most significantly, the prudent Swiss ownership decided to acquire its own vineyard. With an eye to the outstanding Chardonnay grown in the Winery Lake Vineyard of Rene di Rosa, whose grapes they had bought at high prices, Schmidheiny acquired 400 acres of rolling land just across the highway from the di Rosa vineyards in Carneros. Land preparation was costly on this former grazing terrain, but with a system of drip irrigation the 250 acres of carefully nurtured vines matured beautifully. Planted mostly to Chardonnay, the winery now concentrates almost exclusively on this very popular varietal. Thacher ages the wine in French oak. Cuvaison Chardonnay is a rich wine, proving once more, by its Carneros region vines, how important soil is in the determination of ultimate character.

The stained-glass window in Cuvaison's Spanish Colonial winery is featured on their wine labels

Visitors to this small, handsome winery have the opportunity of acquiring some of the Togni-made wines of substantial character and long-aging potentials, especially some quite superb Limousin-oak-aged Cabernet Sauvignons.

SAMPLER SELECTION

Chardonnay (Carneros). The pride of Cuvaison, with vine-ripe grapes from the Carneros region producing fat, rich, buttery wine.

DIAMOND CREEK VINEYARDS

1500 Diamond Mountain Road, Calistoga, California 94515

In his own words, after a "hectic, punishing business career" in the beauty-aid business in southern California, Al Brounstein was ready for a sylvan retreat. He found it on Diamond Mountain, due west of Sterling Vineyards and minutes away from Schramsberg. Twenty acres of the 79-acre estate are planted with 90 percent Cabernet Sauvignon and 10 percent Merlot. They produced the first vintage in 1973.

The arable tracts were of such dissimilar geological natures that Brounstein determined to make three different wines whose names would reflect the differences: Volcanic Hill, Gravelly Meadow, and Red Rock Terrace.

An old-fashioned basket-press is used, with equally old-style open wooden fermenters. The aim is for big wines, long on the skins, to be aged in Nevers, Limousin, and Yugoslavian oak barrels. All the wines have a cedar tinge to the bouquet. While the Red Rock Terrace Cabernet Sauvignon, in Brounstein's opinion, is softer than the other two, each of the three has its adherents who would give it top rank.

SAMPLER SELECTION

Cabernet Sauvignon (Napa Valley). Three vineyard designations, each a big wine, not overly tannic, but requiring aging.

DOMAINE CHANDON

California Drive, Yountville, California 94599

When in February 1973 the late Count Robert de Vogüé of Moët-Hennessy, producers of Dom Pérignon Champagne, bought 875 acres of prime vineyard land in the Napa Valley, the question greeted him everywhere, what would he call his California sparkling wine? Champagne? Heresy for a Champenois!

The debut of the wine occurred in December 1976, and it was named Domaine Chandon Napa Valley Brut. Moët-Hennessy's finest champagne master, Edmund Maudière of Épernay, commuted between France and California to assure the excellence of the first American sparkling wine to carry the name of Chandon, a name synonymous with Dom Pérignon. Moët-Hennessy even sent Lucien Dambron to instruct the Domaine Chandon employees in the art of turning the bottles, known as "riddling," which maneuvers the sediment of wine in secondary fermentation onto the corks, a technique dating back to the time of Dom Pérignon. Dambron can turn 50,000 bottles per day; his apprentices are already up to 20,000 per day.

Domaine Chandon Napa Valley Brut is approximately two-thirds Pinot Noir and one-third Chardonnay, with an undeclared amount of Pinot Blanc. "California Chardonnay," Maudière says emphatically, "it is too strong. It's more a Burgundy Chardonnay than a champagne Chardonnay, but we need Chardonnay because it gives a particular sparkle and zest to our wine." The *cuvée* has a kinship with Dom Pérignon, not only sharing the same champagne master but also being made from similar grape varieties. "It would be a mistake to try to make a French champagne here," Maudière concluded. "It should be Californian." It will always be nonvintage, and this indicates the importance of blending for that elegant *cuvée*.

In 1977, Domaine Chandon began the harvest of their own vines on the Mount Veeder ranch, in addition to taking grapes from Carneros and the 50 acres surrounding the new winery in Yountville. A second wine, a Blanc de Noirs, has a frank and delicately pale apricot blush from its 100 percent rich black-grape origins. Both wines take about eight years to ascend to their peak of perfection, largely because of the domi-

Domaine Chandon flies the flags of the United States, California, Champagne, and France.

nant role of Pinot Noir. The Moët-Hennessy $12-million investment in California, shared with Californians, is a boon whose promise is just beginning to reach fulfillment.

Napa Valley Brut. Nonvintage sparkling wine of a bold and round richness of taste. A silvery-bronze blush of color.

Napa Valley Blanc de Noirs. Long, silky, and elegant. Pale apricot color; dry, classic fruit and yeast bouquet.

FRANCISCAN VINEYARDS

Highway 29 at Galleron Road, Rutherford, California 94573

One of the handsome young wineries in the Napa Valley had a sad beginning. The original investors, in a last-ditch effort at salvation, had to sell Franciscan Vineyards' bottled wines to weekend tourists at deep discount prices. To the rescue came genial former Christian Brother Justin Meyer, in association with Denver financier Raymond Duncan. They soon brought everything together, with energy and funds to spare for a second, single-wine winery, Silver Oak Cellars. In 1979 they sold Franciscan to the Peter Eckes Company of West Germany. Meyer stayed on as winemaker until January 1982, when Tom Ferrell was lured away from Inglenook. Today, Ferrell is president/winemaker and the owners are more than pleased with the brilliant advances he has made.

Ferrell works with an impeccably equipped winery, 900,000 gallons of storage capacity, stainless-steel fermenters and fine oak cooperage, which handle the harvests from the winery's 450 acres of vineyard, equally divided between the Napa and Alexander valleys. The emphasis is wholly upon premium varietal wines.

SAMPLER SELECTION

Sauvignon Blanc (California). Crisp, clean on the palate, with subtle undertones of oak from partial barrel fermentation. A stylish complement to shellfish.

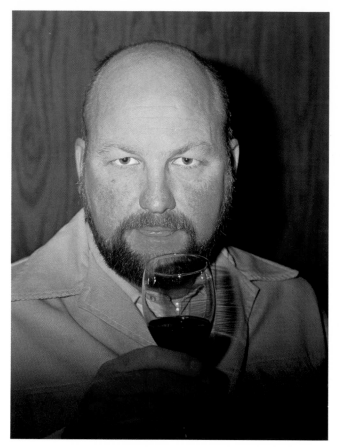

Justin Meyer, every inch the genial friar, savors the bouquet of a Franciscan Cabernet Sauvignon

Chardonnay (Napa Valley & Alexander Valley). Two Chardonnays, one from each appellation, both outstanding in golden complexity.

Cabernet Sauvignon (Napa Valley). From Franciscan's noted Oakville estate vineyard. Deep varietal intensity; fine to drink now and later.

Charbono (Napa Valley). One of the few bottlings of this intriguing big red wine, long a Ferrell specialty.

FREEMARK ABBEY

3022 St. Helena Highway, St. Helena, California 94574

The only association of a religious nature that can be linked with the name of Freemark Abbey (coined from those of its three founders) is the devout faith in its wines held by an ever-growing number of eno-

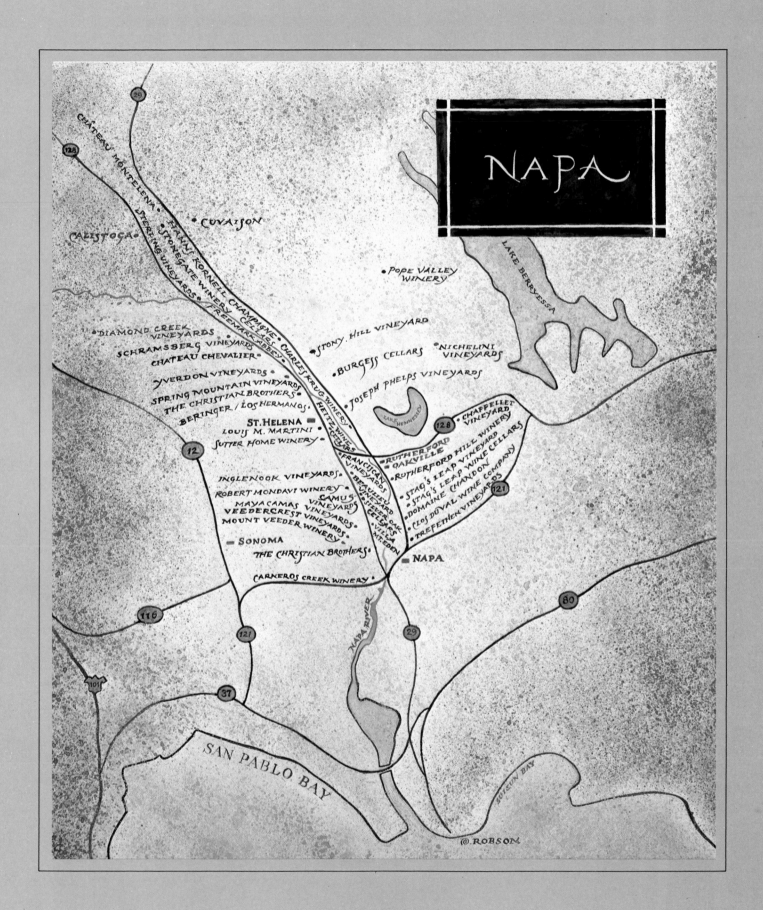

philes who seek their share of its modest 25,000-cases-per-annum production.

The owners of the present Freemark Abbey include Charles A. Carpy, of a pioneer Napa Valley family; vineyardist Laurie Wood; William Jaeger, Jr., also of Napa; and R. Bradford Webb, one of the state's leading biochemists, who had been the creative operator of Hanzell for the late Ambassador Zellerbach.

Production at Freemark Abbey was and is essentially limited to three varietal wines: Chardonnay, Johannisberg Riesling, and Cabernet Sauvignon. Of particular interest to many winelovers are the Cabernet Sauvignon grapes from the John Bosche vineyard, a Rutherford neighbor of the famed Beaulieu Vineyard, where the Georges de Latour Private Reserve wine is

At Freemark Abbey: checking the sugar content of Johannisberg Riesling

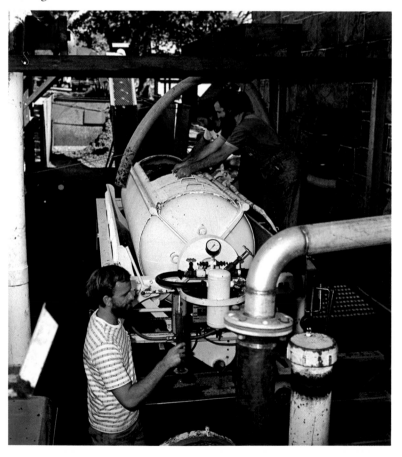

made. The Freemark Abbey Cabernet Sauvignon from these grapes always carries the Bosche designation on its label. Select lactobacillus strains are added to the crush of red wines to assure the malolactic fermentation, with its subsequent reduction of total acidity. New wines are held in stainless steel for racking, with fining and filtration at a minimum. The Cabernet Sauvignon, with 10 percent Merlot, the Pinot Noir, and the Chardonnay are aged in Nevers oak, the Johannisberg Riesling kept softly and gently fragrant in the large American-oak casks.

Riesling grapes with fully developed *Botrytis cinerea* produced the incredible Edelwein not incorrectly likened to a fine German *Beerenauslese*. In 1976, a difficult harvest year, luck smiled again and Edelwein II began its life in the crusher with an incredible refractometer reading of 35 sugar and a total acidity of .95.

After Larry Langbehn took over as winemaker, once again in 1978 the humid warmth in the vineyard produced botrytised grapes whose golden nectar had 15.5 percent residual sugar. This was topped in 1982 by Langbehn with an incredible Edelwein Gold with 21.9 percent residual, a veritable *Trockenbeerenauslese.*

SAMPLER SELECTION

Chardonnay (Napa Valley). Every vintage more firmly establishes this as one of California's greatest landmark white wines.

Edelwein-Sweet Johannisberg Riesling (Napa Valley). Not made every year. Every edition a connoisseur's rich treasure. Always expensive, but with proper storage will hold for a lifetime.

Cabernet Sauvignon (Napa Valley). Like the Cabernet Bosche, these dark, big, tannic wines need time to become drinkable.

HANNS KORNELL CHAMPAGNE CELLARS

Larkmead Lane, St. Helena, California 94574

Hanns Kornell is a third-generation winemaker who began his career in Upper Silesia at the age of four, helping to clean bottles for his grandfather in the family winery. Academic education in enology began at Geisenheim, with on-the-job training in Épernay, Burgundy, and finally in Italy where he learned the secrets of vermouth's aromatic infusion. Before returning home to Germany, there was practical experience with bottling techniques in England.

After fleeing Germany in 1939, Kornell got his first significant break with his appointment as champagne maker for the memorable Fountaingrove Winery of Santa Rosa. With scrimping and saving, by 1952 he had accumulated just enough to lease the Sonoma Wine Company in Sonoma. "Bottle by bottle, I built the business, taking orders for wine by day, filling them by night. I lived on six hundred dollars that first year. I ate a lot of salami."

In 1958, with an inventory of 5,000 bottles, he was ready for his own winery. He found it on Larkmead Lane—a fine old stone winery built in 1845 and operated in the post-Repeal era as Larkmead Cellars.

There was a time when many of the leading California champagnes were brought up to their sparkling finish in the Hanns Kornell Champagne Cellars. But today, the more than two million bottles in those stone cellars are exclusively Kornell wines. Kornell has an abiding affection for Johannisberg Riesling, and his *cuvées* often run a maverick course. Sehr Trocken is just such a maverick wine, having no *dosage* and, unlike most California champagnes, being made primarily from Riesling. Honored with gold-medal awards from tasting competitions at home and abroad, it is a connoisseur's selection—dry, dry, dry, and pungent with the yeastiness of the true "champagne nose." Kornell utilizes Pinot Blanc and Sémillon as well as Riesling. All his sparkling wines are bottled, fermented, aged, then shipped in their original bottles in the classic *méthode champenoise* tradition.

SAMPLER SELECTION

Hanns Kornell Sehr Trocken. Often as much as six years "on the yeast," an intensely dry, crisply brilliant wine.

Hanns Kornell Brut. Drier than many California cham-

pagnes of this *dosage*. A beautiful golden straw color and fine bead.

Hanns Kornell Extra Dry. To many, the favorite for its more gentle mien and fruity roundness, barely edged with sweetness.

HEITZ WINE CELLARS

500 Taplin Road, St. Helena, California 94574

From the day that he received his master's degree in enology from UC–Davis, Joe Heitz has moved toward his winemaking goals with uncomplicated simplicity, uncompromising and, ultimately, highly rewarded. Today his name is synonymous with the finest of California wines. His vintage Cabernet Sauvignons are favorably compared with the finest growths of Bordeaux, and his multi-lot Chardonnays frequently with the best *grand cru* growths of the Côte de Beaune, Meursault, or Montrachet.

Before establishing his own winery, there were significant years in the fifties with André Tchelistcheff in the lab at Beaulieu, and a few years of giving courses in enology at Fresno State College. In 1961 Joe and his bride, Alice, bought a small winery surrounded by 8 acres of Grignolino grapes which the former owner had vinted for his "Only One" winery. With the tenacity for which he has become famous, Joe quickly developed an attachment to Grignolino, giving the Piedmontese variety a Napa Valley distinction the grape has not known before or since. Vintage Grignolino Rosé at a modest $3 is always on the Heitz list of offerings, along with the more noble and expensive varieties that are collectors' items. One example of the interesting wines he has cellared is featured on his list as Cellar Treasure Angelica, a wine too often scorned by wine snobs who don't know what they're missing.

Joe has an answer for critics of the pricing of Heitz wines, many of whom will pay as much or more for European growths of lesser quality. "The wines are limited, require minute attention and long-term aging. I work long, hard hours to make a fine wine, and so I feel I am entitled to a fine price. Our pricing is not

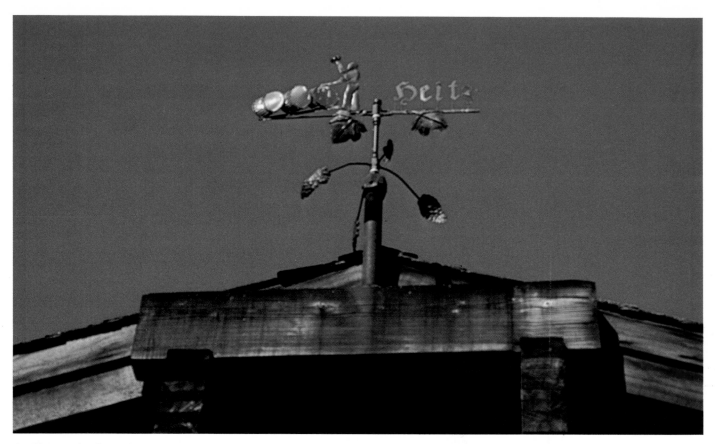

Joe Heitz makes beautiful wines no matter what the weather

based on supply and demand alone, but actually on the kind of quality that I try to get into my wine."

In support of his theory, there is a waiting list of wine merchants all across the land hoping they'll have even a token supply of Heitz wines.

SAMPLER SELECTION

Chardonnay (Napa Valley). Each vintage lot carries its code number and each is dry, golden, wood-aged, distinguished.

Grignolino Rosé (Napa Valley). Characteristically orange-pink in hue, fragrant of its fruit, dry, surprisingly silky.

Cabernet Sauvignon (Martha's Vineyard) Among the finest clarets of the world, each vintage a cellar treasure.

Cellar Treasure Angelica. Rich wine of golden amber color, luxuriously sweet and mellow—music by candlelight.

INGLENOOK VINEYARDS

Highway 29, Rutherford, California 94573

No winery in California has a more romantic history than Inglenook. Its founder, Finnish sea captain Gustave Ferdinand Niebaum, bought the young vineyard in 1879 from the Scotsman who gave the property its name, which means "cozy corner," an apt description of this property tucked protectively into the Mayacamas foothills.

In his corner of the foothills, Captain Niebaum built a grand mansion in 1879, and he spared no expense in building the winery, completed in 1887. The years have softened the majestic exterior with vines that turn a glowing red in autumn. Fermentation is no longer conducted as it was in Niebaum's day, on the top floor, but the raked gravel corridors which tunnel into the shelter knoll still hold 1,000-gallon oak oval casks filled with aging red wines.

A corner of the baronial Inglenook tasting room

Shortly after Repeal, ownership of Inglenook had passed to John Daniel, Jr., a grand-nephew of the founder. Speaking of his red wines, he once told me, "Wines, you know, are like children. Each one develops differently. The wines in all these casks, as you can see from these chalked scribbles, are Cabernet Sauvignon. No two of them are identical. We could blend them all together, of course, but some of them are just too outstanding to lose." Daniel's feeling for the casks of Cabernet Sauvignon resulted in "cask bottling" at Inglenook, a practice which was started in the late thirties and continues today.

In 1964 John Daniel, Jr., sold the winery (but not the mansion and its adjacent vineyard) to Heublein. The mansion was used in a television movie, "Killer Bees," starring Gloria Swanson as the mysterious bee-loving matriarch of a wine dynasty. I played the role of the Episcopal priest summoned for the heroine's last rites. In late 1976, the great mansion became the home of Francis Ford Coppolla, director of "The Godfather."

In 1971 a change of policy brought young Thomas Ferrell to Inglenook as winemaker. A graduate of UC-Davis and a member of the American Society of Enologists, he brought uncompromising standards as well as exceptional talent to the broad spectrum of wines bearing the Inglenook label. A newly constructed and expanded fermentation and aging facility, completed in 1974, provides the present winemaker, John Richburg, with deluxe equipment for fine winemaking.

Inglenook table wines are now grouped into four distinct bottlings: (1) Inglenook Navalle (a contraction of Napa and Valley) are modestly priced generic and varietal wines from California-grown grapes; (2) Inglenook Vintage wines come from grapes of Napa, Mendocino, and Sonoma counties carrying vintage dates; (3) Inglenook Estate Bottled wines are vintage-dated, from the Napa Valley, all top varietals including the famed Cabernet Sauvignon and Charbono, plus exciting new white wines from Chardonnay, Johannisberg Riesling, and Gewürztraminer; (4) Inglenook Cask Bottling, in limited production of Cabernet Sauvignon, Red Pinot (Pinot St. George), and Pinot Noir.

Estate Bottled Chardonnay (Napa Valley). Held on the skins eight hours, fermented at 45° F. A big, oak-aged, virile, white poem.

Estate Bottled Johannisberg Riesling. Allowed two months to complete fermentation. Flowery, fragrant, essentially dry.

Estate Bottled Gewürztraminer. As freshly pungent and fragrant as nasturtiums in a summer garden. Beautiful wine!

Estate Bottled Cabernet Sauvignon. Soft and velvety wine with an intriguing pepperiness. Cask editions worth long holding.

CHARLES KRUG WINERY

Highway 29, St. Helena, California 94574

The Charles Krug Winery was established in St. Helena in 1860 by Prussian-born Charles Krug, who had come from Germany to San Francisco in 1852. There, working at the U.S. Mint under the dynamic Agoston Haraszthy, he was infected by his enthusiasm for winemaking possibilities in California. In 1860, Krug married General Vallejo's grand-niece, Caroline, and, fired by ambition, moved to the Napa Valley, where his bride owned land. The Charles Krug Winery became a great estate of far-reaching fame, but at the time of Krug's death in 1892, phylloxera had devastated his vineyards, and he was deeply in debt.

In 1943 the sadly neglected winery facilities and ranch, owned then by James K. Moffitt's family, were sold to Cesare Mondavi. The $75,000 purchase price included two houses, a dilapidated winery, and 150 acres of land. With enormous energy, thrift, and skill, the Mondavi family made a net profit of $77,000 that first year, solidly establishing this immigrant family as worthy inheritors of the Charles Krug wine traditions. Despite the deplorable conditions of the winery equipment, Cesare Mondavi, with the assistance of his sons, Robert and Peter, bottled bulk wines that at once found a demand in the market.

Cesare Mondavi died in 1959, leaving his widow, Rosa, as the head of the family corporation and Robert

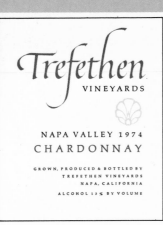

Trefethen
VINEYARDS

NAPA VALLEY 1974
CHARDONNAY

GROWN, PRODUCED & BOTTLED BY
TREFETHEN VINEYARDS
NAPA, CALIFORNIA
ALCOHOL 13% BY VOLUME

Vintage 1971 Napa Valley

CUVAISON
Napa Valley
Cabernet Sauvignon

Alcohol 13.5% by Volume
Produced and bottled by Cuvaison, Inc., Calistoga, California

FRANCISCAN
1973

NAPA VALLEY
CABERNET SAUVIGNON

Produced and Bottled by
FRANCISCAN VINEYARDS
Rutherford, California
Alcohol 12% by Volume

Charles Krug

NAPA VALLEY
CHENIN BLANC
A MEDIUM DRY WHITE WINE MADE
FROM THE CHENIN BLANC GRAPE
PRODUCED AND BOTTLED BY
Charles Krug Winery
ST. HELENA · CALIFORNIA
ALCOHOL 12% BY VOLUME

MOUNT VEEDER WINERY
1974
CABERNET SAUVIGNON
MT. VEEDER–NAPA COUNTY
PRODUCED AND BOTTLED AT
MOUNT VEEDER WINERY
NAPA, CALIFORNIA
ALCOHOL 13% BY VOLUME

SPRING MOUNTAIN
1974
Napa Valley
CABERNET SAUVIGNON
MADE AND BOTTLED BY
Spring Mountain Vineyards · St. Helena, California
ALCOHOL 13.0% BY VOLUME

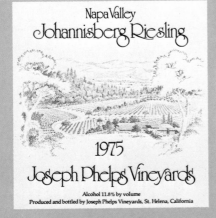

Napa Valley
Johannisberg Riesling

1975

Joseph Phelps Vineyards

Alcohol 11.8% by volume
Produced and bottled by Joseph Phelps Vineyards, St. Helena, California

UNFINED

1969
Napa Valley
CABERNET SAUVIGNON
ALCOHOL 13% BY VOLUME
PRODUCED AND BOTTLED BY
ROBERT MONDAVI WINERY
OAKVILLE, CALIFORNIA

CLOS DU VAL

1973
CABERNET SAUVIGNON
Napa Valley
Made and Bottled by
CLOS DU VAL WINE CO LTD
Napa California
Alcohol 12% per Volume

NAPA WINE LABELS

and Peter as the winemakers. Innovations by Robert, trained in enology after graduation from Stanford in 1937, emphasized longer, cooler fermentation of white wines than was common practice at the time. Glass-lined tanks, purchased from breweries, were used to hold wines before bottling, preventing excessive wood-iness. In 1955 a wine called White Pinot was rechris-tened Chenin Blanc after its 100 percent varietal source. With notable brilliance, fresh perfume from cool fermentation, and a certain residual sweetness, it not only won a gold medal at the Sacramento Fair but was the first California white wine to become so popular that its makers had to place it on allocation to dealers.

Differences began to arise between Robert, who tended to pioneer new enological frontiers, and Peter, who held to more traditional ways. In 1966, Robert left the family firm to establish his own winery at Oakville, while Peter and their mother, Rosa Mondavi, administered the operation of the Charles Krug Win-ery. The August Moon Concerts, since 1965 a popular tourist attraction, are conducted on the lawn beneath the great oaks of the Krug Estate, where members of the Mondavi family live in their own houses within the flower-bordered compound.

The Charles Krug Winery owns 1,200 acres of vine but much of the wine in their 3 1/2-million-gallon storage space is made from grapes bought from other growers. The finest wines, such as the Vintage Selec-tion Cabernet Sauvignon, honoring Cesare Mondavi, and the immensely popular Moscato di Canelli, are listed as "when available," but the regular varietals and CK jug generic wines are sufficient to supply retail customers and the nation's restaurants with depend-ably excellent house wines of fine value at a moderate price. The Chablis, with a significant percentage of Chardonnay press wine, is in my opinion one of the state's best buys in this much-abused category; it is crisp, dry, and with enough Chardonnay character to warrant a Chablis title. And Charles Krug Napa Valley Chenin Blanc is a popular standard, essential on any wine list across the land.

SAMPLER SELECTION

Napa Valley Chablis. Nonvintage wine, always depend-

able, dry, crisp, clean, inexpensive.

Napa Valley Blanc Fumé. A vintage wine carrying the flowery and fruit charms of its Loire namesake.

Napa Valley Chenin Blanc. When well-chilled, the apparent sweetness seems to add to the pleasing silkiness of the wine.

Napa Valley Cabernet Sauvignon—Vintage Selection. Oak-aged to soft maturity in 50-gallon barrels before release.

LOUIS M. MARTINI

Highway 29, St. Helena, California 94574

Both wine and wisdom were in the heritage from the late Louis M. Martini, who was born in 1887 on the Italian Riviera at Pietra Ligure, and died in California in 1974. "Industry without art is brutality," he once told me. "Infallible grace of instinct makes a winemaster of one man, while avarice makes an indus-trial brute of another."

In one of the winery's brochures is the statement "Wine is a food beverage intended to make our meals more enjoyable each and every day." In the wide range of wines offered under the Martini label, from the least expensive generic jug wine to the aged Special Selec-tion varietals and richly mellow dessert wines, the dominant consideration has been the pleasure-giving potential of wine to enhance food.

In 1937, Louis acquired a large vineyard 1,000 feet above the Napa Valley floor, extending across the Napa–Sonoma line in the Mayacamas Mountains. Since it was in both Napa and Sonoma counties and was truly a mountain vineyard, where nonirrigated vines struggled with the elements to produce grapes rich in concentration, low in tonnage yield, it was logical for the Martini labels to read neither Napa nor Sonoma but California Mountain. The phrase moved into the American wine vocabulary quickly after Louis bottled a good red and a good white wine, popularly priced, and labeled the red, California Mountain Red Wine (or Mountain Burgundy) and the white, Mountain Chablis. Today, "California Mountain" means "inexpensive" but the Louis M. Martini Mountain Cabernet Sauvi-gnon is properly named not because it is a low-priced

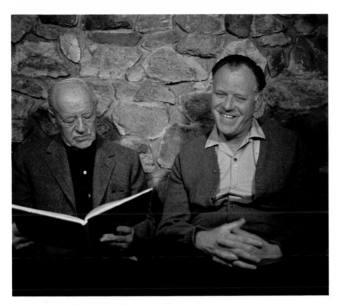

Louis M. and Louis P. Martini, father and son, relaxing in front of their rock-solid winery

wine but because it does indeed come from one of the Martini mountain vineyards.

The Martini vineyards now total more than 1,000 acres, including acreage in the cool Carneros region, a ranch in the Healdsburg area, as well as Monte Rosso, and a new acquisition in Chiles Valley.

It is the red wines of the Louis M. Martini vineyards and winery that connoisseurs treasure: the Cabernet Sauvignon, Zinfandel, Barbera, and Pinot Noir. The Private Reserve labels are the wines regularly offered which have been given added bottle aging, while the Special Selection labels are wines from outstanding years, produced in small lots and having greater quality and aging potential. Louis P. Martini, the son of the founder and now the head of the company, has made some experimental lots, available at the winery only, where the celebrated Moscato Amabile is still enchanting winelovers with its gentle effervescence and delicate perfume.

The Martini white wines, particularly good accompaniments for food, are dry, crisp, and brilliant, always to be enjoyed young. The Gewürztraminer is unique among California examples for its dryness, and in its 100 percent varietal composition, aromatic, spicy, and appetizing. The Johannisberg Riesling is subtle, soft, almost fragile in its delicacy on early release, suggesting a Moselle wine.

Ever since Louis P. Martini graduated, in 1940, from the University of California at Berkeley—in the banner class that included agriculture and enology majors Myron Nightingale, winemaster emeritus at Beringer, Charles Crawford, chief enologist at Gallo, and Zev Halperin of Christian Brothers—he had been unobtrusively active in extending the range and reputation of the Martini name. There is a measure of true greatness in Louis P. that kept him working quietly in the shadow of his father's genius until the older man was ready, at the close of his life, to surrender the reins of management. There are no more highly respected wines made in California today than those of the winery that continues to bear the Martini name.

Third-generation Carolyn and Michael Martini are dynamically engaged in enhancing this splendid heritage.

SAMPLER SELECTION

California Gewürztraminer. Produced in the tradition of Alsace. Spicy and fruity; vintage, and in limited supply.

California Merlot. Pure Merlot of distinctive tartness and familial relationship to Cabernet Sauvignon.

California Cabernet Sauvignon. A wine of consistent elegance and breed from the finest grapes, all mountain-grown.

MAYACAMAS VINEYARDS

1155 Lokoya Road, Napa, California 94558

In 1889 a sword engraver from Stuttgart, Germany, turned pickle merchant in San Francisco, made his way up through the tangled scrub and rocky dells of Mt. Veeder to establish a small vineyard and winery at an elevation of 2,000 feet. This is the kind of terrain that the Roman poet Ausonius called the "land Bacchus loves." Though difficulties—such as swarms of locusts, marauding birds, mountain thunderstorms —abound, when the sun shines bright the vines, nourished by the volcanic soil and natural rainfall, yield grapes that concentrate a wonderful richness.

In 1941 petroleum engineer Jack Taylor and his

wife, Mary, acquired the 400-acre property with its old graystone winery and distillery and its gnarled Zinfandel vines. They renamed it after the mountains that the Indians called Mayacamas ("cry of the mountain lion"), and even today the howl of the cougar is not unknown in this wilderness paradise.

In 1968, Bob Travers, another young petroleum engineer from Stanford, turned to wine production, and, after an apprenticeship with Joe Heitz, he took over Mayacamas Vineyards with a small group of investors. That September the Travers's first child arrived just when the Zinfandel grapes were ready to be harvested. By the time Bob got around to picking them, the must reading registered a dismaying 27.5 sugar, which zoomed to a Balling reading higher than 35°, attributable to some raisined grapes. By rule-of-thumb conversion, this indicated that the alcoholic

The Late Harvest Zinfandel of Mayacamas, with the terraced vines on the upper slopes of Mt. Veeder in the background

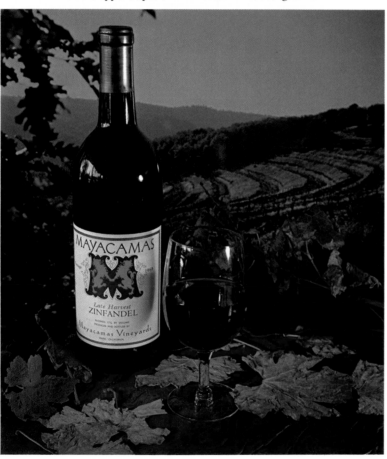

content of the wine might be higher than 17 percent. Any reading higher than the critical 15 percent suggests a "stuck" fermentation, that is, the annihilation of the yeasts by the alcohol before all the sugar is converted. "We kept our cool . . . and prayed a lot," Bob Travers remembers. When with ears pressed to the casks they discerned no more sounds of bubbling within, a reading was taken. The wine was bone-dry, and registering a 17-plus percent alcohol. Impossible! Obviously those yeast cells didn't know they couldn't go on converting grape sugar at over 15 percent alcohol, so they did it anyway!

After many complications, including the payment of higher taxes because of the alcohol content, and a refusal to call the big Zinfandel Port, the wine emerged as "Mayacamas Vineyards 1968 Late Harvest Zinfandel—Alcohol 17 1/2 Percent by Volume." I dubbed it "the Miracle at Mayacamas," and all the world beat a track to the Travers's cellar doors. In 1972, Travers produced another Late Harvest Zinfandel, and again in 1974, but the wines are too big to serve with anything but cheese and fruit after dining. They served primarily to call winelovers' attention to the Chardonnay from the terraced vineyards established by Jack Taylor and to the rich Cabernet Sauvignon developed by Bob Travers. All the Mayacamas wines are 100 percent varietal and emphasize only these three titles.

SAMPLER SELECTION

Chardonnay (Napa Valley). Big wines of true varietal character, aged one year in American oak, six months in French oak.

Zinfandel (Napa Valley). "Late Harvest" editions are not regularly produced. (Sometimes a Zinfandel Rosé is added.) The big robust wines are intensely flavored to last a lifetime.

Cabernet Sauvignon (Napa Valley). Each vintage edition needs at least five years before its stature can be adequately judged.

ROBERT MONDAVI WINERY

Highway 29, Oakville, California 94562

When he broke away from the family winery in

Michael Mondavi at work filling barrels of wine

1966 to put his own winemaking theories into practice, Robert Mondavi's career had its real beginning . . . at age fifty-four. Today the Robert Mondavi Winery, with its grand archway and tower in the California mission style of architecture, is a Napa Valley landmark, housing the equipment for this century's most exciting developments in California winemaking. The proliferation of storage and fermentation capacity to millions of gallons is a minor accomplishment compared with the advances in wine quality brought about by the creative drive of Robert Mondavi. He was assisted in no small measure by his talented sons Michael and young Tim in the formulation of these new trend-setting methods that have influenced the winemaking industry.

To the layman the dazzling stainless-steel fermentation equipment, the horizontal rotating tanks, the centrifuges, the pyramids of French oak, German oak, and Yugoslavian oak barrels, the glass-enclosed laboratories seem implements of modern alchemy. All serve to bring added dimension to the wines, to extract ever more and more from the potential in the grape, to aid in achieving wine's main purpose—its harmony with food at table. There is not a wine country in Europe or Australia that has not been visited by Robert Mondavi. It is as if two thousand years of winemaking, all the techniques developed since Noah, were as nothing before what can be done now.

That exciting "now" has come to pass in the French connection of Robert Mondavi and Baron Philippe de Rothschild. Their vintage Red Table Wine called Opus One made a much-heralded debut in March 1984 with two vintages, 1979 and 1980, both made at the Napa Valley winery under the direction of Baron Philippe's winemaker Lucien Sionneau and Robert Mondavi's son and winemaker, Tim Mondavi. Both wines, of Cabernet accent, are uniquely and elegantly "sculptured" (Mondavi's term), warranting all the advance excitement. Alas, the quantities are limited, the prices high.

SAMPLER SELECTION

Pinot Noir (Napa Valley). Each vintage moves toward a greater realization of the grape's true, full, dry dignity, the translucence a hallmark of quality.

Opus One. A Napa Valley Red Table Wine. The wine will always reflect its Cabernet body, but every vintage, as with French clarets, will be different.

MOUNT VEEDER WINERY

1999 Mt. Veeder Road, Napa, California 94558

This small winery, high in the Mayacamas Mountains, was built in 1973 by San Francisco lawyer Michael Bernstein, who brought it esteem from a succession of fine Cabernet and Zinfandel wines made from his own vines. In 1982, after searching the eastern United States for a vineyard home, Henry Matheson answered an ad in the *Wall Street Journal* from a small California winery in the Napa Valley; Mount Veeder became the Mathesons' idyllic home. Peter Franus stayed on as winemaker and with the new owners is pursuing the goals of fine Cabernet. The 1,400-foot elevation provides the choicest grapes, including Merlot, Cabernet Franc, Malbec, and Petite Verdot, which augment the major planting of Cabernet Sauvignon in this ideal 22-acre nonirrigated vineyard. The last vintage of Zinfandel was 1982; the vines were budded over to Chardonnay in June 1983.

SAMPLER SELECTION

Cabernet Sauvignon (Napa Valley). Estate-grown grapes, impeccably fermented, aged in fine French oak, assure a velvety, complex jewel.

NICHELINI VINEYARDS

2349 Lower Chiles Rd., St. Helena, California 94574

Winemaking has been going on almost without interruption here ever since 1890, when Anton Nichelini came to the valley from Switzerland. Then as now, good, sound table wines from good, sound grapes brought customers to the cellar doors. At 900 feet above sea level, with its own microclimate and soil complexity, the Chiles Valley is attracting more and more attention from vineyardists of Napa, below.

James and Rosemary Nichelini put the welcome mat out in an engaging way, and winelovers may sit on the open terrace and sample wines at leisure, so the detour is worth the effort.

SAMPLER SELECTION

Chenin Blanc (Napa Valley). Fresh and fruity, the zing of the earth giving substance to the dry white wine.

Sauvignon Vert (Napa Valley). Long one of the Nichelini specialties. Crisp, clean, dry; not great, but good.

JOSEPH PHELPS VINEYARDS

200 Taplin Road, St. Helena, California 94574

Driving north on the Silverado Trail, the casual tourist cannot miss the freshly painted green-and-white schoolhouse topped with a belfry. It is a part of the 670-acre former cattle ranch that Joseph Phelps has adopted as a temporary home. An interior valley of gentle knolls is now ribbed with 120 acres of Cabernet Sauvignon, Merlot, Cabernet Franc, Zinfandel, and Syrah, the last a stock—distinctly different from the more common planting of Petite Sirah—imported to California from the Rhône by Professor Olmo.

Phelps, the president of the Hensel Phelps Construction Company, of Colorado, came into wine with innocent inadvertence. On vacation in Italy he became fascinated with both the taste and the production of Italian wines. His company's commission to build the two Souverain wineries, one in Napa and the other on a multi-million-dollar scale at Geyserville in the Alexander Valley, reinforced his desire to build a winery of his own. Phelps located his double-winged winery, built from recycled lumber, on a rise of land above the oak-shaded meadow, without losing a single tree.

As winemaker, Phelps secured young Walter Schug, a graduate of the famous center for the study of viticulture and enology in Geisenheim in the German Rheingau. It is not surprising that the first wine released from the winery was Johannisberg Riesling of the 1973 vintage. Under full production, the goal is 40,000 cases of wine annually.

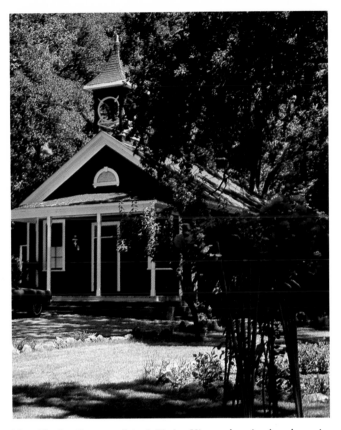

The old schoolhouse at Joseph Phelps Vineyards, a landmark on the Silverado Trail

On my first visit I tasted the 1975 Special Selection Johannisberg Riesling, which remains in my memory as perhaps the finest vinification of this grape I have ever experienced in California. Statistically, it had 10 percent residual sugar, which is very sweet, but the sweetness was balanced with .94 total acidity, while a light 10 percent alcohol by volume allowed a delicacy hauntingly reminiscent of fine *Beerenauslese* of the Rhine. But the color, a brilliant lemon yellow, was equally striking. Totally botrytised grapes were used, and the slow, cool fermentation was conducted by Schug with the care of a conscientious baby-sitter for four and a half months at 58° F. Any cooler and fermentation would have stopped.

Already available in eighteen states, Joseph Phelps wines are bound to become highly prized members of California's growing family of premium wines.

Johannisberg Riesling (Napa Valley). A 100 percent flowery varietal wine of delicacy and clean brilliance.

Gewürztraminer (Yountville). Aged briefly in Schug's style—in German-oak ovals, with 1 percent residual sugar.

Chardonnay (Napa Valley). A generous, big wine of full bouquet with its oak aging not overshadowing the fruit.

Cabernet Sauvignon (Stanton Estate). Blended with 5 percent Merlot; ready in the early eighties. Aged in French-oak barrels.

POPE VALLEY WINERY

6613 Pope Valley Road, Pope Valley, California 94567

In 1972 the James Devitt family undertook to restore this gravity-flow winery, built into the side of a slate hill in 1910. Wine is being made here as it was early in this century at almost every winery: grapes are delivered to the crusher on the top (third) floor; the juice flows naturally to the fermenters on the second floor; the finished young wine flows, still by gravity, to aging and storage tanks on the cool ground floor. Devitt, an electronics engineer (as are many other California winemakers), began his alliance with vines and wines as an avocation. Now it is a full-time, rewarding occupation. Making fine wine has become his primary ambition, leading to the acquisition of new stainless-steel fermenting tanks, modern presses, and European-oak barrels for aging. None of the rustic charm of the place has been lost, and visitors may enjoy picnic lunches under giant oaks while delighting in the rural quiet of old California.

In line with the goals of fine winemaking, James and Robert Devitt (the latter is in charge of winemaking) supplement the grapes from their own 65 acres of vines with premium grapes from the Dry Creek area of Sonoma.

Sauvignon Blanc (Pope Valley). Light, dry, soft wine of modest price; pleasing with shellfish and trout.

Cabernet Sauvignon (Napa and Sonoma). One of the finest wines produced by the James Devitt family; richly complex.

RUTHERFORD HILL WINERY

Souverain Road at Silverado Trail, Rutherford, California 94573

"Wineries used to be perennials, with dependable flowering each new vintage season," an astute observer of the California wine scene remarked to me. "Now, they're row crops . . . in and out!" Tucked away in the hills just east of the Silverado Trail, this handsome, modern winery designed by John Marsh Davis was built in the early 1970s after Pillsbury of Minneapolis had bought the property then known as Souverain Cellars. Pillsbury sold their interest in 1976 to a group of seasoned vineyardists and winemakers that included William P. Jaeger, Jr., Charles Carpy of Freemark Abbey, Brad Webb, who brought his considerable skills in wine technology, and Phil Baxter, their winemaker.

Rutherford Hill Winery has achieved its own distinctive identity, quite apart from its ownership ties to Freemark Abbey. Winemakers, like artists, are famed for their individuality, and Baxter is an artist-winemaker. You have only to bring a glass of his Chardonnay to your nose to appreciate his sensitive handling of the grape in its translation to golden wine. The same is true of his Gewürztraminer, Sauvignon Blanc, and medal-winning Merlot. Each is a model of its kind.

Merlot (Napa Valley). With a generous addition of Cabernet Sauvignon, this garnet-hued wine has incredible depth, softness, and charm.

SCHRAMSBERG VINEYARDS

Schramsberg Road, Calistoga, California 94515

Jack Davies and his wife, Jamie, came to Calistoga

Jamie and Jack Davies enjoy a private tasting of Schramsberg champagnes

as young wine enthusiasts. When they found Schramsberg it was all there, not only the tradition and the history, but the house, the caves, some old vines—a relic of the great winemaking days a century or more ago. The Davies's transformation began in 1965. The caves hewn from the rocks by Chinese laborers in the last century would henceforth house only sparkling wines. New vineyards of Chardonnay, Pinot Noir, Pinot Blanc, and Napa Gamay were planted; an additional 25 acres were acquired, and planted. Over the last few years, the aging tunnels, too, were expanded, with digging machines boring a quarter mile of passageways into the hillside—additional space that will help the Davieses reach a new goal of 50,000 cases. Already those auxiliary tunnels are filled with stacks of wines *en tirage,* expensive resting inventory. For every bottle marketed, there must be three in reserve if the wine is to be three years on the yeasts. In short, millions of bottles! But that's why the Schramsberg label is synonymous with quality and is found only on the best restaurant wine lists in the land.

André Tchelistcheff became the first consultant at Schramsberg, and he recalls well the day of their first harvest, when the automatic press failed to work. "Madame," he announced to Jamie, "your duty is clear!" The slight, bewildered mistress of the house gasped, "Not me!" But there was no denying the gallant winemaster, who insisted, "Oui, madame!" and escorted her into the grapes . . . minus her stockings.

All Schramsberg champagnes are produced by the classic *méthode champenoise* technique, the secondary fermentation occurring in the same bottle that goes to market, after hand riddling, racking, and disgorging have removed the claw of sediment. The Blanc de Noirs, an absolute *tour de force* of brilliant pale-gold wine without a tinge of color from the black skins, often appears daringly in a clear bottle.

There are six Schramsberg wines: the Blanc de Blancs, predominantly from Chardonnay; Blanc de Noirs from free-run Pinot Noir, with a little Pinot Blanc for silky body; Cuvée de Pinot, a salmon-pink wine of free-run Pinot Noir with some added Gamay; Reserve, composed of select lots of each vintage left longer on the yeasts; Cremant Demi-Sec, a dessert champagne from the hybrid Flora.

Each of the above, like the *grande marque* sparkling wines of France, reflects handcrafting techniques, with close attention to the creation of each *cuvée,* giving the wine its *élan.*

SAMPLER SELECTION

Blanc de Blancs (Napa Valley Champagne). Substantial fruit in the bouquet; dry, crisp. The 1981 was chosen by President Reagan as the toasting wine for the formal banquet he hosted on his 1984 visit to China.

Blanc de Noirs (Napa Valley Champagne). Three years on the yeasts. Classic richness and elegance. Improves with age.

Crémant (Demi-Sec Napa Valley Champagne). California's most distinguished dessert sparkler. Fragrant, sweet, golden.

Cuvée de Pinot (Napa Valley Champagne). Pale salmon-pink in color, recommended for fine luncheon service.

SILVER OAK CELLARS

915 Oakville Crossroad, Oakville, California 94562

"To make exceptional Cabernets was my winemaker's dream for many years," Justin Meyer told me. "Ten years ago, when Ray Duncan and I created Silver Oak Cellars, my dream began to materialize." In 1979, with the sale of Franciscan Vineyard, Meyer was free to pursue his particular dream. With Alexander Valley grapes (which he believes are even finer than Napa Valley Cabernets), study, hard work, patience—he ages his wine three years in oak, two in bottle, before release—it seems that his dream is coming true.

In the spring of 1983 I tasted all the released wines —'73, '74, '75, '76, '77, and '78. All reveal Justin's styling, with age in both American and French oak. Look for the water tower on a silver label, a landmark design, a landmark wine!

SAMPLER SELECTION

Cabernet Sauvignon (Alexander Valley). The only wine under the Silver Oak label, always five years old before release, always outstanding.

A Victorian stained-glass window in the Tiburcio Parrott house, home of Spring Mountain's Michael Robbins

SPRING MOUNTAIN VINEYARDS

2805 Spring Mountain Road, St. Helena, California 94574

If it is true that every man at some time would like to have a yacht, an oil well, a mistress, or a restaurant (not necessarily in that order), a winery with a mansion would also fit into this inventory of Walter Mitty fantasy. In 1968 Shirley and Michael Robbins of southern California found a small but stately mansion with a terraced vineyard just north of Beringer and its Rhine House, bought it as a second home, began restoration, and found themselves entering the wine business, as it were, by the back door.

This soon led to a wish for a larger place. The first house became St. Clement Vineyard when sold to a San Francisco eye surgeon. The Robbinses bought a much grander wine estate, the nineteenth-century Tiburcio Parrot home, with 110 acres of hillside vines and some old cellar tunnels. Given full restoration, a handsome Disneylike "Town Hall" facade for the winery, thoroughly equipped for fine winemaking, this multi-million-dollar project ended the Robbinses' marriage —and began the winery's own double life. It inspired the logo and is the location for the popular television series "Falcon Crest."

Needless to say, sales of Spring Mountain wines began to climb, leading to an even more dramatic second label, Falcon Crest, which sells especially well in tourist shops across the land.

SAMPLER SELECTION

Sauvignon Blanc (Napa Valley). A vintage selection, always bone-dry, crisp and golden, suggesting a Graves of Bordeaux.

Chardonnay (Napa Valley). Each successive vintage has rated high in critical esteem. Aging in French oak. Soft, splendid.

Cabernet Sauvignon (Napa Valley). Grapes from contracted acres produce wine in the French tradition, requiring long aging.

Spring Mountain's Falcon Crest Napa Valley Chardonnay. The same fine vintage Chardonnay, though of a separate lot, from Spring Mountain Vineyards, obviously bottled to capture fans of the prime-time television series.

STAG'S LEAP VINEYARD

6150 Silverado Trail, Napa, California 94558

A private road leads from the Silverado Trail to a small secluded valley just below the stony peaks of the mountains on the eastern border of the Napa Valley. A great sixteen-point Roosevelt elk once fell or leaped to his death from those stone cliffs to the slopes below. For years the great set of stag horns ornamented the stone manor house built in the last century by Howard Spencer Chase for his bride, Minnie Mizener, sister of the legendary Wilson and Henry Mizener. Hard times became Chase's master and in 1909 he sold the entire place to Clarence and Frances Grange.

Carl Doumani and a small group of investors purchased the property from widowed Frances Grange in 1970, and have slowly begun restoration of the manor house and replanting of the vineyard and gardens. From the 100 acres of vines replanted in Pinot Noir, Cabernet, and Merlot, some fine wines may emerge. From the existing Petite Syrah and Chenin Blanc vines, a token production already gives reason for great expectations.

SAMPLER SELECTION

Chenin Blanc (Napa Valley). Lovely, silky wine, not bitingly dry, tinged with residual sweetness.

Petite Syrah (Napa Valley). A big, beautiful wine of great substance; a wine of majestic quality, after long airing.

STAG'S LEAP WINE CELLARS

5766 Silverado Trail, Napa, California 94558

The legendary stag's leap of this area is enshrined in the names of two separately owned and operated wineries, a circumstance sometimes confusing to con-

The mansion at Spring Mountain, familiar to television viewers as the fictional "Falcon Crest"

Warren Winiarski of Stag's Leap Wine Cellars

sumers. It is Stag's Leap Wine Cellars, purchased in 1973 by Warren Winiarski, whose esteemed bottles are eagerly sought—and all too rarely found—by wine-lovers in all parts of the United States.

Winiarski completed his first crush in his new winery in 1973, a Cabernet Sauvignon that dazzled the wine world at a Paris tasting in May 1976. A completely French jury placed it first over a clutch of stellar First Growth clarets of Bordeaux. Shock waves from that event are still rippling in the sea of controversy surrounding California/French wine comparisons. In Winiarski's own estimation, and that of many, including myself, his 1974 edition was even better.

After years of apprenticeship, at Souverain with Lee Stewart, at Beaulieu with André Tchelistcheff, and at the Robert Mondavi Winery in Oakville, Winiarski, with his wife, Barbara, their children, and a group of partners, operates his own vineyards and winery, where he can produce wines according to the highest

ideals of winemaking. The 45-acre property contains his Cabernet Sauvignon and Merlot vines. White Riesling grapes come from the Birkmyer Vineyard of Wild Horse Valley. Fermentation of the Riesling is in oak tanks (for a softer wine), Cabernet Sauvignon and Merlot in stainless steel. A Chardonnay, his first, was made in 1976, and, released in 1978, rounded out the offerings of intense varietal wines.

SAMPLER SELECTION

Johannisberg Riesling (Birkmyer Vineyard). A long wine of delicate complexity, masculine in its solidity.

Gamay Beaujolais (Napa Valley). A combination of Napa Gamay for softness and Pinot Noir for intriguing fruitiness.

Cabernet Sauvignon (Stag's Leap Vineyards). So rich in substance you can almost chew it. Velvet-soft, full varietal fragrance.

Merlot (Stag's Leap Vineyards). In keeping with the winery policy, the varietal is emphasized, though touched with Cabernet Sauvignon.

STERLING VINEYARDS

1111 Dunaweal Lane, Calistoga, California 94515

Peter Newton and Michael Stone were in the avant-garde of California winelovers in the decade preceding the wine boom of the 1970s. They had ambitious plans for the hilltop winery and the surrounding vineyards below. Their parent company, Sterling International, which dealt in the manufacture, conversion, and sale of paper products, funded their lofty objectives. Trellised vineyards were planted in 1964; the dazzling white winery, resembling a Greek monastery, was completed in 1973.

The first wine from Sterling's own grapes, a 1968 Merlot, was rich and balanced, reflecting the under-cropping techniques that result in fewer berries of more concentrated complexity. Its signal success inaugurated a period of new importance for Merlot in California, which still continues.

The whirligig of time, however, brings changes. In August 1977, Coca-Cola of Atlanta bought the winery,

Cabernet Sauvignon and Merlot vines lined up beneath the high rocks where the legendary stag is said to have made his famous leap

159

appointing Gregory De Lucca as president in charge of operations. That included the acquisition of additional acreage, making it possible for all Sterling wines to be estate-bottled. Viticulturist Tucker Catlin supervised the cultivation of the splendid Diamond Mountain hillside vineyards in Sterling's 1,000-acre domain. T-budding of varieties outside those needed for Cabernet Sauvignon, Merlot, Chardonnay, and Sauvignon Blanc was completed.

In October 1983, Coca-Cola's wine holdings, including the flagship winery, Sterling Vineyards, were acquired by Seagram. De Lucca and winemaster Theo Rosenbrand, a Tchelistcheff disciple from Beaulieu Vineyard, have remained under the new administration, eagerly awaiting the inauguration of the winery's partnership with the French Champagne house G.H. Mumm & Co. of Reims. Guy de Vaux, formerly of Gold Seal, is the director of this exciting development. There has been no official announcement of the name for the sparkling wine made at Sterling, but an educated guess suggests it will be Domaine Mumm, with a Napa Valley appellation. All Sterling's good news can ring out on the bronze bells atop the hill, acquired from London's St. Dunstan's-in-the-East. This landmark winery continues its saga of prestige.

SAMPLER SELECTION

Sauvignon Blanc (Napa Valley). Every vintage has classic Graves silkiness from added Semillon grapes, bringing softness and charm.

Chardonnay (Napa Valley). An intense wine of hillside grapes and Napa Valley complexity; classic balance of wood and fruit.

Merlot (Napa Valley). Elegant, dark garnet in color, with tea and cherry fragrance. Pleasant to drink early, yet long-lived.

Cabernet Sauvignon (Napa Valley). With added Merlot for fragrant complexity; requires aging for full appreciation.

STONEGATE WINERY

1183 Dunaweal Lane, Calistoga, California 94515

West of Calistoga, the highway over the mountains to Sonoma curves upward through hillside farm-ing plots which even before the turn of the century were planted to orchard and vine. On these steep slopes in 1969 James and Barbara Spaulding planted Cabernet Sauvignon and some Chardonnay and Merlot in place of gnarled old Mission vine stumps. Grape growing led naturally to winemaking. In 1973 they bonded a very small winery adjacent to a bungalow on Dunaweal Lane. On an outside concrete pad stands their compact, modern winemaking plant—crusher and thirteen jacketed stainless-steel tanks for controlled fermentation. Their son David now shares the increased responsibilities that have come with an additional 16 acres of vines surrounding the tiny winery. Annual production is geared to 5,000 cases, with the purchase of choice grapes from independent growers to round out their offerings. Robert Stemmler, who has had German training and California experience, is consultant.

SAMPLER SELECTION

Sauvignon Blanc (Napa Valley). Aged in Limousin-oak barrels, the estate-bottled wine has eloquent varietal bouquet.

Chardonnay (Napa Valley). The first from their own winery and hillside grapes was produced in 1975. Big, racy, fine.

Petite Sirah (Maryroy Vineyard). From a nearby vineyard on the Silverado Trail, purple-black; a huge wine with peppery finish.

Cabernet Sauvignon (Napa Valley). Aged in Nevers oak. Estate-bottled production of a rich wine of complex varietal bouquet.

STONY HILL VINEYARD

P.O. Box 308, St. Helena, California 94574

The annual supply of Stony Hill Napa Valley Pinot Chardonnay is the equivalent in cases of half of the entire production of Montrachet in a good year. The excellence of Le Montrachet and of Stony Hill's Pinot Chardonnay cannot be denied, though in most instances the argument must rest upon faith...faith in

Grand opera against a backdrop of vineyards, one of Sterling's summer attractions

those lucky few whose tasting experience permits them to report on the glory of those wines.

In January 1977, Frederick Hoyt McCrea—the founder, with his wife, Eleanor, of Stony Hill Vineyard—died at the age of seventy-nine. He was among the first of the city dwellers to move into a second career of winemaking from a corporate boardroom, having retired to the Napa Valley in 1943 from McCann-Erickson of San Francisco. A thrifty man of pragmatic intelligence, he aimed at having his small winery make nothing but the finest product. He and Eleanor produced their first wine in 1952, and twenty-five succeeding vintages proved his decision to be right.

With the family and Michael Chelini, the vineyard and winery manager, Eleanor is continuing the noble legend of Stony Hill. "Because of the two-year drought, we may have to strip the vines of their fruit to save the life of the vines," she told me recently. "Last year you could *feel* the lack of rainfall in handling the bunches of berries, they were so light in weight." Even those lucky enough to be on the Stony Hill mailing list (the only way to buy their wines) will be strictly rationed in the amounts they can purchase.

In the lowest part of the vineyard is a tiny plot of Sémillon grapes, cuttings from the Sauternes vines pioneered in California at the Wente vineyards in Livermore. Eleanor and Fred embarked upon an experiment not unrelated to the *vino santo* techniques of Tuscany or the *recioto de Soave* using the loft-dried grapes of the Veneto. Picked at 26° Balling of sugar, the grapes were laid out on prune-drying trays for five to ten days in the sun, after which the sugar content would soar to 36°. (The first year the raccoons found these trays a marvelous buffet set out just for them!) Cool fermentation, stopped at 8 percent residual sugar and 13 percent alcohol by volume, produced a straw-gold wine of extraordinary richness not unlike a Château d'Yquem. Wine merchant Darrell Corti of Sacramento is the fortunate and exclusive purveyor of this wine, which Fred declared "a curiosity, not commercial" even though Corti customers gladly pay $6 a tenth, when they can get it.

No man can have a greater monument to his memory than his created works. As such, the Stony Hill Vineyard wines maintain Fred McCrea's ideal of perfection for winelovers everywhere.

SAMPLER SELECTION

Chardonnay (Napa Valley). Subtle differences exist between vintages. All are long-lived, full-bodied, glorious.

White Riesling (Napa Valley). First editions were made dry, later with slight residual sugar. Very fruity, intense flavor.

Gewürztraminer (Napa Valley). A fresh, clean wine of spicy bouquet from 100 percent varietal fermentation.

SUTTER HOME WINERY

277 St. Helena Highway South, St. Helena, California 94574

In 1946, the Trinchero family purchased the large, barnlike winery building constructed in 1874 and later bought by Jacob and John Sutter, cousins of the gold-rush pioneer of Sutter's Fort. Access to the streams of tourists on the central highway of the valley gave the Trincheros reason to buy the old building. To qualify them as dealers in bulk wine were six generations of winemaking in the Asti region of Piedmont. Bring a container and John or Mario Trinchero would fill it with almost any kind of wine in the book, at a bargain price. But the story changed when Mario's son Louis, known as Bob, entered the picture. Risking his father's scorn, in 1968 he bottled a fine Zinfandel with a Sutter Home label, and priced it well above the winery's going price. At $1.25 a fifth it sold out quickly, because it was fine wine.

The 1968 Sutter Home Deaver Vineyard Zinfandel became the fulcrum, turning and lifting Sutter Home into the ranks of front-line attention from winelovers. Sutter Home Zinfandels are produced with as little cellar treatment as possible. They are among the most sought-after Zinfandels of California today, of great depth of flavor, fruitiness and spice, capable of lasting ten to twenty years.

White Zinfandel (Amador County). From the white juice of black grapes; 2 percent residual sweetness.

Zinfandel (Amador County). Vintage selections from vines growing at 1,500-foot elevations. Always dark, rich, fragrant.

Moscato Amabile. A dessert wine produced from the Muscat grape. Popular, but a pallid pretender to this noted title.

TREFETHEN VINEYARDS

1160 Oak Knoll Avenue, Napa, California 94558

An old 1886 winery has been saved from oblivion and returned to its early prestige by industrial executive Eugene Trefethen, who acquired the 600-acre ranch in 1968. The eighty-year-old vines and the apple and walnut orchards were uprooted, and, under the direction of viticulturist Anthony Baldini, Cabernet Sauvignon, Merlot, Chardonnay, Pinot Noir, White Riesling, Gewürztraminer, and Zinfandel were planted. The microclimates of the property, previously determined by careful weather-station findings, were found to be well suited to those varieties. The new concrete flooring and modern winemaking equipment were in place literally only moments before the first grapes came in from harvesting in 1973.

The first Trefethen wine, a 1974 Napa Valley Chardonnay, produced under the direction of enologist David Whitehouse, made its debut in February 1977 as a 100 percent varietal. With son John as general manager and daughter-in-law Janet in charge of marketing, Trefethen Vineyards is a family enterprise, strongly dedicated to the respected European concept of making wine only from the estate's own vineyards. In this château tradition, all the wines will be 100 percent Trefethen grapes, and production will be limited to but three wines: Chardonnay, White Riesling, and Cabernet Sauvignon blended with some Merlot. Our tasting has been limited to the first two.

In 1979 the Trefethen 1976 Chardonnay scored a stunning first-place victory in the Gault-Millau Olympiades du Vin and a repeat victory in a second tasting competition staged by Robert Drouhin in Bur-

John and Janet Trefethen, one of the many young couples who have found winemaking in California an attractive way of life

gundy. He doubted, but was convinced by his own French jury.

Chardonnay (Napa Valley). Clean, dry, and fruity. President Reagan selected Trefethen Chardonnay to serve to Queen Elizabeth on her 1983 West Coast visit.

White Riesling (Napa Valley). Estate-grown grapes produce one of California's most luscious, silky examples of this German varietal.

VEEDERCREST VINEYARDS

1401 Stanford Avenue, Emeryville, California 94608

This small winery, managed by A.W. Baxter and owned by a group of partners, has a larger winemaking facility projected for completion in 1980. In the meanwhile, wines are being produced from choice lots of grapes from René di Rosa's Winery Lake Vineyard in the Carneros district in the southern part of Napa

Valley, some exceptional botrytis-touched White Riesling from the Steltzner Vineyard in Yountville, and Merlot, White Riesling, Chardonnay, Malbec, Petit Verdot, and Cabernet Franc from Veedercrest's own vineyard in the Mayacamas Mountains, where the vines grow in the volcanic soil of Mt. Veeder.

Considerable international fame accrued to the relatively new Veedercrest label with the triumph of the 1972 Chardonnay at a tasting at Maxim's in Paris, where it scored a victory over a fine French white Burgundy. Shades of Robert Louis Stevenson's prediction to his European readers: "The smack of Californian earth shall linger on the palate of your grandson."

SAMPLER SELECTION

Johannisberg Riesling (Spätlese). Rich wine, with a unique touch of Gewürztraminer.

Chardonnay (Cask designation). Very well balanced, with hints of vanillin from the wood mingled with the fruit.

Cabernet Sauvignon (Gamay Acres). Label legends, as with all Veedercrest wines, are explicit as to origin and content.

VILLA MT. EDEN

Mt. Eden Ranch, Oakville Crossroad, Oakville, California 94562

Two Stanford graduates, Anne and James McWilliams, have joyously undertaken the vintner's profession, bringing back into productive use a frame winery built on their Napa Valley property in 1881. Young Nils Venge, a UC–Davis graduate in viticulture and enology, is their winemaker. With previous experience at Charles Krug and Sterling Vineyards, Venge has worked at Villa Mt. Eden since early 1973.

The 80 acres of fine varietal vines grow on an alluvial fan that slopes gradually toward nearby Mt. Eden. Temperature-summation studies show this slightly rising land to be cool, with varying microclimates favorable to the planting of Chardonnay and Pinot Noir as well as Cabernet Sauvignon. Field-crushing, to bring full fruitiness to the must, is well exemplified in both the Chenin Blanc and the Gewürztraminer.

SAMPLER SELECTION

Chardonnay (Napa Valley). The second-leaf wine, aged in Nevers oak, already indicating the great potential of this label.

Gewürztraminer (Napa Valley). In true Alsatian style, bone-dry, golden, long on the palate; appetizing character.

Cabernet Sauvignon (Napa Valley). Estate-bottled from second-leaf vines, showing intensive varietal character.

Napa Gamay (Napa Valley). Field-crushing of the Beaujolais grape brings an almost raspberry freshness to the wine.

YVERDON VINEYARDS

3787 Spring Mountain Road, St. Helena, California 94574

Yverdon is the name of the village at the southern tip of Lake Neuchâtel in Switzerland where Californian Fred Aves's grandparents were winegrowers. Aves's desire to make wine as his family had, asserted itself, so he sold his automotive business. With his son Russell, he moved in 1970 to a vineyard at a 2,000-foot elevation on Spring Mountain in the Napa Valley.

The two men engaged in more than one new trade as they became their own builders, stonemasons, carpenters, coopers—all essential to being self-sufficient vinegrowers and winemakers. The Yverdon house, which is pictured on the label, was designed by Fred after a château with mansard roof remembered from travels in France. An additional 90 acres of vineyard on Tubbs Lane near Calistoga now provide Gamay, Johannisberg Riesling, Chenin Blanc, and Cabernet Sauvignon. All the Aveses' wines are 100 percent varietal, made exclusively from their own grapes.

SAMPLER SELECTION

Johannisberg Riesling (Napa Valley). A wine of stunning flower-freshness, full varietal bouquet; sweet-edged.

Cabernet Sauvignon (Napa Valley). Vintage, estate-bottled wine of bold varietal character, needing considerable aging.

VINEYARDS AND WINERIES: BAY AREA AND CENTRAL COAST COUNTIES

"There is no link with the past as eloquent as an ancient wine, and its impact on the senses is intensified by the historic climate in which it was born."

—H. Warner Allen

On the morning of April 5, 1806, a stanch copper-bottomed 206-ton sailing vessel, the *Juno*, flying the Russian flag, sailed into San Francisco Bay. Under the command of Baron Nikolai Petrovitch Rezanof, accompanied by the naturalist George Heinrich von Langsdorff, the *Juno* had sailed southward from Sitka with a cargo of merchandise which the baron hoped to barter for much-needed grain. California's great historian Hubert Howe Bancroft explains: "The contrast between sunny California and the dreary Sitka with its storms and starvation introduced discontent to the *Juno*'s crew. Life in California—where to eat, to drink, to make love, to smoke, to dance, to ride, to sleep, seemed the whole duty of man—must have seemed to these cold, sea-salted men a pleasant dream." When four members of the crew asked to remain and were denied permission by Governor Argüello, they were put onto an island in the bay, an early Alcatraz, until the time of departure, lest they run away and remain in California illegally. In 1816 an English seaman, Robert Livermore, not unlike some of the *Juno*'s crew, found this area of New California such a paradise that he deserted ship. Ultimately, he found his way to the coastal valley and its golden hills, the Valle de Oro, married the daughter of a Spanish grandee, and, from money saved from a variety of endeavors, acquired ownership of the Rancho Los Positas, which he renamed Livermore Valley.

Naturalist Von Langsdorff accepted the invitation of Franciscan Father Cueva to visit the Mission San Jose. It would be the first time a foreigner would navigate the difficult and winding channels of the South Bay approach to the mission or see the fertile development of that region southeast of the bay.

Mission San Jose had been founded on June 11, 1797, by Father Fermin Francisco Lasuen. Von Langsdorff found the splendid mission, with its fine buildings, its extensive fields of corn, barley, wheat, and beans, its kitchen gardens, and its vineyards and orchards of vegetables and herbs, "extremely well laid out, and kept in very good order; the soil is everywhere rich and fertile, and yields ample returns."

In the Mission San Jose area today, where from the steel scaffolding surmounting the outdoor fer-

menters of the Weibel Champagne Cellars one can look to the west and see the winding channels of Von Langsdorff's approach, the early-nineteenth-century naturalist's observations remain significant and true. "Some vineyards have been planted within a few years, which yield excellent wine, sweet, and resembling Malaga. The situation of the establishment is admirably chosen, and according to the universal opinion this mission will in a few years be the richest and best in New California. The only disadvantage is that there are no large trees very near. To compensate for this disadvantage, there are in the neighborhood of the mission chalk-hills and excellent brick-earth, so that most of their buildings are of brick." Today's visitors to Weibel will step inside brick walls housing the winery begun by Leland Stanford.

Very near Mission San Jose, natural warm springs served Spanish colonial settlers as a place for washing linen. By the 1860s Rancho Agua Caliente had become a fashionable watering place for wealthy San

Stony fields are surprisingly hospitable to vines—in California as in Bordeaux

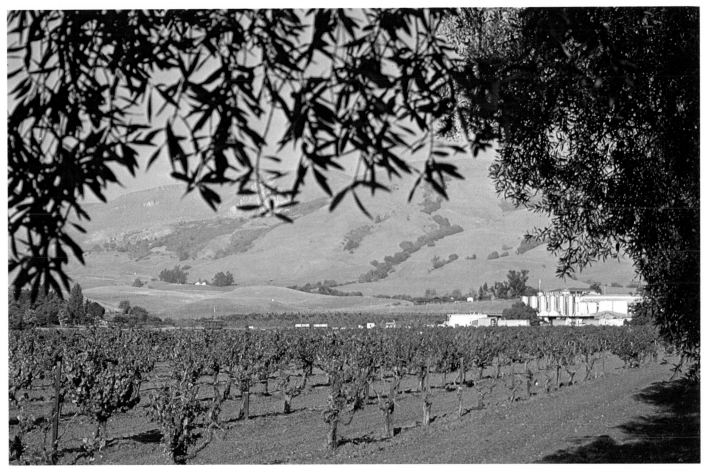

The Weibel Champagne Cellars and vineyards near Mission San Jose

Marker commemorating English-born Robert E. Livermore, who settled in the valley that bears his name

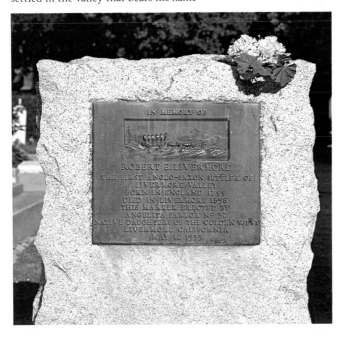

Franciscans. In 1870, only a few decades after Von Langsdorff's visit, railroad tycoon and former governor of California Leland Stanford acquired a square mile of orchards and vineyards surrounding the warm springs. He assigned ownership of the property to his brother Josiah, who tripled the vineyards' acreage, enlarged the brick winery, and inaugurated a brandy distillery.

Alameda County does not have the scenic charm of green, tree-clad hills found in Napa and Sonoma, so alluring to casual tourists. Its treasures consist in the all but invisible qualities of the land. The vines flourish in stony fields where little else could thrive. During the day the rocks become reservoirs of the sun's heat, and they hold the ripening warmth through the cold nights. Drainage, equally essential to the vine's well-being, is provided by the stones and pebbles in the earth, producing an environment for vine roots similar to the gravelly soil of Graves and Sauternes in Bordeaux.

It was San Francisco journalist Charles Wetmore who, following a visit to France in 1879, called attention to the area, with reports supporting California wine production. His entry into the fracas between champions of native wines and champions of imports led Wetmore himself directly into winemaking. In 1882 he acquired 480 acres of almost barren grazing land in the Livermore Valley, planted select vines, and built a winery, naming it Cresta Blanca after the chalk cliff into which the aging tunnels were dug. In 1884 he wrote the first ampelography for the benefit of winegrowers, "A Discussion of Vines Now Known in the State Together with Comments on Their Adaptability to Certain Locations and Uses." Even by today's standards, this 22-page pamphlet is a work remarkable for scholarly application and accuracy. Though Wetmore generously attempted to avoid "a pride of opinion," humbly stating his study of vines to be "kaleidoscopic" and "sometimes confusing," his study not only "brought order out of chaos" but set the industry on the path that was to bring it recognition in Europe.

The Marquis de Lur-Saluces, owner of Château d'Yquem, had sent to California cuttings of Sémillon, Sauvignon, and Muscadelle de Bordelais vines, the varieties comprising the classic blending of the famed Sauternes. Planted in Louis Mel's El Mocho Vineyard, which he shared with Wetmore, they were to earn for the pebbly fields of Livermore the sobriquet "Sauternes district of California" and two gold medals for Cresta Blanca from the Paris Exposition of 1889. The once proud property in Livermore is, alas, no longer productive. As a separate subdivision of Guild Wineries and Distilleries, a growers' cooperative discussed elsewhere, Cresta Blanca wines are now produced largely from Mendocino County grapes at a winery in that area. But El Mocho is a working part of the Wente vineyard.

Throughout these three counties—Alameda, Contra Costa, and Solano—agricultural land has been encroached upon by industry and housing. In the mid-forties, before legislation could be enacted designating existing farmlands as "agricultural preserves," many California wineries disappeared, virtually confiscated through taxation. Rezoned from low agricultural tax rates to prime residential rates, wineries and vineyards had but one alternative—relocation. With tract homes and industrial plants crowding the borders of their vineyards, including the famed El Mocho Vineyard, Wente Bros. acquired acreage in Monterey County. The Cadenasso Winery of Fairfield in Solano County, famed for fine Pinot Noir and Zinfandel, is almost a solitary holdout.

The vineyard domain south of San Francisco is as rich and colorful in its vintage history as the more celebrated regions north of the Bay Area. During the gold-rush days, when more than seven hundred ships swept through the Golden Gate in nine months, passengers and crews scrambled ashore, asking only for directions to the goldfields. Many, finding no gold, stayed on to plant vineyards and make wine on land that had already been proven suitable by Mission Period colonials. In 1850 the price of wine in San Francisco was as high as a king's ransom. Thirsty miners

San Francisco Bay divides the North Coast from the other wine areas of California

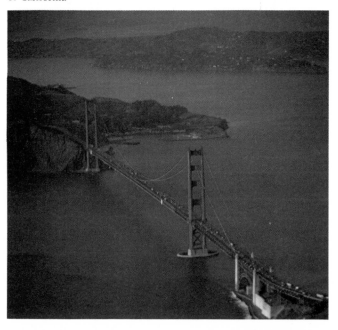

The 3,500-acre Almadén empire at Paicines

At Paul Masson: an old basket-press, now retired to the inactive list

3 acres of the famed La Questa Vineyard, planted by Emmett Rixford in 1883, remain and may endure. In the high folds and slopes of the Santa Cruz Mountains, nourished by subterranean springs, forested with trees, young Paul Masson in 1905 planted his own vineyard of Petit Pinot vines for champagne making. At 2,000 feet, free from fog, with double the rainfall of the valley floor, facing eastward toward the morning sun, the *chaîne d'or* (golden ridge), as Masson called it, was an ideal terrain. It remains so today for a small group of winemakers as dynamic and intense as was Masson. Urban encroachment is not likely to displace them.

ALMADÉN VINEYARDS

1530 Blossom Hill Road, Los Gatos, California 95118

Almadén's reputation as the largest of the premium wine producers often troubles the budding enophile, who tends to wonder how the company can make truly fine wines and at the same time satisfy the consumer of good, inexpensive table wine. The answer is to be found in the conscientious administration of a wine empire whose range of products was scarcely dreamed of by its founders more than a century ago.

Stand in the shoes of Étienne Thée in 1847, as he acquired a dominion of 350 acres of fertile land near Mission San Juan Bautista. The humble Bordelais vigneron had survived the rough sea voyage around the Horn to arrive in a new world that seemed patterned after Paradise. In Bordeaux, Talleyrand's Château Haut-Brion had but 92 acres, Château Margaux 155, while Thée now owned more than the two combined. The neighboring Franciscan friars gave him vine cuttings with which to establish more than a home—a small winemaking kingdom.

Similar visions drew another Frenchman to plant a vineyard in the area in 1852. Charles Lefranc, a tailor from Passy, brought with him, besides a determination to make wine, a large basket-press and some white-oak puncheons coopered from German oak. The young immigrant, a bachelor, took great delight in the company of Thée's daughter. Within a short time, they were married and the properties joined. Lefranc chose

consumed 60,000 gallons of California wine, mainly from Los Angeles and Santa Barbara counties. The wiser immigrant vignerons, eschewing the unfamiliar and chancy labor of goldmining, wanted vineyards near the city instead, where a cask of wine would bring them a good-sized bag of gold.

It was inevitable that the swift growth of San Francisco and its environs would crowd agriculture, including the vineyards, on the peninsula. San Francisco is still given as the place of origin on the labels of many wines, although the vineyards just south of the city long ago headed for the hills.

Green-belt legislation did not come soon enough to Santa Clara County to save the Almadén vineyards surrounding the original homestead of the founder, Étienne Thée. The winery still stands, with a few token vines around it, as a historical landmark, but the rest of the vineyards are now real estate subdivisions and tract homes. On the peninsula in San Mateo County,

The Charles Le Franc Late Harvest Riesling, lusciously sweet, leaves rich "tears" on the sides of the glass for their vineyard the name Almadén ("The Mine"), which the Spanish had given this region because of its quicksilver deposits. Ambitious to produce better wines than Thée was making from the Mission grapes, Lefranc acquired cuttings of choice European varieties. This was the beginning of finer winemaking in Santa Clara County.

In 1878, at the age of nineteen, Paul Masson emigrated to California because of the phylloxera devastation in his Burgundian homeland. He was hired as a bookkeeper by his fellow countryman Lefranc, and with his knowledge of vines and wines the arrangement was a felicitous one. In 1888, Masson married Lefranc's daughter, Louise, and in 1905 he struck out on his own, to the hills above Saratoga, with the intent of making champagne. In this early history can be traced the common background of today's two rival companies, Almadén and Paul Masson, both sharing the original vineyard's founding date of 1852.

The present status of Almadén Vineyards as a winemaking empire had its true beginning in 1941, when the Los Gatos property was acquired by Louis Benoist of San Francisco. A 1,400 percent increase in land taxes forced Benoist to establish new vineyards about 80 miles to the south, where he bought 3,000 acres at Paicines in San Benito County. Early in the 1940s Benoist had called upon Frank Schoonmaker to guide Almadén's winemaking policies. Schoonmaker brought in as winemaker Oliver Goulet from the Novitiate of Los Gatos. Peter Jurgens, as director of merchandising, increased the sales of Almadén wines from thousands of cases to millions, statistics that still boggle the mind.

In 1967 Benoist sold Almadén to National Distillers. Some of Almadén's most significant advances in premium wine production came when John McClelland was made president, in 1976, and general manager of the winery, in 1981. During his regime, with Klaus Mathes as winemaster, a program of small-lot premium wines honoring founder Charles Lefranc was launched. Almadén wines bear the prestigious Charles Lefranc label only when the vintages are of exceptional merit. These wines are Almadén's answer to the unfounded belief that fine wines are made only in small lots. The

In the La Cienega barrel house, part of Almadén's 23,000,000 gallons of cooperage seems to stretch to infinity

buttery-rich Lefranc Chardonnays and Fumé Blancs are made in lots of fewer than 3,000 cases. A Lefranc Zinfandel Royale is equally worth seeking out for its rich intensity of berryness and mellow softness.

From the original 350 acres to the present 15,000 acres in five counties—Alameda, Santa Clara, San Benito, Santa Cruz, and Monterey—winemaster Mathes has an enviable choice of fine varieties. Gold medals attest to the quality of the Almadén varietals, fine wines though modestly priced.

In conjunction with Laurent Perrier of Tours-sur-Marne, a brilliant California vintaged Chardonnay is now made in still, *côteaux champenois* style, marketed by Almadén under the Caves Laurent Perrier label. The wine is crisp, clean, and bone dry, and, like its French counterpart, has nary a trace of wood.

SAMPLER SELECTION

Blanc de Blancs Champagne. Vintage; the *cuvée* from the largest Chardonnay vineyard in California. Crisp, clean, dry.

Gewürztraminer (Monterey). Produced in vintage or nonvintage examples; exceptionally big, spicy wine.

Pinot Noir (Mountain). From the tiny, classic clusters, a pungent, regal wine true to Burgundy in bouquet.

BARGETTO WINERY

3535 North Main Street, Soquel, California 95073

Philip Bargetto, hearing the good report of California as a wine country, came from Asti, in Piedmont, to work with the pioneer viticulturist Antoine Delmas of San Jose in 1887. He was joined by his brother John in 1929, and together they planned their rustic creek-side winery in anticipation of Repeal. Today, John's son Lawrence and his family maintain the winery in this cool coastal region above the north rim of Monterey Bay.

While he is capable of translating the pure, fragrant essence of raspberries, apricots, peaches, plums, strawberries, cherries, and even olallieberries into extraordinary, prize-winning fruit wines, Lawrence Bargetto's training and skill as a winemaker really shine when choice varietal grapes arrive at the red-barn winery. Inside these humble walls there is all the sophistication of first-rate winemaking procedures, with careful aging in Yugoslavian and Nevers oak for Pinot Blanc, Sylvaner, Johannisberg Riesling, and Chardonnay produced from grapes grown in the Santa Cruz Mountains. When warm Indian summers allow full ripening in the 17-acre Vine Hill Vineyard (saved from subdividers by comedian Dick Smothers), these white wines are worth journeying far to taste. The lower-than-2-tons-per-acre yield limits the availability even in the best years.

With distribution planned for select markets on the Eastern seaboard, from Maine to Florida, and representation in Ohio, Wisconsin, Washington, Oregon, and Colorado, Bargetto is a label to look for.

SAMPLER SELECTION

Chardonnay (Vine Hill) Santa Cruz Mountain vintage wine, oak-aged, long, soft, silky, balanced, superb.

Johannisberg Riesling (Vine Hill). An incomparable, silky subtlety sets this wine apart. Very little available.

Raspberry Wine. The berries cost more than premium grapes. Try this instead of Cassis with your next Kir. Jewel-toned.

Chaucer's Mead. Classic golden honey wine, fragrant as clean straw in the sunlight. A sweet touch out of medieval times.

DAVID BRUCE WINERY

21439 Bear Creek Road, Los Gatos, California 95030

On a hot summer day in the 1950s, dermatologist David Bruce, then a young intern, joined in the search for a small boy lost in the Santa Cruz Mountains. In the house of the vineyardist to which he brought the rescued child, Dr. Bruce, hot and thirsty from negotiating the rugged terrain, had his first taste of wine—and became a convert. One day, in a wine shop, Bruce found a bottle of Martin Ray's Pinot Noir that had

Dr. David Bruce holds his unfiltered, unfined vintage Chardonnay to the light

Today, in his 6,000-square-foot, two-story winery, completed in 1968, with rows of European-oak barrels, plus some mechanical contrivances of his own devising, the unique and individual winemaker is creating some of the best wines in the mountains. A handsome new label proclaims on its sidebar, "David Bruce wines are distinguished by their out-of-the-ordinary properties and ranges of tastes." You can count me among those who revel in the huge dimensions of his oak-ribbed Chardonnays and extraordinary deep and dark Amador County Zinfandels, so fat they can be chewed. I also subscribe to his own expressive descriptions of his wines, sent out to a loyal mail-order clientele. David Bruce wines require palates prepared for big adventure and, more often than not, for rich excitement.

SAMPLER SELECTION

Chardonnay. Always vintage, never filtered or fined. Requiring long rest and careful decanting. Oaky overtones, big and dry.

Zinfandel. Deep purple-black, sometimes with traces of residual sugar. Intense flavor suggesting chocolate. Aged in Limousin oak.

Cabernet Sauvignon. Vintage wine, 100 percent varietal, aged two years in new and used Nevers oak. Big, powerful.

Pinot Noir. Mouth-filling wine of extraordinary darkness of color and long-lasting aftertaste of fruit. Requires aging.

CONCANNON VINEYARD

4590 Tesla Road, Livermore, California 94550

In 1983, Concannon celebrated a centennial of continuous fine wine production in the Livermore Valley. The dynamic founder, James Concannon, was a son of Erin from County Galway. In 1874, when he was twenty-seven, he brought his bride to San Francisco, where he worked at whatever offered the most promising returns. From Archbishop Joseph Alemany he learned of the Church's need for altar wines. In 1883 he purchased 47 acres of land in the Livermore Valley. It was here that Robert Livermore had planted the first vineyards of the area and that in 1882 Charles Wetmore

come from those same Santa Cruz Mountains, high above Los Gatos and Saratoga. He paid the extravagant price for it, out of curiosity.

"It was a wonderful wine," he told me. "I decided right then that we'd start looking for some acreage, and plant some vines!" In 1961 he found just what he was looking for, high on a ridge overlooking the whole *chaîne d'or*, fog free at 2,000 feet, complete with an old farmhouse and a few ancient vines. The family project now embraced all the chores of planting, attending, and nurturing 25 acres of Chardonnay, White Riesling, Cabernet Sauvignon, and Pinot Noir. Office hours in San Jose had to compete with the long hours of study and research demanded by the new career in the vineyard and winery. All the skills of the laboratory scientist merged with the devotion of the ardent enophile. Bruce bottled his first Chardonnay unfined, from the wood, accepting a slight cloudiness for fear any further racking might diminish the majesty of the flavor and bouquet.

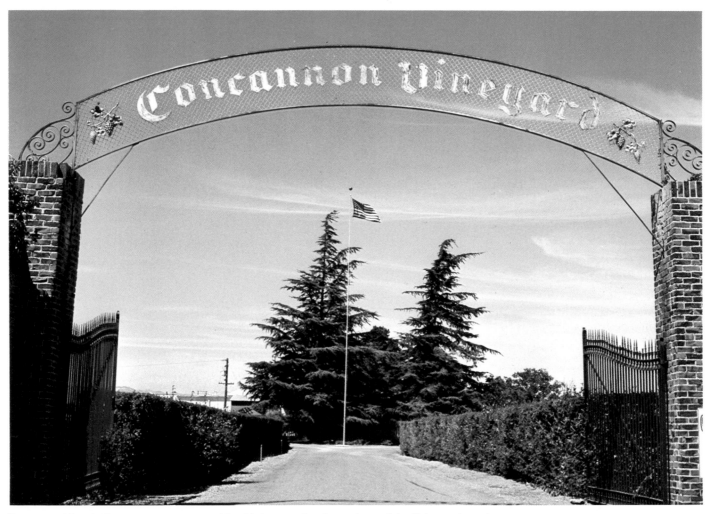

Gateway to historic Concannon, now operated by third-generation descendants of the Galway winemaker

had drawn attention to the great potential of the deep gravel soil and established his famous Cresta Blanca winery. Following the lead of these pioneers, Concannon built a frame-and-brick winery that still endures. Vineyard and family both expanded. There were five boys and five girls, and eventually 300 acres of vineyard. Joseph Concannon assumed management of the winery upon his father's death, in 1911, and continued to produce altar wines during Prohibition. In 1965, with Joseph's death, ownership passed to his sons Joe and Jim, who continued the family operation of the winery until Joe died, in 1978. To settle the complicated claims of the many heirs to the estate, Jim sold the winery in 1983 to the Distillers Company Ltd., of Edinburgh, but he has continued as president of the winery, which is beginning its second century in full operation.

Concannon Vineyard has an intensely loyal following of winelovers for its gentle, velvety red wines and delicately complex white wines. When Dr. Sergio Traverso became winemaker, in 1981, the emphasis on finesse and elegance of the house style was further increased, though the number of wines was reduced. Sadly, the rare Rkatsiteli, a unique Russian varietal grown only by Concannon—a brilliant golden wine of beguiling charms—was discontinued, the vines T-budded over to Sauvignon Blanc. Jim wistfully and wisely noted, "We have to go with what sells well."

SAMPLER SELECTION

Sauvignon Blanc (Livermore Valley). In French style, blended with Semillon and aged judiciously in French Nevers oak.

176

Petite Sirah (Livermore Valley). The wine is a Concannon specialty, the Rhone varietal here of exceeding grace with proper aging.

Cabernet Sauvignon (Livermore Valley). Strength and softness coexist in this splendid estate-grown wine.

ENZ VINEYARDS

1781 Limekiln Road, Hollister, California 95023

Robert and Susan Enz belong to that growing list of city dwellers seeking a better life on the land. In 1966 they found their answer in the Cienega Valley of San Benito County—a 150-acre spread with some vines that had been planted in 1895. In 1970, Robert turned his talents as a civil engineer to transforming an old redwood barn into a twentieth-century winery. With 30 acres newly planted, and with Almadén's winemaster, Klaus Mathes, to guide them, the Enzes hope to make Cienega Valley a significant appellation.

SAMPLER SELECTION

Golden Chasselas (Cienega Valley). The Enzes couldn't resist making a vintage wine of these misprized golden grapes. Dry and clean.

Zinfandel Rosé (Cienega Valley). A beautiful deep pink color, dry, fragrant, almost spicy, with the tang of earth.

Pinot St. George (Cienega Valley). An estate-grown vine of remarkable bouquet and finesse. Needs some aging.

FELTON-EMPIRE VINEYARDS

379 Felton Empire Road, Felton, California 95081

Thirty-five years ago, Chafee Hall, a San Francisco corporation lawyer, set out 5 acres of Cabernet Sauvignon and 9 acres of White Riesling in virgin soil. Hallcrest, the progenitor of today's proliferating boutique wineries, produced some of the earliest of the rare, custom-made wines. Today, a trio of young men have acquired the once-celebrated vineyard and winery—Leo McCloskey, an enologist with experience at Ridge and David Bruce wineries, Jim Beauregard, a viticulturist, and John Pollard, an airline pilot with an M.B.A. degree.

In addition to grapes from the Hallcrest vines, Felton-Empire uses Cabernet Sauvignon, Zinfandel, White Riesling, and Chardonnay from the Vine Hill Vineyard, as well as Riesling from the Robert Young Vineyard of Sonoma County.

SAMPLER SELECTION

White Riesling (Santa Cruz). Made in the German style with late-harvested grapes; soft yet strong, with residual sugar.

Zinfandel (Santa Cruz). Big, dark, rich wines of tannic strength and regional character, expertly made. Full varietal nose.

Cabernet Sauvignon (Santa Cruz). In the tradition of the area, the wine, long on the skins, is full-bodied, fragrant.

GEMELLO WINERY

2003 El Camino Real, Mountain View, California 94040

It is by word of mouth that astute winelovers discover the rich, rugged red wines of Mario J. Gemello. The Cabernet Sauvignons and Zinfandels inevitably end up in high scorings at competitive winetastings. Founded in 1934 by Mario's father, John Gemello, who came from Piedmont, Italy, the small winery on the highway was a family affair until Louis Sarto joined as a partner in 1969. Their search is always for exceptional grapes for exceptional wines, and their quest for the elegance of red-wine grapes has taken them to the Santa Cruz Mountains and into the Carmel Valley.

SAMPLER SELECTION

Cabernet Sauvignon. The 100 percent varietal vintage selections usually stipulate the source of the mountain-grown grapes.

Zinfandel. Earthy, rich, full-bodied, and aged in oak puncheons and barrels to mellow roundness. Wines to last for years.

Barbera. Trust a winery with an Italian lineage to give real meaning to this secondary Piedmontese grape in California.

EMILIO GUGLIELMO WINERY

1480 East Main Avenue, Morgan Hill, California 95037

Emilio Guglielmo established this small Santa Clara Valley winery in 1925, producing unpretentious table wines that, following Repeal, found their way into Italian grocery stores in the Bay Area at modest prices. Today, son George, trained at Fresno State, is the winemaker. A tasting room has been opened, and with considerable expansion some finer varietal wines have been added to the locally popular generics under the Emile's Private Stock label. One of the state's richest and finest Italian-style Vermouths is produced here.

SAMPLER SELECTION

California Chablis. (Emile's Private Stock). In fifths or jugs, one of the best buys in California country wine. Crisp, dry, clean.

Grignolino Rosé. Estate-bottled under the Mount Madonna label, fragrant, fresh, vintage; from Santa Clara Valley grapes.

Petite Sirah. Grandson Gene Guglielmo's pride among the varietal reds under the Mount Madonna label.

Emile's Sweet Vermouth. Too good to waste by mixing with whiskey in cocktails. Superb body; herbs, spices, barks, petals.

KIRIGIN CELLARS

11550 Watsonville Road, Gilroy, California 95020

Instead of retiring, after a full working life as chief wine chemist for such wineries as Almadén, San Martin, Perelli-Minetti in California, and Canandaigua in New York, Nikola Kirigin Chargin decided to start his own winery with his son, Nick Jr. In December of 1976 they bought the long-established Bonesio Winery, located on the old Spanish land grant Solis Rancho. The house, built in 1827, is among the historic landmarks of Santa Clara County.

Stainless-steel, temperature-controlled fermentation tanks were installed, and an additional 10 acres of white-wine varietal grapes will be added to the present acreage of Cabernet Sauvignon, Pinot Noir, and Zinfandel. With the new professionalism, the modern equipment, and the Croatian winemaking heritage of the Chargin family, there'll be even finer wines.

SAMPLER SELECTION

French Colombard. Produced as a dinner wine. Almost totally dry, it still retains the fruity bouquet of the grape.

Malvasia Bianca. Produced 100 percent from their own vines. Dry, with a bouquet suggesting orange blossoms, apricots.

Pinot Noir. A vintage, estate-bottled wine of light body and pleasing bouquet with true varietal character.

LLORDS & ELWOOD WINERY

Fremont, California 94538

Twenty years as one of the leading wine and spirits merchants of Hollywood and Beverly Hills led the late J. H. ("Mike") Elwood into researching the

Irene Elwood carries on the family wine business with her son Richard

ALMADÉN

CALIFORNIA SPARKLING WINE

Eye of the Partridge

ŒIL DE PERDIX

CUVÉE 1974

A superb, bottle fermented, sparkling wine with great bouquet and distinctive character. Made from grapes of the Pinot varieties, it has the unique bronze pink color found in the "eye of a partridge".

PRODUCED & BOTTLED BY ALMADÉN VINEYARDS
LOS GATOS, CALIFORNIA
ALCOHOL 12½% BY VOLUME • 4/5 QUART

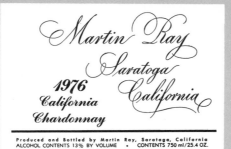

Martin Ray

Saratoga

1976 *California*

California

Chardonnay

Produced and Bottled by Martin Ray, Saratoga, California
ALCOHOL CONTENTS 13% BY VOLUME • CONTENTS 750 ml/25.4 OZ.

Pedrizzetti

CALIFORNIA

PINOT CHARDONNAY

Produced and Bottled by Pedrizzetti Winery
Morgan Hill, California • Alcohol 12% by Volume

1974

CALIFORNIA

CHARDONNAY

VINE HILL VINEYARD
SANTA CRUZ MOUNTAINS

ℬ

Bargetto

PRODUCED AND BOTTLED BY BARGETTO'S SANTA CRUZ WINERY, SOQUEL, CALIFORNIA • ALCOHOL 13% BY VOLUME

ENZ VINEYARDS ®

CIENEGA VALLEY
GOLDEN CHASSELAS
ESTATE BOTTLED
1975

Grown, Produced and Bottled by
Enz Vineyards of San Benito County,
Hollister, California

ALCOHOL 12.2% BY VOLUME

VINEYARDS SINCE 1895

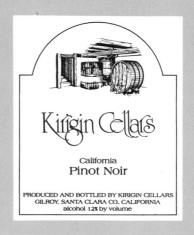

Kirigin Cellars

California
Pinot Noir

PRODUCED AND BOTTLED BY KIRIGIN CELLARS
GILROY, SANTA CLARA CO. CALIFORNIA
alcohol 12% by volume

1960
VINTAGE

Gemello's

GEMELLO'S
V
G.W. means Good Wine

CALIFORNIA
CABERNET SAUVIGNON
An Elegant, Mountain Grown Red Dinner Wine
ALCOHOL 12½% BY VOLUME
MADE AND BOTTLED BY
GEMELLO WINERY
MOUNTAIN VIEW, CALIFORNIA

PAUL MASSON.

1852

CALIFORNIA

RARE SOUZÃO
PORT.

Cellared & Bottled by Paul Masson Vineyards,
Saratoga, California, U.S.A.

| Alcohol 18 percent. By Volume. | CUVÉE NO. | Net Contents 750 ml. (25.4 fl. ozs.) |

Emile's
PRIVATE STOCK

CALIFORNIA
CHABLIS

In 1925 on fifteen fertile acres, Emilio Guglielmo's first harvest was nurtured to perfection. For three generations the Guglielmo family has celebrated this ritual and shared the finest wines with family and friends. This dedication to produce and share fine wines has made our family owned and operated winery more than a business—a way of life.

Emilio Guglielmo

ALCOHOL 12% BY VOLUME
PRODUCED & BOTTLED IN SANTA CLARA VALLEY, MORGAN HILL, CA. BY
EMILIO GUGLIELMO WINERY

BAY AREA AND CENTRAL COAST WINE LABELS

how's and why's of finer wines. By 1955, Elwood was determined to produce good sherries and to blend and bottle nonvintage table wines of superior merit that consumers could enjoy immediately. Since fewer and fewer California houses had anything approximating proper storage facilities for wines, the need for cellar aging was a serious disadvantage. He sold his chain of stores and became a winemaker, producing, blending, and bottling ten wines: a champagne, five varietal table wines, three sherries, and a port. They won many awards and immediate market acceptance. When Elwood died, in 1974, his widow, Irene, and his son Richard carried on the small family business. Their own experienced palates are responsible for the continued reliability of the wines.

SAMPLER SELECTION

Castle Magic Johannisberg Riesling. Mike Elwood was among the first to produce a Riesling with the sweet edge of a German *spätlese*.

Great Day D-r-ry Sherry. Truly comparable to some of the finest dry *fino* sherries of Spain. Full-bodied, smooth.

Dry Wit Sherry. Nutty taste, medium dryness; comparable to solera-aged *amontillado* wines of Jerez de la Frontera.

Ancient Proverb Port. A tawny wine of expanding bouquet, rich body, and ingratiating flavor.

PAUL MASSON VINEYARDS

13150 Saratoga Avenue, Saratoga, California 95070

The overlapping early history of today's rival companies, Almadén and Paul Masson, has been touched on above (see page 171). By the year 1905, young Paul Masson, driven by his consuming ambition to make champagne, was planting his La Cresta Vineyard on the hilltops of the *chaîne d'or* above Saratoga, putting down his "Petit Pinot" vines—Pinot Blanc, Pinot Noir, Pinot Chardonnay, Folle Blanche (for brandy), Cabernet Sauvignon, and Gamay. Masson's Vineyard in the Sky is the well-known locale of the "Music at the Vineyards" weekend concerts and operas presented each summer at the winery.

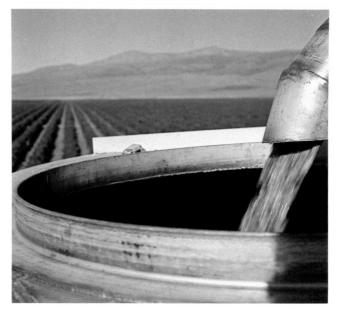

Wine in the making at Paul Masson's Pinnacles Vineyard in Monterey County

In 1936, in need of money, Masson sold the 350-acre property and its 70 acres of vines to a young Saratoga stockbroker, Martin Ray, keeping only the Vineyard in the Sky. An equally idealistic wine zealot, Ray retained the founder as president until Masson's death in 1940 at the age of eighty-one.

During his brief tenure, which ended in 1941, when fire destroyed the winery, Martin Ray produced some exceptional Pinot Noir and Cabernet Sauvignon and had a brief marketing association with Frank Schoonmaker during which they launched varietal table wines under the Paul Masson Champagne Co. label.

In 1943, through a suggestion made by Alfred Fromm, the winery, which Ray had rebuilt after the fire, was bought by Seagram, and an expansion program was instituted which has continued, successfully, to this day. In 1962, the first of more than 5,000 acres of varietal vines planted on their own *Vitis vinifera* roots were set out at the Pinnacles Vineyard near Soledad in Monterey County. One of the state's finest winemaking facilities was completed, for handling the

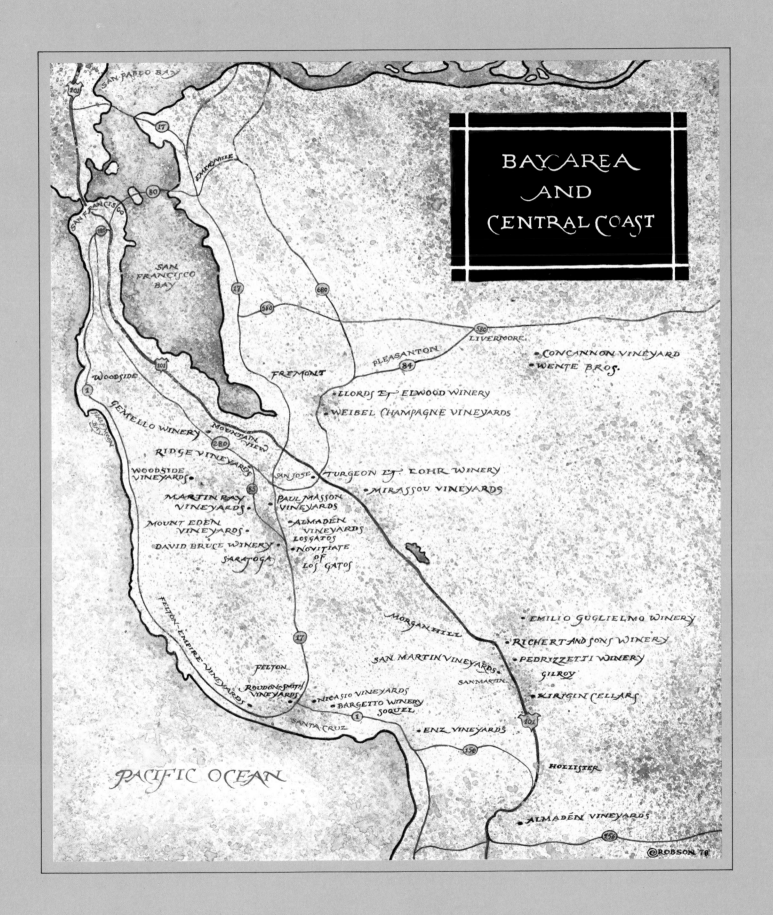

BAY AREA
AND
CENTRAL COAST

SAN PABLO BAY

SAN FRANCISCO

SAN FRANCISCO BAY

EMERYVILLE

LIVERMORE

•CONCANNON VINEYARD
•WENTE BROS.

PLEASANTON

FREMONT

WOODSIDE

•LLORDS ET ELWOOD WINERY

•WEIBEL CHAMPAGNE VINEYARDS

GEMELLO WINERY

MOUNTAIN VIEW

RIDGE VINEYARDS

WOODSIDE VINEYARDS•

SAN JOSE •TURGEON ET LOHR WINERY
•MIRASSOU VINEYARDS

MARTIN RAY VINEYARDS•

PAUL MASSON VINEYARDS

MOUNT EDEN VINEYARDS•

•ALMADÉN VINEYARDS
LOS GATOS

•DAVID BRUCE WINERY
SARATOGA

•NOVITIATE OF LOS GATOS

MORGAN HILL

•EMILIO GUGLIELMO WINERY

•RICHERT AND SONS WINERY

•PEDRIZZETTI WINERY

FELTON–EMPIRE VINEYARDS

FELTON

SAN MARTIN VINEYARDS•

SAN MARTIN

GILROY

•KIRIGIN CELLARS

ROUDON–SMITH VINEYARDS•

NICASIO VINEYARDS
•BARGETTO WINERY
SOQUEL

SANTA CRUZ

•ENZ VINEYARDS

HOLLISTER

PACIFIC OCEAN

•ALMADÉN VINEYARDS

©ROBSON 78

ever-increasing grapeloads from the Gavilan benchland vineyards. In 1965, the President's "E" award flag came from the United States Government for the excellence of leadership in industry—an export program that sent Paul Masson wines to the principal countries of the world.

Under Seagram's management, the wine merchandising policy at Paul Masson has emphasized non-vintage table wines, in the belief that consumers enjoy wines that are drinkable at the time of purchase and consistent in taste. The shortcomings of one vintage year can be compensated for with artful blending from wines of other years. While this is a boon to steady sales, it limits the potential height that a wine from the wealth of varietal plantings in the Pinnacles Vineyard of Monterey County might achieve. I have tasted the winery's 100 percent varietal Pinot Noir, Chardonnay, and Gewürztraminer, drawn from wood and steel, any or all of which might one day lift the label to more distinguished ranks. A varietal vintage program was initiated in the fall of 1977.

No winery in California has more splendid vineyards or up-to-date technology available for premium winemaking. The Paul Masson Pinnacles Vineyard and Winery in Monterey County at Soledad has the potential for greater production of premium vintage varietal wines, but with the relocation of the winery offices in New York, and emphasis upon generic wines for volume sales, there is need for reorientation if the founder's ideas are to be achieved. High quality still and sparkling wines are still being made, along with the finest aperitif and dessert wines, but in the roster of 45 titles, the stars at the top of the line could be allowed to shine more brightly.

SAMPLER SELECTION

Fumé Blanc (Monterey County). A Pinnacles Selection, vintage Sauvignon Blanc, with gentle aging in French oak. Fine wine.

Pinot Noir (Monterey County). The true clone of the regal Burgundian grape is estate grown for this Pinnacles Selection.

Rare Souzão Port. One of the finest port wines produced in California from Portuguese varieties. Well-aged, rich wine.

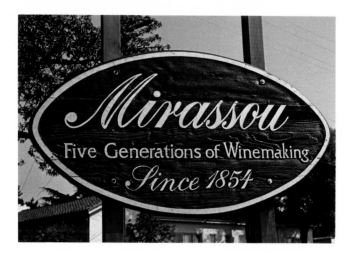

MIRASSOU VINEYARDS

Aborn Road, San Jose, California 95121

Billed as "America's Oldest Winemaking Family," the Mirassous bring more than a touch of showmanship to their sophisticated merchandising. The fifth generation of a family of vintners who first came to California in 1848, the youthful Mirassou clan—Daniel, Steve, Jim, Peter, and brother-in-law Don Alexander—are making up for lost time in bringing the Mirassou name, virtually unknown until 1966, to the attention of American winelovers. For their fathers, Edmond and Norbert, it had been a safe and steady cash business to sell wines in cask and barrel to other premium wineries, under whose alien labels they would emerge. The young Mirassous are interested in building their own name and are prepared to take the risks involved.

Innovation is part of the strategy, as exemplified by Peter's harvester-crusher, which obviates potential oxidation by turning the berries into juice almost instantly while still in the field. Creative merchandising and creative winemaking are exemplified by two of their best-sellers, White Burgundy and Monterey Riesling. No one seems to be attracted to Sylvaner as a wine, but everybody is drawn to Riesling. The fifth-generation Mirassous decided to dub their Sylvaner wine Monterey Riesling and let it have a modicum of sweetness. It has become a star overnight.

Similarly, White Burgundy has more going for it than Pinot Blanc, from which this retitled wine is made. I was sorry to see their Fleuri Blanc, a creative blending

Mirassou's first generation: Pierre and Henriette Pellier Mirassou

of Gewürztraminer, Johannisberg Riesling, and Pinot Blanc slide from the repertory; its unique zing and novelty didn't bring on the mass buyers.

Dan Mirassou became president of the winery in 1982, while his brother Peter remained in charge of production, concentrating on the Monterey County vineyards, a veritable garden of impeccably attended premium varietals. With annual sales now reaching 300,000 cases and still climbing, the fifth generation seems well advanced along a firm merchandising route.

The Fifth Generation (as they are called on their labels) work closely with their fathers, taking full responsibility for 650 acres in Monterey County and dividing responsibility equally for the homesite acreage near San Jose. With annual sales reaching 126,000 cases in 1975, and still climbing, youth's gamble seems to be winning.

SAMPLER SELECTION

Champagne (Monterey County, Au Naturel). Vintage wine, on the yeasts four years, plus. Superbly crisp, dry, clean.

Monterey Riesling. Vintage wine of the Alsatian Sylvaner in a fragrant, sweet-edged, popularly styled wine.

Chenin Blanc (Monterey County). An almost overwhelming wine of pungent fruitiness and regional distinction.

Johannisberg Riesling (Monterey County). Early editions were of uneven quality. Present vintages are fresh, fruity, silky.

Chardonnay (Monterey County). The regular and Reserve editions are top-quality white Burgundy: rich, elegant, fine.

MOUNT EDEN VINEYARDS

22000 Mt. Eden Road, Saratoga, California 95070

"The challenge of trying to make a truly great wine lights a fire in the soul that time won't put out. Time merely fans the flame, intensifies your determination—and humbles you by granting so very few chances for real achievement."

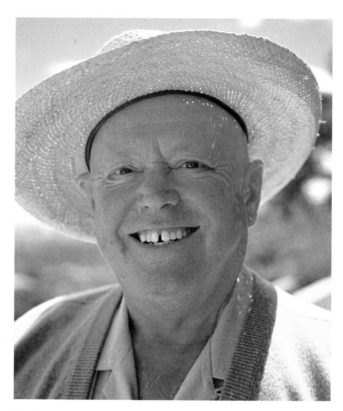

The late Martin Ray, wearing his straw hat like a crown

This comment of Martin Ray's explains something of the spell that he cast on California winemakers. The irascible iconoclast realized a boyhood dream on March 15, 1936, when he bought Paul Masson's La Cresta Vineyard and winery for $200,000. The son of a Methodist minister in Saratoga, Ray first worked at the famous Vineyard in the Sky earning five cents for every gopher he trapped on the vine slopes. His father, pointing to the windows of the chalet on the hill, brightly lighted late into the night, would call it "the devil's own domain here on earth." This only served to intrigue the six-year-old, who, at his first opportunity, scrambled up the hill to glimpse the famed champagne baron of the mountain. "He was wearing white flannel trousers, white socks and oxfords, a nice jacket, a great big brimmed hat, with his eyeglasses dangling on a ribbon. Standing there beside that château, he was a splendid sight!" In later years, the freckled, red-haired "Rusty" Ray affected a similar wide-brimmed straw hat, his own crowning insigne as ruler of the domain.

In 1945, after he sold the original property to Seagram, he bought the higher hilltops immediately to the north, where old Paul Masson had told him even finer wines might be made. Before Martin Ray's death in 1976, the Mount Eden Vineyards had been sold and the way cleared to produce some great wines from its acres. A small group of investors took over, the M.E.V. Corporation, headed by Robert Nikkel with Dr. Don Alcott, William Hanna, and Dr. Frank Dutra as officers and young Bill Anderson as winemaker.

In the first years, winemaker Richard Graff of Chalone was invited to assist the new group. "I'm convinced," he told me, "that this hill will produce the greatest Cabernet of California!" Superlatives are a normal part of the conversation of those making wines on the *chaîne d'or*. And not without reason.

The first Cabernet Sauvignon of Mount Eden Vineyards was made in 1973, fermented in stainless steel, aged in Nevers-oak barrels, fined with fresh egg whites in the Bordeaux tradition before bottling. The ruby-hued wine has great promise, a subtle peppery undertone, and a body of balanced substance auguring a good long life. The Chardonnays of '72 and '73, while overpriced, were of a majesty justifying high hopes for the new winery of legendary origin.

SAMPLER SELECTION

Chardonnay. Rich, golden, estate-bottled wine from the 2,000-foot-elevation vineyard. Well-balanced with oak aging.

Cabernet Sauvignon. Expensive. An interesting invest-

Steel tanks, wooden barrels, and cardboard cartons mark the progress of a wine on its way to the consumer ment for the connoisseur, bound to be a conversation piece.

NICASIO VINEYARDS

14300 Nicasio Way, Soquel, California 95073

Six miles north of Soquel, in the Santa Cruz Mountains, electronics engineer Dan Wheeler dug a cave into the hillside for storing the wines he produces. "Wines by Wheeler" are unfiltered, unfined, and virtually unsulphured. He buys most of the grapes, being careful to retain the recognized regional excellence, and he has developed his own technique for the retention of fruitiness in wine, a secret he is unwilling to share. It accounts for some of the outstanding difference in his white wines, particularly Chardonnay and Riesling, and gives a lilt to his dry Zinfandel Rosé. Because of his own dislike for woody tastes in wine, Wheeler takes his red wines from fermentation in wood into his cave in 5-gallon glass jugs in which they are stored before bottling. Until recently, the loyal customers who consume his 300 cases per year have been accommodated through mail order only.

SAMPLER SELECTION

Champagne of Chardonnay. Vintage champagne, au naturel, aged *cuvée*, no *dosage*, produced in classic bottle-fermentation procedure.

Zinfandel Rosé. Dry pink wine, very fruity, of Santa Cruz Mountain grapes from the Beauregard vineyards.

Zinfandel. Each vintage briefly aged in French brandy barrels and 5-gallon glass jugs before bottling. Big, bold wine.

NOVITIATE OF LOS GATOS

300 College Avenue, Los Gatos, California 95030

Ever since 1888, the fathers and brothers of the Novitiate of the Sacred Heart of the Society of Jesus in Los Gatos have grown and produced the finest sacramental wines of California. Not very many seasons ago, among the novices tending those vines was former California governor Jerry Brown.

There has been some expansion of the vineyard holdings in the San Ysidro district of the Santa Clara Valley. With an 800,000-gallon storage capacity, and 80,000-gallon fermentation facility, Father Louis B. Franklin, the general manager of the Novitiate, has found it expedient to expand the market for their table wines, since the Novitiate has a supply comfortably beyond their needs of altar wines for the Church.

The most famous of the Novitiate wines is Black Muscat, a unique rich liqueur-type dessert wine of the Muscat Hamburg grape. Beyond this renowned and stellar selection, aged in old, dimly lit caves, are some 2,300 oak casks mellowing other prize aperitif and dessert wines, including a rich Angelica, Muscat Frontignan, Cocktail Sherry, Flor Sherry, and varietal Tinta Port. But the focus is now upon Cabernet Sauvignon, Pinot Noir, Chenin Blanc, Johannisberg Riesling, and Pinot Blanc. The wines are modestly priced, with all proceeds going to finance the education and training of Jesuit priests.

SAMPLER SELECTION

Château Novitiate. A rather distinguished blended wine of Sémillon and Sauvignon grapes in the sweet Sauternes style.

Pinot Blanc. Full-bodied, dry white wine in the white Burgundy tradition.

Cabernet Sauvignon. A limited-bottling edition of this claret varietal, wood-aged and ready for drinking.

Black Muscat. From the Muscat Hamburg grape. So rich in body and flavor, it is suggested as a dessert wine-liqueur.

PEDRIZZETTI WINERY

1645 San Pedro Avenue, Morgan Hill, California 95037

The Santa Clara Valley between Morgan Hill and Gilroy is still largely vineyard country. A cooling fog blanket rolls in from the Pacific regularly after sundown, and grape growers in this area are grateful because it makes for a better climate for the better varietals. And it is better varietals that Ed and Phyllis Pedrizzetti are making today.

The winery, with its 60-acre vineyard in rocky riverbed soil, was bought in 1945 by John Pedrizzetti, and from this unpretentious country winery a bulk-wine business was built. Ed and Phyllis Pedrizzetti took over the management in 1963. The Courtyard Tasting Room is in the domain of Phyllis, while Ed is upgrading the wines, made from their own and purchased grapes, that carry the family name.

SAMPLER SELECTION

Pinot Chardonnay. With grapes from Santa Barbara County; a dry, long, and silky wine, free of oak taste.

Chenin Blanc. Monterey County grapes give the intense fruitiness to this pleasing wine of 7 percent residual sweetness.

Barbera. A really distinguished 100 percent varietal from the Pedrizzettis' own mature vines. Beautiful wine, soft and fragrant.

Petite Sirah. Another estate-bottled wine. Deep and dark in color, bold, a little peppery, appetizing.

MARTIN RAY VINEYARDS

22000 Mt. Eden Road, Saratoga, California 95070

On November 14, 1976, Eleanor Ray, Martin Ray's widow, sent out a letter headlined, *Peter Martin Ray Takes Over Martin Ray Vineyards and Brings in a Magnificent 1976 Vintage!* A professor of biology at Stanford, with specialized knowledge of plant physiology, Peter Martin Ray is also a veteran of more than a few winemaking skirmishes with his ebullient stepfather through the good years and the troubled years that divided Martin Ray's empire. Today, five shareholders have formed a corporation to carry on the winemaking traditions in what many people think of as an ivory tower among the vines.

There are only 5 acres of Chardonnay, Pinot Noir, and Cabernet Sauvignon in the Martin Ray Vineyards, but Peter buys select supplementary lots of those varietals. In 1976 the Chardonnay and Pinot Noir came from René di Rosa's Winery Lake Vineyard in the Carneros region of the Napa Valley.

The style of the Martin Ray Chardonnay owes its traditional richness of taste to a triple pressing of the must, which extracts the very essence of the grape. The new wine gains complexity from aging in Burgundian oak barrels acquired from the renowned seigneur of the Côte d'Or, Louis Latour.

A bottle-fermented champagne of Chardonnay and Pinot Noir is contemplated by Martin Ray Vineyards but not yet in *cuvée* blending. It will be called Madame Pinot and will doubtless not only qualify as a successor to the legendary wine of that name but be even finer.

SAMPLER SELECTION

Chardonnay (Winery Lake Vineyard). This first release of the 1976 vintage is a big wine; in current distribution.

RICHERT & SONS WINERY

18980 Monterey Road, Morgan Hill, California 95037

Walter Richert, with his degrees in chemistry and food science from the University of California, and his experience as editor of *Wine Review* and *Wines & Vines*, was a logical candidate for winery ownership in 1953, and he dubbed the budding enterprise Richert & Sons in the strong hope that his three sons, Robert, Eric, and Scott, would ease him into retirement. These hopes have been realized now that Robert and Scott have come home from college with appropriate degrees and with the desire to continue the highly specialized focus of the winery upon port and sherry. Richert chooses his grapes and methods to suit his own positive ideas of good-tasting sherry, and his success is measured by numerous awards and gold medals from competitive tastings. He uses Palomino grapes, of course, plus some Pedro Ximenez for cream sherries, but believes the Flame Tokay of the Lodi area and the misprized Mission grape have valuable roles in contributing their taste to the best sherries. The family label with trademark of four barrels, standing for Walter Richert and his three sons, is familiar to California connoisseurs, and it deserves to be known by a wider audience.

Full Dry Sherry. As the name suggests, it is a wine of full body, golden richness of color, dry on the palate.

Triple Cream Sherry. The medal winner, full-bodied, full-flavored, mellow in the mouth, rich and smooth.

Ruby Port. A glorious jewel-colored wine, with a haunting reminiscence of its grape origins in the full bouquet.

RIDGE VINEYARDS

17100 Monte Bello Road, Cupertino, California 95014

It began quite informally in 1959 as a hobby when Professor David Bennion persuaded some of his Stanford colleagues, electrical-engineering Ph.D.'s, to join him in purchasing a ramshackle old winery 10 miles south of the campus, high on a ridge of Black Mountain at an elevation of 2,300 feet. By 1967 Bennion had become full-time winemaker at Ridge Vineyards. Associates from the university retained

David Bennion, founder of Ridge Vineyards

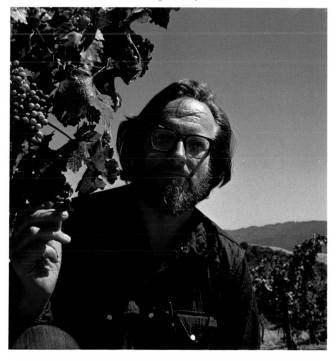

their investment and interest, but in 1969 they invited a trained enologist, Dr. Paul Draper, to join them. Industrialist Richard Foster of southern California was invited also, to assist in the shaping of what would certainly become a commercial enterprise.

In 1970 the nucleus of Ridge Vineyards as a winery was moved higher up the mountain to the old stone Monte Bello Winery, which was refurbished and provided with stainless-steel fermenters and a laboratory to accommodate the microbiologist. The legendary primitive complexity of the Ridge Cabernet Sauvignon, Zinfandel, and Petite Sirah was adroitly refined, to keep it satisfying to purist fans appreciating unfiltered wholeness, but possibly to advance the time of drinkability.

Ridge was among the earliest of the California wineries to use wrap-around labels offering each wine's full pedigree, from source of grape to bottling information, for the winelover's cellar book. Zinfandels, made in separate small lots, from as many as ten different vineyard sources, from Mendocino in the north to San Luis Obispo in the south, and from the prized old gold-mining areas of the Sierra, have become collectors' prizes. English wine authority Harry Waugh describes Ridge Cabernets and Zinfandels as "the Mouton Rothschilds or Latours of California." He rightfully adds that "at times they can be too powerful." The names of the Zinfandels have a California ring—Fiddletown, Langtry Road, Jimsomare, Coast Range, and Geyserville. The wines also have the individuality and earthy excellence that has earned Ridge Vineyards a reputation for bold integrity.

Chardonnay (Monte Bello). The grapes from the original vineyard yield but one ton per acre, for a rich, big wine.

Cabernet Sauvignon (Monte Bello). Classic fining with egg white is used for elegant balance.

Zinfandel (Jimsomare). Every vintage is huge, with almost overwhelming perfume of the grape. An enduring prize.

Zinfandel (Occidental). Another cellar treasure, from a cool Region I area. Strongly built; needs aging.

The big wines of Ridge come, in part, from their vineyards 2,300 feet above sea level on the Monte Bello ridge

ROUDON-SMITH VINEYARDS

513 Mt. View Road, Santa Cruz, California 95065

Many of California's new professional "nonprofessional winemakers" are inevitably moved into their second careers with the most ardent devotion. Ignace Paderewski, the great Polish pianist–statesman, took the greatest pride in the Zinfandel made at his mountain vineyard in Paso Robles. Richard Graff, with a degree in music from Harvard, took enological training at UC–Davis before embarking on his almost monastic existence as a winemaker at Chalone. The founding Stanford professors of Ridge Vineyards were all electrical engineers, and Bob Travers of Mayacamas was trained as a petroleum engineer, as was his predecessor on that mountain, Jack Taylor. Cardiologist Stanley Hoffman of Beverly Hills brought new life to the Paso Robles vineyards by putting down Pinot Noir vines, which face the Paderewski vineyard.

The list is long, and the foregoing few examples are cited merely as preamble to another young winery of laudable ambitions in the Santa Cruz Mountains. Founded in 1972, the winery was to provide an alternate life-style for electronics engineers James Smith and Robert Roudon. Roudon took courses in enology at UC–Davis, expanding on some background in chemistry. Not to labor the point, he is also a musician.

The young 12-acre vineyard surrounding the winery in Scotts Valley is planted in White Riesling, which thrives in the cool region. They are currently buying other grapes: Zinfandel from Lodi, Chenin Blanc, Chardonnay, Barbera, and Pinot Noir, as they work toward a 5,000-case annual goal. At present their small-batch, high-quality varietals are sold directly to consumers and a few local restaurants, but in the near future, as wine enthusiasts spread the good word, Roudon-Smith Vineyards' wines will be appearing in cellars beyond California.

SAMPLER SELECTION

Sauvignon Blanc. A light, graceful, dry wine from grapes grown in the nearby region of Hollister. A hint of oak.
Zinfandel (Lodi). In the tradition of the region, this is a big wine of late-harvest grapes, wholly dry.

New techniques in the winery are as important as growing conditions in the vineyard for the quality of California's wines

SAN MARTIN VINEYARDS

13000 Depot Street, San Martin, California 95046

At the height of the wine boom of the 1970s in California, when diversification was the key word in conglomerate structuring, changes of vineyard ownership and direction were the order of the day. Changes at San Martin Vineyards, a fourth-generation family winery established by Bruno Filice in 1892, continue to this moment. A new winemaker of energetic talent and a strong academic background, Ed Friedrich from Trier, Germany, assumed general management for the new owners, Norton Simon's Somerset Wine Company, in the spring of 1977. Somerset's wine affiliates also included the renowned Alexis Lichine.

The San Martin Vineyard's tasting room on Highway 101 south of San Jose has been a tourists' delight ever since Repeal. But there are no longer those wonderful fruit wines, the memorable Aprivette and the Satsuma plum wine called Sum-Plum. I loved them for their true translation of fruit into wine. San Martin's whole emphasis today is upon fine varietal wines and a

192

San Martin's Monterey County vineyards are watered by 28 miles of irrigation canals with pump stations like this one

tradition of "soft" wines inherited from Ed Friedrich's devotion to getting berryness into wines. Ed left in 1982 to make wine in Georgia. His successor as general manager and winemaker, Ron Niino, continues the soft wines, which have a mere 7–9 percent alcohol, and berry-fresh sweetness.

In June 1984 negotiations were concluded for the sale of Somerset Imports to the Distiller's Company Ltd., bringing San Martin into the DCL holdings in the United States, which also include the Concannon Vineyards of Livermore.

Winemaker Niino now buys his grapes on the open market. The number of titles has been reduced from twenty to ten, while the San Martin varietals reflect several premium winegrowing regions. Somerset remains as a marketing sales arm for the not inconsiderable sales of 250,000 cases per year.

SAMPLER SELECTION

Johannisberg Riesling (San Luis Obispo). One of the "soft" wines—gentle, sweet, and charming.

Chardonnay (San Luis Obispo). Fine wine, edged with aromatic hints of American oak in its aging. Cool-fermented, appetizing.

Chenin Blanc (Monterey County). Another of the "soft" wines, as fresh as a ripe grape crushed right in your mouth.

Cabernet Sauvignon (San Luis Obispo). Fine breed from well-selected grapes, carrying a California styling.

Zinfandel (Amador County). For lovers of the big Zin, this is a collectors' item, of depth and seductive fragrance.

TURGEON & LOHR WINERY

1000 Lenzen Avenue, San Jose, California 95126

Civil engineer Jerry Lohr, with a master's degree from Stanford, and Bernard Turgeon embarked on a multi-million-dollar winery project with twenty-five other partners in 1972. In that year they planted 280 acres of vines in the Salinas Valley, the fabled Steinbeck country near Greenfield. In 1974 they bought a substantial part of the abandoned Falstaff Brewery in downtown San Jose. As winemaker they hired Peter

Stern, a UC–Davis graduate in enology with experience at both Gallo and Robert Mondavi. He initiated the layout for the 55,000-gallon winery and the aging facilities, which include American, French, and Yugoslavian oak barrels. Eventually Turgeon & Lohr hope to sell 100,000 cases annually. Stern's scholarly handwritten histories of each released wine indicate his recognition of the present trend toward enlarging the consumer's technical comprehension of a wine's complexity. For his 1975 Monterey Rosé of Cabernet Sauvignon, the back label reads: "On November 3rd and 4th, 1975, we harvested the first crop from our own-rooted Cabernet Sauvignon vineyards. The grapes were in excellent condition due to the long, cool growing season we experienced this year. This rosé was made entirely from Cabernet grapes averaging 22.9° Brix at the time of crushing. After crushing, the juice remained in contact with the skins for an average of ten hours before pressing. At pressing, the juice was inoculated with a pure yeast culture and fermented at between 50° F. and 55° F. You will find this wine to be slightly sweet with a bright pink-red color. It is distinctly young, having the refreshing aroma of cassis and a hint of yeastiness. It is perfect for immediate consumption. Peter M. Stern, Winemaker, Turgeon & Lohr Winery."

SAMPLER SELECTION

Jade (Monterey County). A delicate, light white wine, predominantly Johannisberg Riesling, blended specially to be served with Chinese food.

Pinot Blanc (Monterey County). A dry white wine of well-balanced acidity, touched with oak; fresh and clean bouquet.

Pinot Noir (Monterey County). The area is cool, and the soil of a nature best suited to this often difficult grape.

WEIBEL CHAMPAGNE VINEYARDS

1250 Stanford Avenue, Mission San Jose, California 94538

In 1936 the Swiss family Weibel came to America, where Rudolph Weibel and his son Frederick hoped to

Weibel champagnes: Crackling Rosé and Chardonnay Brut Blanc de Blancs

The Wente Bros. tasting room

produce splendid champagnes. In 1945, when they found the old pre-Prohibition Leland Stanford Winery and surrounding vineyards, this seemed to be the time and place to begin.

Today Fred Weibel heads the company whose champagne cellars remain in the enlarged brick winery built by Leland Stanford near Mission San Jose. The search for grapes took Weibel to the area north of San Francisco, and there in Mendocino County, at Redwood Valley, 6 miles beyond Ukiah, he built a winery for making fine varietals.

"You dig your hands into the soil, smell the rich earth. Live with your grapes day and night. And you pray. And if nature is good to you, the sun, the rain, the cool night air . . . then the winemaker's art can bring out the soul in his wines." Fred Weibel's words tell much about the wines he makes. His delectable Champagne Chardonnay Brut Blanc de Blancs, bottle-fermented in the classic *méthode champenoise*, scored

higher than many other California champagnes in a tasting with leading French champagnes of *grande marque*. But possibly because of its clean fruitiness and softness, purists have been inclined to downgrade its ranking. Less-sophisticated consumers, however, who often find the acid bite and yeastiness of bouquet of brut champagne barely tolerable, enjoy Fred's soft, fine sparkler. The Weibel Champagne Vineyards maintain fine winemaking traditions, including those for their splendid sherries.

Because they have been erratically merchandised, Weibel wines are often hard to find, particularly the excellent, wood-aged Pinot Noir. The champagne cellars produce every kind of sparkling wine—Charmat bulk process, transfer method, and classic *méthode champenoise* bottle-fermented champagnes. Many appear under private labels. The clue is in the bottom line; you will know they are Weibel's if the cellar indicated is Mission San Jose.

SAMPLER SELECTION

Green Hungarian. A popular, very fruity, sweet-edged wine, blended with Chenin Blanc to give it greater appeal.

Chardonnay Brut Blanc de Blancs Champagne. Softer than most brut champagnes. Fruity, clean, silky, charming.

Pinot Noir. The well-aged, vintage selections are well worth seeking for their true varietal depth and complexity.

Solera Flor Dry Bin Sherry. Produced from Palomino grapes with yeast cultures. Comparable to fine Spanish *fino* sherry.

WENTE BROS.

5565 Tesla Road, Livermore, California 94550

Young Carl Heinrich Wente arrived in California from Hanover in 1880. Aware of the winemaking excitement in the state, he determined to make wine his life work. After an apprenticeship with Charles Krug in the Napa Valley, he bought 50 acres of young vines in the Livermore Valley in 1883, and built a modest frame house on Tesla Road. Cuttings of Sémillon and Sauvignon Blanc, the Sauternes varieties imported by Louis Mel, dominated the vineyard when it expanded to 300 acres.

Wente's eldest son, Carl F. Wente, eschewed farming for accounting and in later years became president of the Bank of America; Ernest, after studying at the College of Agriculture at UC–Davis, took charge of the vineyards; Herman, following his studies in enology at UC–Berkeley, became the winemaker. Bulk wines were sold to San Francisco wine merchants until Prohibition, when, through an arrangement with Georges de Latour of Beaulieu Vineyard, production of altar wines was continued. In 1934 the first wines to bear the Wente Bros. label appeared under the proprietary designation Valle de Oro (Valley of Gold), the name the early mission settlers had given the Livermore area.

When Frank Schoonmaker came to California in search of fine wines to augment his imported wine selections, he soon became an ardent advocate of the Wentes' white wines and urged them to differentiate their pure varietal wines from the commonly marketed Sauterne and Chablis. He was convinced that these outstanding wines, of positive individual character, with regional taste distinction, should be marketed without leaning upon European comparison. In the late 1930s, through Schoonmaker's enthusiasm, and with support from winemakers like Louis M. Martini, the Korbels, and even the maverick Martin Ray, varietal labeling of California wines was inaugurated. Wente Dry Semillon and Sauvignon Blanc, among others, became the most popular and dependable wines of California.

Schoonmaker was at the winery on the day the Marquis de Lur-Saluces paid his famous visit to the Wentes in May 1939. Herman set out for him a series of successive vintages of Sauvignon Blanc, a pure 100 percent varietal wine, which is not produced as such in Bordeaux. It was the first time the owner of famed Château d'Yquem had ever tasted California wines produced from cuttings from his vineyard. All of us watched anxiously while he went through the tasting . . . silently. Before the Marquis could comment on the bone-dry Sauvignon Blanc, Herman produced a bottle of Semillon. It brought a quick smile to the visitor's face, like meeting an old friend. "These are beautiful wines," he said. "I am delighted to find such splendid work going on here! It makes me happy to see my 'children' doing so well in California in this setting where they are so appreciated."

Herman Wente died in 1961. With the growing popularity of the wines, a cautious expansion of the winery facilities took place, and Wente Bros. wines were distributed to every state in the union. Ernest supervised the changeover into the new technology of both harvesting and winemaking, while his son Karl headed the family winery as president. On my first visit to the enlarged winery, with its new stainless-steel fermenters, representing the investment of millions of dollars, Ernest whispered to me, "You know, Robert, we did this ourselves." It was said with modest pride, underscoring a statement in the Wente Bros. brochure: "Of the many distinguished California wineries established in the 1800s, only a small handful are still owned and operated by the original families. Wente is one of these."

Karl Wente died suddenly at forty-nine, in January of 1977. Under his careful and well-considered guidance, 300 acres of varietal vineyards were pioneered in 1962 in Monterey County at the upper end of the Carmel Valley, 15 miles inland from the ocean.

Fourth-generation Wentes Eric, Philip, and Carolyn celebrated the winery's centennial in 1983 with the debut of a *méthode champenoise* Monterey County sparkling wine, Wente Brut.

SAMPLER SELECTION

Pinot Chardonnay (California). Of Livermore and Monterey grapes. California's first great Chardonnay. Fruity, dry, noble.

Le Blanc de Blancs. A blend of Ugni Blanc and Chenin Blanc. Semidry, fruity, modestly priced, universally popular.

Grey Riesling. Light, white, dry wine from the Chauché Gris grape; never disappointing, of standard excellence and value.

Wente Brut (Monterey County). Classic vintage sparkling wine, of a Chardonnay/Pinot Noir *cuvée*; bright, crisp, dry, clean.

WOODSIDE VINEYARDS

340 Kings Mountain Road, Woodside, California
94062

When Robert and Polly Mullen took up wine-making as a hobby in 1960, they had no idea that they would become not only guardians of a revered legacy, but the mainstays of a community project that keeps residential Woodside alive to the joys of wine. There remain only about 3 acres of the celebrated Cabernet Sauvignon vines of Emmett Rixford's La Questa vineyard, planted in 1883. Some of those ancient vines, of diminishing yield, and newer ones in the same venerated soil, are tended by the Mullens. Their enthusiasm has enlisted six Woodside neighbors, who also grow modest plots of Cabernet Sauvignon, Chardonnay, and Pinot Noir. Even the village church benefits: it has Woodside Vineyards wines for Communion.

The Mullens have their own 3-acre vineyard with 800 vines lovingly cared for. Their Chenin Blanc vines have been grafted over to Chardonnay, which, like Pinot Noir, seems to be better adapted to this moderately cool area. The Cabernet Sauvignon, however, remains the prize and pride of Woodside. It is aged in American oak for two years and spends another two years in bottle before release.

Though in 1973 the Mullens expanded the winery, virtually doubling its size, annual production averages only 1,500 gallons.

SAMPLER SELECTION

Chardonnay. The Burgundian grape is given cool fermentation to capture bouquet, with aging in American oak.

Pinot Noir. Careful handling of the small clusters of tiny black grapes, in open fermentation, brings forth fine wine.

Cabernet Sauvignon. Perpetuating the La Questa label, the wine carries a unique "dusty" bouquet prized by claret lovers.

VINEYARDS AND WINERIES: SOUTH CENTRAL COAST COUNTIES

"Wine opens the heart. It warms the shy poet hidden in the cage of the ribs. It melts the wax in the ears that music may be heard. It takes the terror from the tongue that truth may be said."
—Christopher Morley

MONTEREY, SAN LUIS OBISPO, SANTA BARBARA

Monterey County is a winegrower's dream. Franciscan padres planted the first vineyard at Soledad, but it was not their blue-black Mission grape that sparked today's interest in the famed lettuce-growing region, John Steinbeck's long green valley of *East of Eden*. Reports of a *Vitis vinifera* vineyard planted in the high benchlands of the Gavilan Mountains in the 1880s focused attention on the bleak area called the Chalone Bench. A Frenchman by the name of Tamm had recognized in the geology of the area a similarity to the prized soil of Burgundy and Champagne. Accordingly, he planted grape varieties that prospered in those French regions—Pinot Blanc, Petit Pinot (now known as Pinot Noir), Chardonnay, and some Chenin Blanc. Will Silvear, a mineralogist, patiently tended the Tamm vineyards after 1919. The Wentes bought Silvear's grapes for a number of years and prevailed upon Professors Amerine and Winkler to visit Silvear. The enologists believed that with less than eight inches of rainfall and no possibility of water, the Chalone Bench would not be good for vineyards. Later they advocated the Soledad District, where water was available.

But subsequent studies by Amerine and Winkler in their temperature-summation studies endorsed the region after water wells were constructed and fed from the underground Salinas River. Following the first plantings by Masson, Mirassou, and Wente in 1962, sophisticated overhead sprinkler systems of artificial rainfall were developed: computerized irrigation that could send moisture to those vines that needed it, as determined by sensitized instruments in the ground. Today Monterey County can boast over 33,000 acres of vines, almost as many as Napa and Sonoma combined. The area is classified as Regions I and II. An afternoon breeze blowing in from the broad northern fan of valley that opens to the sea cools the area. The moisture carried by that dependable breeze the "Monterey mistral" has fostered the development of the fungus *Botrytis cinerea*, prayed for by French vineyardists of Sauternes and German viticulturists of the Rhine. The noble rot concentrates sugar in ripen-

An irrigation canal 27 miles long winds through San Martin Vineyards in Monterey County

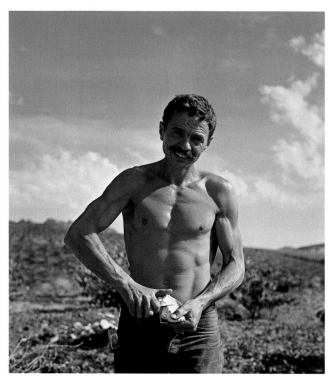

Richard Graff coaxes rich Burgundian wines from his rocky Chalone vineyards

Barely whispered among winelovers is the existence of a Pinot Noir from Chalone Vineyard which, as made by Dick Graff, has all the majesty of a Chambertin or Musigny of Burgundy. The very first pure Pinnacles Selection bottlings of the variety from the Paul Masson plantings gave the same true scent, recalling wines of the Côte d'Or. Monterey County is still young, the full promise yet to be achieved. The same is true of the limestone hills of the Paso Robles area, with new pioneering of Pinot Noir at the Hoffman Mountain Ranch, and in the Santa Ynez Valley, inland from Santa Barbara, at The Firestone Vineyard.

There are 10,000 acres of premium varietal grapes growing in the Santa Maria region, some from Rancho Tepusquet, which has become a highly regarded source of grapes. Scouts from Beringer, Sebastiani, Robert Mondavi, Louis M. Martini, Château Montelena, and ZD of Sonoma have found Chardonnay, Johannisberg Riesling, Gewürztraminer, Pinot Noir, and Merlot from this microclimate worthy of their own more exalted labels.

ing grapes, giving wines made from botrytised berries richer glycerines and subtle nuances of flavor. While it is a boon for white wines, it is a bane for red-wine varieties, calling for special spray controls.

The superlative early estimates of Monterey County as California's great vineyard bonanza caused cultivation to be extended southward into San Luis Obispo County. The boom of the seventies revived interest in Santa Barbara as grape-growing country.

Regional characteristics of the wines are only now becoming apparent as vine roots penetrate deeper and deeper into the soil, extracting a recognizably different mineral complex. Vinification by Mirassou and Wente is designed to avoid the *goût de terroir*, which can be strong enough to suggest an earthiness tinged with cabbage, garlic, and overwhelming herbal odors in white wines where delicacy is being sought. But balancing this occasional risk is an extraordinary affinity of the Monterey region for those two vines that demand a cool climate, Pinot Noir and Riesling of the Rhine.

CHALONE VINEYARD

Stonewall Canyon Road, The Pinnacles, Soledad, California 93960

There is an old Gallic saw that declares: "To produce a great wine, the vine must suffer a little." In many of the world's most renowned vineyards, vines thrive where nothing else will grow. Impossible conditions seem to favor the wine vine. The site of Chalone Vineyard, first planted by the Frenchman Tamm and tended by Will Silvear, was acquired by the Graff family almost twenty years ago. Before that, most people had been deterred by its many difficulties: inaccessibility, lack of water, lack of modern conveniences such as the telephone.

Enter Richard Graff, music major from Harvard, young, sinewy, with some UC–Davis theories clamoring to be tested, plus his father's indulgence for his proposal to make something of the Chalone Vineyard. On my first visit, half a dozen years ago, I followed Dick's pickup truck from the verdant rows of the Paul

The first harvest from Firestone Vineyard is blessed and weighed en route to becoming an elegant wine

Masson Vineyards on the lower slopes, where sprinklers like the fountains of Versailles were showering the vines with water. We wound upward into the hills, the earth growing more and more arid and desolate, the parched red soil a veritable hot waste out of Dante's Inferno. As we turned into an upper valley, I saw some straggling vines, each row with empty spaces where vines had died. We pulled up to a ramshackle cottage with the spavined boards of a porch sagging above a broken stairway. Graff leaped out of the pickup with a merry smile. "We're here!" he said, to which I could only reply, as I vaulted onto the porch, hoping the boards would support me, "We certainly are!"

Once inside, the whole scene changed. A modern Scandinavian iron fireplace held center stage, and as my eyes took in the room, they moved from a three-rank Mason & Hamlin organ to a life-size oil portrait of Dick's grandaunt in flowing silks and taffeta painted in the style of Sargent. In an adjacent dining room a table was set with Baccarat crystal and fresh flowers. Young Graff poured a golden wine into one of the goblets, and from its generous bowl emerged a scent unmistakably Chardonnay, as regal as any Montrachet or Meursault of my tasting experience. In a daze of disbelief, I walked with him to the makeshift winery, a small whitewashed adobe outbuilding, half submerged in the earth. Graff flipped a switch, and a Diesel generator whirred into life, giving electricity to light the interior and also power for fans blowing over blocks of ice trucked up from Salinas to provide the needed air-cooling in the blistering heat of autumn harvest days and nights.

With equal ingenuity, Graff had bought an antique tank truck, made a goat-trail roadway up the side of a hill above the vineyard, installed a redwood storage tank for water hauled up the mountain from Salinas, and, with plastic lines to each of thousands of old and new vines, inaugurated a drip system for irrigation years ahead of other California vintners. In 1975 and 1976, with no help but that of his brothers, he built a two-story winery into the side of the hill. There, with modern stainless-steel equipment plus French-oak cooperage, some of the finest wines of California are being made. A group of investors headed by Richard Graff, and William P. Woodward, with Michael Michaud as winemaker, assures a fine future for Chalone Vineyards, and, it is to be hoped, greater availability of its outstanding wines.

SAMPLER SELECTION

Pinot Blanc (Estate Bottled). In French bottles, from French oak, a substantial wine of woody incense and long-lasting flavor.

Chenin Blanc (Estate Bottled). Made completely dry. A wine of stature, crisp, clean, and with unusual elegance. Oak-finished.

Chardonnay (Estate Bottled). Easily one of the most superb vinifications of this grape in California. French-oak-aged.

Pinot Noir (Estate Bottled). A collectors' prize. Proof that the difficult grape *can* produce elegant, translucent wine here.

THE FIRESTONE VINEYARD

Zaca Station Road, Los Olivos, California 93441

The first crush for the vineyards planted in 1972 by Ambassador Leonard Firestone and his son Brooks

André Tchelistcheff, the dean of California enologists, has been Firestone's consultant since its inception was blessed and dedicated on the morning of September 23, 1975. The 75,000-case winery, with its 300 acres of vines, has been an expensive gamble involving an enormous investment. But the first "third leaf" wines affirm the wisdom of the endeavor, in which the Firestones are joined with Suntory, Ltd., of Japan, and André Tchelistcheff, who has been the consultant from the beginning. Winemaker Alison Green declares: "I try for elegance." She is succeeding.

The labels that launched the first wines, with their sketches of Firestone under construction by California artist Sebastian Titus, will be souvenirs for coming generations. Cellared bottles of the good red wines, for those lucky enough to find the vintages of '75 and '76, might well be laid down for twenty-one years against the coming of age of a fortunate child. They will surely last that long.

SAMPLER SELECTION

Johannisberg Riesling (Santa Ynez Valley). Clean, light, gentle. Late-harvest, botrytised editions are richer, fuller, sweeter.

Chardonnay (Santa Ynez Valley). A big, unique wine of dry-weed scent, classic chalky taste, complex hints of wood and fruit.

Cabernet Sauvignon Rosé (Santa Ynez Valley). Silky and dry, with hints of the noble grape from which it was made.

Cabernet Sauvignon (Santa Ynez Valley). A big wine of deep color and taste, French-oak-aged, loganberry aftertaste.

HOFFMAN MOUNTAIN RANCH VINEYARDS

Adelaide Road, Paso Robles, California 93446

The first new winery in San Luis Obispo County in nearly fifty years is set on the rolling terrain of a 1,200-acre walnut and almond ranch in the Santa Lucia Mountain range, 1,700 feet above sea level. It borders the ranch that once belonged to the great Polish patriot and pianist, Ignace Jan Paderewski, whose Zinfandel wines were widely praised many years ago.

Winemaking history in this Central Coast region was well served with the development of the Hoffman

Mountain Ranch Vineyards in 1965, the first major planting of premium varietal vines. Currently there are 18 wineries thriving in this good wineland.

Consultant André Tchelistcheff described the HMR vineyards as "a jewel of ecological elements." One of the first Chardonnays from the 1973 vintage, made under the regime of the widely respected and beloved Dr. Stanley Hoffman, was awarded a Gold Seal diploma by the Club Oenologique in an International Wine Competition at Ockley in Surrey, England. On every hand there were plaudits also for each vintage edition of HMR Pinot Noir, made by the Hoffman family with sons Michael and David dividing the responsibilities of grapegrowing and winemaking, field and cellar.

Financial problems, which beset many young wineries in California, brought about changes of direction at HMR, but "still the vines, their ancient ruby yield." In 1983, the Hoffman family were divorced totally from the operation; a sale in April 1982 to Intra-Leisure, Inc., of Redondo Beach, continues the winery operation with a "dba HMR, Ltd." Chris Johnson is the winemaker in the handsome multilevel winery set among the vines.

SAMPLER SELECTION

Franken Riesling. HMR wine of the Sylvaner grape has a silky softness, with a well-balanced residual sweetness.

Chardonnay. A round, mouth-filling wine of varietal depth, dry, fragrant, rich, with moderate bouquet in its finish.

Pinot Noir. Vintage, estate-bottled wine from the true clone of Burgundy. Translucent ruby with penetrating bouquet.

Cabernet Sauvignon. Vintage, estate-bottled wine of deep, dark garnet color. Certain to require long aging. Full bouquet.

LOS ALAMOS WINERY

Route 135, Los Alamos, California 93440

Attorney Samuel D. Hale, Jr., is a self-taught winemaker who, like many another city dweller, was caught up in the fascination of grape growing. In the

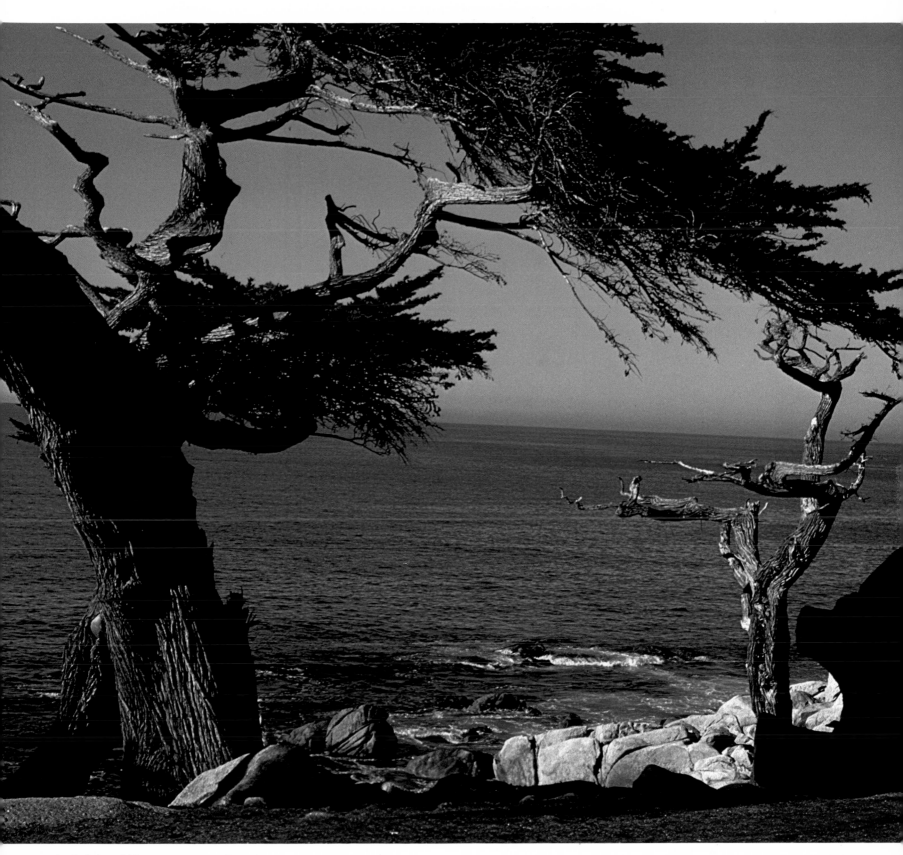

A wind-shaped Monterey cypress at Carmel

newly developed region below Santa Maria, in Santa Barbara County, Hale planted 330 acres of six choice varietals in 1972, with a sensitivity to the distinctly different microclimates favorable to each. His Chardonnay, Johannisberg Riesling, and Pinot Noir grow in the cool areas, while on the slopes of the back canyons of his estate, where it is much warmer, are his Cabernet Sauvignon, Merlot, and Zinfandel. By his own admission, the "second leaf" wines were a little disappointing. But vines and winemaker had matured for the "third leaf" harvest of 1975: the Chardonnay of that year won a bronze medal at the Los Angeles County Fair; the Zinfandel was allowed to gain a fuller stature by leaving the grapes longer on the vine. With a unique and rather baroque label, gleaming with burnished gold, Los Alamos Winery takes its place among the new boutique wineries worthy of consumer recognition.

SAMPLER SELECTION

White Riesling. A lilting freshness and ingratiating lightness give this wine, too often heavy, indications of fine promise.

Chardonnay. Early editions were made by Dr. Richard Peterson at The Monterey Vineyard before the Los Alamos Winery was completed.

Zinfandel. The late-harvest 1975 wine showed fine potential for the newly planted area to produce this varietal as a big wine.

THE MONTEREY VINEYARD

800 S. Alta Street, Gonzales, California 93926

Twenty-eight Monterey County properties, growing 9,600 acres of choice varietal grapes for a 500,000-case winery, alas came apart at the seams in the first wave of the 1974 recession's effect upon California's wine world. Pay-back schedules for the multi-million-dollar financing were predicated upon the grape prices of the early seventies. When prices fell in 1974, the grim handwriting was on the wall, not only for many marginal grapeland investors but also for such seemingly well-funded enterprises as The Monterey Vineyard.

Winemaker and president of the winery division of the enterprise was, and still is, Dr. Richard Peterson, who left the security of Beaulieu Vineyard to head the challenging Monterey County operation. There was deserving praise for the white table wines assisted toward their perfection by Dr. Peterson's $100,000 adjustable centrifuge.

In the rapid dissolution of the original corporation, the grape growers had to look elsewhere for support. Many were able to salvage their future through advantageous contracts for their grapes with Gallo. In December 1977 the large winery was bought by Coca-Cola of Atlanta, whose wine holdings were purchased by Seagram in November 1983. Dr. Peterson, as winemaster/director, declared that the winery will continue to operate as in the past, producing vintage-dated varietal wines for its own label.

The winery uses grapes from 600 acres of choice varietals and operates virtually as a small boutique winery. Among the new titles already in demand is a rich botrytised Sauvignon Blanc, Monterey's golden answer to Château d'Yquem—elegant, honey-sweet, and flowery-clean in bouquet.

Beyond premium varietal wines, a major category of The Monterey Vineyard labels are the California Classic Table Wines: Red, White, and Rosé, modestly priced and outstanding values.

Taylor California Cellars wines are also produced here in high technology winemaking facilities which they share with Monterey, though the two contiguous wineries operate individually, under Seagram ownership.

SAMPLER SELECTION

Chardonnay (Monterey County). Light in style, almost delicately crisp, clean, a fine companion to seafood and shellfish.

Cabernet Sauvignon (San Luis Obispo) French Camp. An outstanding, vineyard-designated Cabernet of rich varietal breed and good aging potential.

Johannisberg Riesling (Monterey County). Perky, fresh, and crisp wine; taste suggests grapefruit.

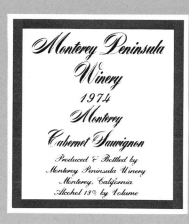

Monterey Peninsula Winery 1974 *Monterey* *Cabernet Sauvignon* *Produced & Bottled by Monterey Peninsula Winery Monterey, California* *Alcohol 13% by Volume*

1975
CHALONE
VINEYARD

CALIFORNIA
CHARDONNAY
ESTATE BOTTLED

This vintage produced 5387 bottles and 60 magnums of which this is No. 5109

A table wine grown, vinified and bottled on Mount Chalone by Chalone Vineyard, The Pinnacles, Soledad, Monterey County, California. For sale in California only.   Net cont. 1 pt. 8 fl. oz.

SANTA BARBARA WINERY

CALIFORNIA
PINOT CHARDONNAY
1975 SANTA BARBARA COUNTY

YORK MOUNTAIN

California
MERLOT ROSÉ
ALCOHOL 12% BY VOLUME
PRODUCED AND BOTTLED BY
YORK MOUNTAIN WINERY, TEMPLETON, CALIFORNIA
ESTABLISHED 1882

THE MONTEREY VINEYARD

MONTEREY COUNTY
Grüner Sylvaner
DRY WHITE MONTEREY WINE
Produced and Bottled by The Monterey Vineyard Gonzales, California USA
ALCOHOL 11½% BY VOLUME

ESTATE BOTTLED 1974
Los Alamos Vineyards
CALIFORNIA
Cabernet Sauvignon
From the Los Alamos Valley of Santa Barbara County
Produced and Bottled by Los Alamos Vineyards Los Alamos, California
alcohol 12% by volume

HMR
California
PINOT NOIR
Estate Bottled
Produced and bottled by
Hoffman Mountain Ranch Vineyards
Santa Lucia Mountain Range, Paso Robles, California
Alcohol 13% by Volume

THE FIRESTONE VINEYARD

Winery Under Construction
Santa Ynez Valley, California
ROSÉ OF CABERNET SAUVIGNON
1975
PRODUCED AND BOTTLED BY THE FIRESTONE VINEYARD
LOS OLIVOS, CALIFORNIA   ALCOHOL 13.1% BY VOLUME

SOUTH CENTRAL COAST WINE LABELS

MONTEREY PENINSULA WINERY

2999 Monterey–Salinas Highway, Monterey, California 93940

The rich red wines of the Monterey Peninsula Winery are a magnet to wine buffs seeking the purist approach to winemaking. There is no fining, no filtering. Each wine is produced in a separate small lot. Under winemakers Dick Nuckton and Roy Thomas some huge blockbuster Zinfandel wines have been produced. The small stone winery is the only one in the romantic bayside city of Monterey. In October, music, wine, and good times are to be had at the "Wine Stomp," when 300 people gather to crush 10 tons of grapes with their bare feet.

SAMPLER SELECTION

Chardonnay. A 1974 vintage lot came home with a bronze medal for winemakers Roy Thomas and Dick Nuckton.

Cabernet Sauvignon (Monterey). Gold medals from the Los Angeles County Fair are evidence of the virtues of these small-lot, truly big wines.

Zinfandel (Lodi). The bigness of this dark, deep, mouth-filling wine suggests another decade ahead for its full enjoyment.

SANTA BARBARA WINERY

202 Anacapa Street, Santa Barbara, California 93101

Trained as an architect, a businessman with diversified interests, Pierre Lafond seems to gain a modicum of aesthetic satisfaction from his chores as a devoted winemaker. At the informal cinder-block winery, in the heart of downtown Santa Barbara, Lafond receives choice grapes from Santa Barbara and San Luis Obispo counties, ferments them in stainless steel, and ages the wine in Yugoslavian-oak tanks. Under a Mission label he provides house wines for many of the local restaurants and fruit wines and mead for the Danish colony at nearby Solvang. The premium varietals are modestly priced and a good value.

SAMPLER SELECTION

Pinot Chardonnay. Cool-fermented over four to five weeks at 45° F., the wine retains a fresh fruitiness and varietal character.

Muscat Alexandria. A vintage wine, with residual sweetness and the full, exotic perfume of the grape.

Zinfandel. Substantial red wine with fine varietal berryness of nose and taste. Vintage selections are the choice here.

YORK MOUNTAIN WINERY

York Mountain Road, Templeton, California 93465

In 1970, Max Goldman, an enologist and champagne maker from New York, bought from Wilfred York the historic property founded in 1882 by Andrew York, and with his son, Steven, a University of Colorado art major, has been bringing it back to an aesthetic and practical level commensurate with its potential. The old vines have been replaced with Pinot Noir and Chardonnay, for a possible future champagne *cuvée*, and there are Cabernet Sauvignon and Merlot for classic claret. But as Max Goldman rightly says, "This is Zinfandel territory." (Paderewski used to send grapes from his San Ignacio Ranch to the York Mountain Winery to be made into the ruby Zinfandel that became so famous.) Veteran winemaker Max Goldman is pleased with the varietal character the good earth is lending to his 10 acres of new vines.

VINEYARDS AND WINERIES: CENTRAL VALLEY AND SOUTHERN CALIFORNIA

"Let those who drink not, but austerely dine,
Dry up in law; the Muses smell of wine."
                                        —Horace

SACRAMENTO, AMADOR, SAN JOAQUIN, FRESNO, KERN, MADERA, MERCED, TULARE, LOS ANGELES, RIVERSIDE, SAN DIEGO, SAN BERNARDINO

The Central Valley, which extends about 400 miles from north to south, is best known, in terms of wine production, for its yields of heavy-tonnage wine grapes—quantity rather than quality. Every harvest season truckloads of grapes go from the Bakersfield area to North Coast wineries, to be used for a significant amount of the cheaper wines released from those distinguished wineries, many of which depend for economic survival on the volume sale of jug wines. As wine country the region has suffered in comparison with the North Coast counties of Napa, Sonoma, and Mendocino. At this writing, California winemakers are locked in an emotionally charged battle for legal definitions of wineland boundaries. Regional appellations within narrower boundaries are being urged by small wineries. The larger wineries argue for one blanket designation—North Coast—for the entire coastal region from Santa Barbara to Ukiah, reflecting the elitism that attaches to the North Coast counties as compared to the highly productive Central Valley.

There is reason for a revised and upgraded opinion of the Central Valley as a region of potential for fine wines. Without any question, California's greatest Zinfandels are coming to market today boasting Lodi or Amador County as their birthplace. The San Joaquin Valley has unrecognized pockets of earth where fine wine grapes *can* grow. In the sandy loam, mineral content is high, the soil is well-suited to grape culture, and drainage, a most important factor, is excellent.

In this region, which was once semi-arid desert, healthy and productive *Vitis vinifera* grows as well as in any other wine country of the world. Today Central Valley wines are shipped not only around this country but overseas to Japan and Germany. But the legend of San Joaquin as wine country is just taking shape. I would suggest suspended judgment until some of the wines hereinafter listed are explored.

The great San Joaquin Valley was noted as early as 1772 for its profusion of wild grapevines. This is the heartland of California agriculture. Eighty percent of all the vegetables sold in the United States are grown here. Although Kern County is the largest oil-producing county in California, oil is secondary to agriculture in the economy of the region. Viniculture is a major element in the valley's economic structure, with the largest producing winery in the world, E. & J. Gallo, at Modesto, and the largest continuous agricultural holding in the state, the 280,000 acres of historic Tejon Ranch, which by 1981 may be producing 15 million gallons of wine.

There are many reasons for a changed viewpoint about this hot wine country. Hybrid vines such as Ruby Cabernet and Emerald Riesling produce better-quality wines in a warm climate than was possible heretofore. Mechanical harvesting and field-crushing, properly understood and expertly controlled, bring juice into the wineries with minimal oxidation; it comes not into old frame wineries, where even the coolest shade was withering to man and wine alike, but to refrigerated environments equivalent to the cool Rhineland. San Joaquin Valley varietals, given premium viticultural attention, are characterized by softness and delicacy. The white wines are fresh, fruity, with distinct grape taste. The reds often lack depth and mature rapidly, but they constitute a vast reservoir of pleasant and dependable table wines for daily use. Central Valley gives us an abundant heritage of great value, worth reappraisal and increased appreciation.

In San Bernardino County, at the foot of the Sierra Madre Mountains, there was at one time a vineyard—the largest in the world—that dazzled beholders and delighted photographers. But today, as a result of the inroads of subdivision and the devastating effects of smog, only gnarled stumps remain in the unharvested, untended vineyard that was formerly the pride of the Guasti family. The winery names that dominate the region—Brookside and San Antonio—still produce some local wines, but the best of their production is from grapes purchased outside the blighted areas—from North Coast counties or the new

From December through February, skilled pruners cut away canes, improving both the quantity and the quality of the next harvest

vineland in San Diego County near Temecula and the Rancho California district.

Branch wineries of San Antonio and Brookside are neighborhood tasting centers where, instead of wines, converts to the pleasures of wine are made by the thousands. Across the tasting bars, they learn the charms of wines made from descendants of the Mission vines first planted in San Diego by Padre Junípero Serra in 1769.

BARENGO VINEYARDS

3125 E. Orange Street, Acampo, California 95220

Shortly after Repeal, this brick granary was converted into a 1,650,000-gallon winery by a group of grape growers headed by Cesare Mondavi. When Mondavi sold it in the 1940s, Dino Barengo became the new owner. In 1949, he was the first to make and bottle a Ruby Cabernet from the hybrid developed at UC–Davis, and his wines continued to bring deserved recognition to the variety.

In 1973, the new owners opened a number of Barengo Vineyards retail tasting rooms, new labels were designed, and the winery was off to acquiring a slick new image. There were the good generic wines of modest price and some classic varietals of excellent value under the Barengo Reserve label. The winery was sold again, in 1976, to the present owner, Ira Kirkorian, of Campbell. UC–Davis-trained Brad Alderson is the new winemaker.

If you should come upon it in a food store, the Barengo Vineyards Wine Vinegar will do wonders for your salads.

SAMPLER SELECTION

Pinot Chardonnay. Under the "Reserve" label, this wood-aged wine is light, well-balanced, tart, and good value.

Muscadelle du Bordelais. Fresh, light, delicately sweet; well-chilled, it makes a pleasant summer luncheon feature.

Ruby Cabernet. With the Cabernet perfume, a light claret body, and good ruby color, it makes a bid for daily wine service.

BEAR MOUNTAIN WINERY, now LA MONT WINERY, INC.

Comanche Road, DiGiorgio, California 93217

Few top varietals were being grown in the Tehachapi area until, in the 1950s, Keith Nylander, the manager of the DiGiorgio Wine Company, realized the possibilities of the region for fine table wines. Then, in 1966, when the DiGiorgio Corporation decided to get out of the wine business, the local grape growers joined together and founded the Bear Mountain Winery.

The 130-member co-op continued as the fourth-largest in the state until 1978, when the whole facility was sold to John La Batt, Ltd., of Canada, who changed the name of the winery to that of its most

Bottles bearing the M. La Mont label are restaurant favorites

A vertical still at Bear Mountain Winery

prestigious label, the French-sounding La Mont. With a storage capacity of some 36,000,000 gallons, fermenting facilities capable of handling 7,800,000 gallons from 5,000 tons of grapes per day, and bottling lines that can turn out 20,000 cases per day, it is apparent that the La Mont Winery remains one of California's large producers.

Much of the wine is sold on the Eastern seaboard, where it appears as the house wine in restaurants. The brands of vermouth and brandy recall some of the state's most historic labels: A.R. Morrow, Aristocrat, Ambassador, and Guasti.

The M. La Mont label continues to be the best seller in California as well as in Texas, New Jersey, and New York. Gross sales for the winery surpass one million cases per year.

SAMPLER SELECTION

French Colombard (California). Fresh, clean, fruity wine, crisp though sweet-edged for popular-appeal drinkability.

Chardonnay (California). Locally grown grapes provide a light table wine, with no wood aging, for a modest price.

Ruby Cabernet (California). Made from the hybrid especially developed for this warm-weather growing region.

BISCEGLIA BROS. WINE CO.

25427 Avenue 13, Madera, California 93637

In 1888, Alfonse F. Bisceglia came to California from Calabria, to make wine with his three brothers, Joseph, Pasquale, and Bruno. During the Depression, the Bisceglia brothers bought the famed Greystone Cellars of the Napa Valley for the bargain price of $10,000. It proved to be a huge white elephant, as it had been for several previous owners. However, since The Christian Brothers, to whom the Bisceglias sold it, began making sparkling wines there, its worth has escalated into six figures.

But winemaking in the San Joaquin suits the Bisceglia brothers. Operated now by Bruno T., son of the founder, and Joseph, one of the original four brothers, the company makes and sells bulk wine to other wineries. In their tasting rooms, they offer private-label reserves, made in small quantities and handcrafted in Old World style. There are generic wines, fruit and berry wines, sparkling wines, vermouth, and brandy. Their finest wines honor the founder, Alfonse F. Bisceglia.

SAMPLER SELECTION

Grenache Blanc. An essentially dry white wine with the delicate acidity plus the varietal zing of the French grape.

Château d'Or. Billed as "a salute to Château d'Yquem," it is a golden wine of Sauternes sweetness, albeit much lighter.

Château Noir. A blended red wine of deep ruby hue, dry and full-bodied, to accompany lamb, beef, or spaghetti dinners.

J F J BRONCO WINERY

6342 Bystrum Road, Ceres, California 95307

South of Modesto, surrounded by fields of maize, cotton, and corn, and peach orchards, is Ceres, where John, Fred, and Joe Franzia have built a million-gallon winery, not to make wine but to receive and package bulk wine from the excess inventories of other wineries. As "seconds" these wines are often of outstanding quality, with bargain-bin pricing, a bonanza to the alert buyer. The shrewdness and life-long wine experience of the Franzias were rewarded at the end of their first year in business with sales of 1 1/2 million cases. Blending to the Franzias' own style is involved, and that style is unquestionably one reason for their success. They have also pioneered the light metal cap for sparkling wines, a boon to airline flight attendants, for safety and ease of opening, and of course to caterers, since less help is needed for opening champagne bottles during large receptions.

In the early months of 1977 Bronco and the Getty Oil Company announced a joint venture to build and

operate a wine-grape conversion and storage facility capable of processing 30,000 tons of grapes annually. Bronco will be the sole operators of the winery, with their bulk table wines available to other vintners.

The young Franzia clan—two brothers and a cousin—are the third generation of the Franzia family that had entered San Joaquin Valley agriculture with Giuseppe Franzia's arrival from Italy in 1890. They resigned from the family winery and formed the Bronco company suddenly in 1972, when the Coca-Cola Bottling Co. of New York acquired the family winery. Volatile Fred Franzia says *bronco* is the colloquial Italian term for "grape stump," a likelier definition than "untamed horse." Bronco's quart carafes can be found in fifteen states, and for a good Cabernet Sauvignon, Napa Gamay, or Gamay Beaujolais they are bargains.

SAMPLER SELECTION

Rhinewein. Cellared and bottled by John, Fred, and Joseph. Sold in quart carafes. Brilliantly clear, sweet-edged, and a bargain.

Sangria. Fruit-flavored red wine in handy carafes, ready to pour over ice cubes and be garnished with a slice of orange.

California Champagne. An Extra Dry *cuvée*, modestly priced, clean, well-made, very, very pale, bland, inexpensive.

BROOKSIDE VINEYARD COMPANY

9900 Guasti Road, Guasti, California 91743

The founding date of 1832 makes Brookside Vineyard one of the oldest in the state. In 1916 the original Brookside in Redlands was sold, and the grandsons of one of the founders went to work for Garrett and Company, which included the Guasti winery. One of the grandsons, Philo Biane, in 1952 reestablished the Brookside Vineyard Company at Ontario, and four years later he purchased the historic Guasti property from the California Wine Association. The old Guasti winery, with native fieldstone walls more than 3 feet thick and cellars measuring 600 by 100 feet, affords Brookside underground aging

facilities that are among the largest in the United States.

Though Brookside was sold in 1972 to Beatrice Foods, Inc., a Chicago conglomerate, management remains with the Biane family. Brookside produces some sacramental and commercial wines with the Benedictine monks of Assumption Abbey at Richardton, North Dakota. Some of the Bianes' finest varietal wines, from vineyards near Temecula, are put out under the Abbey label.

A unique aspect of Brookside's operation is their retail outlets, in which they are licensed to serve free samples of wine of their own production.

SAMPLER SELECTION

Saint Emilion (Assumption Abbey). A dry white wine from the Ugni Blanc grape, packaged in a Burgundy bottle! Clean, silky.

Zinfandel (Assumption Abbey). From well-established vines of the Sierra Madre slopes; aged and blended for present service.

Malmsey Madeira (Vin de Biane Fres.). A blending created by Philo Biane; mellow, rich and satin-smooth.

Sherry d'Oro (Assumption Abbey). From well-aged reserves, a medium-dry sherry; modest price and fine value.

CALIFORNIA GROWERS WINERY

38558 Road 128, Cutler, California 93615

California Growers was established as a cooperative by the Setrakian family in 1936. For many years, while it produced bulk wines for sale to other wineries, it specialized in sherries and brandy. Under its own label, Growers Old Reserve Sherry developed a considerable following among discriminating buyers. In the boom years of the early seventies, Robert Setrakian expanded both the winery and the vineyards, planting 800 acres of popular table-wine varieties, adaptable to the warmer growing region, including Chenin Blanc, Emerald Riesling, Ruby Cabernet, and Barbera. Storage capacity, mostly in stainless steel, now amounts to 12,134,000 gallons.

California sherry, port, and Madeira can hold their own with the table wines

Robert Setrakian has his own wineries in nearby Yettem for the production of premium dessert and table wines, sparkling wines, and brandies to be released under the Robert Setrakian Vineyards label.

SAMPLER SELECTION
Pale Dry Sherry. This Growers-label wine with its 99¢ price tag is better than wines at twice the price; comparable to some Spanish sherries.
Cabernet Sauvignon. Also modestly priced, and of more modest quality. Good everyday wine.

BELLA ROSA WINERY
(CALIFORNIA WINE ASSOCIATION)

Pond Road & Highway 99, Delano, California 93216

In 1969, enologist Antonio Perelli-Minetti, a 1902 graduate of the Conegliano Institute in Italy, purchased the California Wine Association and all its brands and labels: A. R. Morrow and Aristocrat (brandies); Ambassador, Eleven Cellars, Greystone, and Fruit Industries (table wines). There was an inventory of 5 million gallons of brandy alone, a statistic that gives an idea of the scope and scale of C.W.A.'s combined operation.

Antonio Perelli-Minetti died in 1976 at the age of ninety-four. Aside from the company bearing his name, he left a most extraordinary heritage, the discovery of a grape variety (which he named "101" and patented) from which wines will be made for generations to come.

The taste is wholly unique, quite spicy over and above the *goût de terroir* that may be drawn from the ground. It is Antonio's lasting contribution. His sons and family are continuing the large winegrowing enterprise, which, while utilizing local grapes for brandy, dessert wines, and some table wines, brings Cabernet and other cool-region varietals from the Napa Valley.

Antonio's son Fred Perelli-Minetti remains as general manager and winemaker of Bella Rosa Winery, and with its ample reserves of well-aged mellow brandies, Bella Rosa owns a rare resource soon to come on the market.

Future plans for Bella Rosa also include the marketing of some table wines with proprietary labels, possibly reflecting the new ownership's rose-growing interests—maybe even a Blanc de Noir wine with just a pale blush of color, though it's too soon to say "everything's coming up roses."

CALLAWAY VINEYARD & WINERY

32720 Rancho California Road, Temecula, California 92390

When Ely Callaway, the former president of Burlington Industries, decided to dedicate his autumn years to winemaking in a remote region of southern California, few among his associates, beyond his devoted young wife, shared his enthusiasm. Rancho California? Temecula?

In ten years the Callaway Vineyard & Winery of

Ely Callaway depends on his own weather station to record temperature, moisture, and sunlight

Temecula has become a principal case study for the enological school at UC–Davis and for connoisseurs across the country.

The microclimate of this high plateau, 23 miles inland from the Pacific Ocean, has the advantage of cooling sea breezes almost daily. In his 135-acre vineyard, Ely Callaway has his own weather station to record the all-important moisture affecting the surfaces of the vine leaves and the skins of the grapes. Temperature and sunlight records confirm Callaway's belief that the environmental factors here duplicate those of the more celebrated North Coast winelands. Even the White Riesling of the Rhine thrives here, and has successfully produced wine of extraordinary depth, brilliance, freshness, and complexity.

Callaway brought his administrative thoroughness and perfectionist drive from textiles to wine-growing. His viticulturist is John Moramarco, a tenth-generation vinegrower, who personally does the final pruning on every single vine at Callaway; he also supervises the cluster-thinning, limiting each crop to about two tons or less per acre where others might push the vines to ten tons per acre. His objective is richly concentrated berries, at the peak of their varietal character. Chenin Blanc, Sauvignon Blanc, White Riesling, Cabernet Sauvignon, Petite Sirah, and Zinfandel planted in 1969 brought in their first commercial crop in 1974, when the winery was completed.

The interior of the winery was laid out by Karl Werner, former winemaster of Schloss Vollrads of the Rheingau, and he designed much of the equipment, all, like the Spessart oak cooperage, imported from Germany. At harvest time, small gondolas, deliberately only half-filled, come leaf-free to the crusher within minutes after hand-harvesting in the adjacent vineyards. Fermentation begins with whole populations of yeasts, selected by Werner in Geisenheim and flown to California. A Westphalia centrifuge cleans the white-wine musts prior to fermentation.

Oak aging barrels are steam-leached to remove excess flavor-producing agents; emphasis in Callaway's almost exclusively white-wine production is on delicacy and clean crispness, qualities uppermost among the winemaker's goals.

In 1981, Ely Callaway sold the winery to Hiram Walker & Sons Ltd., of Canada, but remained as consultant and neighboring grape grower. On Sunday, July 24, 1983, a major celebration brought hundreds of wine writers and friends of the winery to mark the completion of the winery's latest and largest expansion program. This included additional capacity of 140,000 gallons in new stainless-steel tanks and 40,000 square feet of new aging and warehouse space. The original staff of twelve in 1974 was increased to eighty-five employees. From initial production of 16,000 cases, the phenomenal success had taken the winery to 110,000 annual case sales in 1983.

Everyone came to cheer, celebrate, and particularly to honor the winemaker, Stephen J. O'Donnell, who was in full charge during the period of growth from 1976 on. Four days later, O'Donnell died in his sleep, at the age of forty-two. His contributions remain very much a part of the continuing operation through his successor, his former assistant, Dwayne Helmuth.

Ever since the Callaway 1974 White Riesling was served to Queen Elizabeth at a Waldorf Astoria luncheon in 1976, Callaway white wines have had their special cachet. Dwayne Helmuth recognizes this uniqueness, resulting from Temecula's soil and microclimate, and he attempts to accent this distinction in each of the white wines, especially the Chardonnay. It is cold-fermented, allowed to rest on the lees for four weeks under constant vigil, then fined, cold-stabilized, and bottled. No oak.

Temecula can no longer be considered a dry, arid desert region. It is one of California's newly discovered areas for quality wine—much of which is proudly labeled Callaway.

SAMPLER SELECTION

Fumé Blanc (Temecula). Sauvignon Blanc-Dry. As the label declares, this is the dry one, with just a bare hint of wood, from 7-year-old German oak.

Sauvignon Blanc (Temecula). Some prefer this wine, which is equally delicate, touched with less than 1 percent (0.65) residual sweetness.

Chardonnay (Temecula). Charming wine in which a
fresh fruitiness is preserved, though the time on
the lees gives an added complexity.

Chenin Blanc (Temecula). Late-harvested editions of
this wine, often fully botrytised, are subtitled
"Sweet Nancy." Very sweet, exotic.

D'AGOSTINI WINERY

Shenandoah Road, Plymouth, California 95669

The label carries the winery's founding date of
1856, although Enrico D'Agostini acquired the
historic vineyard and winery in 1911. Following
Repeal, his four sons continued the tradition of
keeping the beautiful oval oak casks filled with the
good country wine from their Zinfandel, Mission, and
Carignane vines. The estate-bottled Zinfandel from
this pioneer winery of Amador County is well worth a
pilgrimage into the Sierra foothills.

SAMPLER SELECTION

Burgundy. The Reserve California Burgundy, modestly priced, is a blend of Zinfandel and Carignane.

Zinfandel. Estate-bottled hearty wine from well-
established vines.

DELICATO VINEYARDS

12001 S. Highway 99, Manteca, California 95336

The Delicato Vineyards were established in 1924
by Gaspare Indelicato and his brother-in-law
Sebastiano Luppino. With grape-growing experience
gained in their native Sicily, they supplied wine
grapes for the Eastern market. Today Indelicato's
three sons operate an 8-million-gallon winery, in
addition to selling bulk wine to other wineries. They
produce generic and varietal table wines under the
Delicato label, as well as sparkling wines, fruit and
berry wines, ports and sherries.

SAMPLER SELECTION

Chenin Blanc. Light, fresh, fragrant, with an edge of
sweetness.

Zinfandel. Produced and bottled from the company's
own 67-acre vineyard. Redwood-aged. Good
country wine.

EAST-SIDE WINERY

6100 East Highway 12, Lodi, California 95240

In 1934, a group of 130 local grape growers
founded this cooperative winery, named for its
location on the east side of town. The popular tasting
room, made from a 50,000-gallon redwood storage
tank, carries *Das Weinhaus* on the marquee, reflecting
the German origins of most of the founders. Herman
Ehlers was the winemaker for thirty-seven years, until
his retirement in 1970. In addition to encouraging
growers to plant the better varietals adapted to the
region, including Ruby Cabernet, Ehlers produced a
superb brandy that came forth anonymously from a
famous Russian River winery which boasted of its
merits as if it was their own. If you find Conti-Royale
Brandy, one of the co-op's premium labels, pay tribute
to its ten years of age and 80° proof softness with your
finest crystal snifter.

Among the treasures of the 4 1/2-million-gallon
winery, today run by Ernest Haas, is a mellow Angelica
Antigua Mission 1773 produced from Mission grapes,
aged in wood for eight to ten years. The Royal Host
label for generic wines is well known in the Eastern
market, but the premium wines are bottled under the
Conti-Royale label. The Dry Sherry won a Grand
Sweepstakes Award in 1972 at the Los Angeles
County Fair, a distinction that is not granted easily or
often.

SAMPLER SELECTION

Grey Riesling. A fresh and fruity edition of the
Chauché Gris French varietal, matching more
famed rival brands.

Petite Sirah. Under the Conti-Royale label, this sturdy
red wine with Rhône Valley characteristics is dry
and full-bodied.

Ruby Cabernet. The hybrid vine was especially
created for the growers in this area; they make
some of its best wine.

Angelica Antigua. This "Mission 1773" example of the mellow, sweet wine from Padre Serra's grape makes one a believer.

FICKLIN VINEYARDS

30246 Avenue 7 1/2, Madera, California 93637

The late Walter Ficklin, Sr., came to Fresno as a grape grower in 1911. With the encouragement of viticulturists of UC–Davis he planted some acres of Portuguese port-wine varieties—Tinta Cão, Tinta Madeira, Souzão, and Touriga—as an experimental lot among his table grapes. With his sons David and Walter, Jr., he planned to make the first California port wine exclusively from Portuguese varieties. The

David Ficklin, whose Tinta Port ranks with the finest

grapes were hand-harvested in separate clusters, only the finest going to the crusher for open fermentation on the skins. With hand plungers the pomace was punched down to extract color, old brandy was added at just the precise moment indicated by the sugar readings, and the wine was aged in oak barrels for several years. Like the British blenders in Oporto, young David soon acquired, with passing harvests, a large inventory of aging wines. Every lot had its own number. He knew every cask, oval, and barrel as a parent knows his children, and like children, some day they would mature and be married.

In the early fifties, Walter Ficklin came to Los Angeles with the first Ficklin Tinta Port, with its label printed by the prestigious Grabhorn Press. A wine merchant in those days, I accepted the privilege of introducing it with great pleasure. Today, Ficklin Port is well known and is appreciated for its excellence. David's son Peter, now in his early twenties, is the third generation of the family to continue along the winemaker's path.

SAMPLER SELECTION

Ficklin Tinta Port. Every bottle could be poured the day you buy it, but further age brings greater bouquet. In the glass the wine is rich, ruby red, slightly bronzed on the edges.

FRANZIA BROTHERS

Highway 120, Ripon, California 95366

After arriving from Italy, in the 1890s, Giuseppe Franzia began his life in the New World as a truck farmer near Stockton. In 1906 he acquired the present Franzia Ranch to grow grapes for the Eastern market. With his five sons, Joseph, John, Frank, Louis, and Salvatore, in 1932 he established the winery known as Franzia Vineyards and Champagne Cellars, which in the ensuing decades was to become one of the largest in the state. The goal was sound, standard wines at popular prices.

A contract to supply bulk-process Franzia Champagne to Western Airlines for their highly advertised "Champagne Flights" zoomed the volume and propelled the image of Franzia into prominence. In April 1972 the company went public with one of the first stock offerings to come from a California winery. An offer from the Coca-Cola Bottling Co. of New York caused some rumblings in the family before the sale took place: three young Franzias split off to form the J F J Bronco Winery; two sons of Giuseppe remained with the new corporate organization. Under the new ownership the 4,000 acres of the Franzia Ranch are being planted to premium varietals with an eye on steeper competition ahead.

SAMPLER SELECTION

Chablis Blanc. In magnums and gallons, this is the "house wine" of many restaurants. Fair-quality, standard wine.

Robust Burgundy. Aiming for its "Hearty" competitor's business. Standard red wine with a slightly sweet edge.

E. & J. GALLO WINERY

600 Yosemite Boulevard, Modesto, California 95353

The Gallo brothers, who were brought up in their father's vineyard west of Modesto, made their

Julio Gallo and chief enologist Charles Crawford in Gallo's laboratory

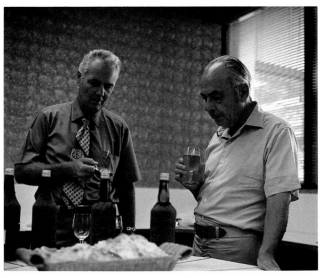

first wines in 1933 in a small rented warehouse. Their present accomplishments represent hard work and intelligence. Ernest and Julio are today the owners of a winery with a 226-million-gallon fermenting and storage capacity, and annual sales in excess of $200 million. The warehouse for wine storage is big enough to swallow a whole freight train, including the caboose. There are batteries of insulated storage tanks, some holding a million gallons. Gallo makes its own bottles in an inferno where caldrons of molten glass feed an assembly line 24 hours a day, 365 days a year.

The newest incredible happening at Gallo is a man-made "cave" 20 feet high, with a total area of 100,000 square feet, all under 5 feet of earth. It will contain 650 4,000-gallon oak tanks made in Yugoslavia. The "cellar" will have total cooperage for 2.6 million gallons of oak-aged premium varietals.

Howard Williams, semiretired vice-president of Gallo, told me, "Until the late 1950s, the wine business was mostly port, sherry, and muscatel, with table wines a scant 25 percent. Table wines were delicate, hard to handle. What was needed was a proven package. Ernest Gallo alone taught the trade how to sell wine, through his distributors in one city after another." Today Gallo sells more than a third of the wine consumed in America.

The varietal wine program, launched in 1974, was the result of almost thirty years of planning. It involved scientific agriculture in experimental vineyards started in the 1940s, a continuous process of testing, planting over 500 varieties of grapes, reclaiming hundreds of acres and transforming them from wasteland to productive vineyard and orchard. The varietal program was initially delayed because the finer varieties such as Barbera, Ruby Cabernet, and Zinfandel were being blended into existing generic wines. Hearty Burgundy got better and better; today it even has some—not much, but some—Cabernet Sauvignon from the Napa Valley in addition to Petite Sirah, Ruby Cabernet, Carignane, Zinfandel, and Barbera. But a full program of varietals—Cabernet Sauvignon, Pinot Noir, Chardonnay, and Johan-

Barengo

California
**Muscadelle
des Bordelais**
Reserve

PRODUCED & BOTTLED BY
BARENGO VINEYARDS
ACAMPO, CALIFORNIA ALCOHOL 12% BY VOLUME

Estate Bottled

D'Agostini
WINERY
EST. 1856

CALIFORNIA
ZINFANDEL
ALCOHOL 13% BY VOLUME

PRODUCED AND BOTTLED BY
D'AGOSTINI WINERY • PLYMOUTH, AMADOR CO., CALIF.

FRANZIA
SERVE CHILLED
CALIFORNIA

Chablis Blanc

*This distinguished white wine
is celebrated for its harmonious balance of
natural fruitiness, flowery fragrance, and a lingering
hint of sweetness. Made and
bottled by Franzia Brothers,
Winemakers, San Francisco, Calif.
BW 3654 Alcohol 12% by vol.*

GIBSON'S

PREMIUM SELECT

**CALIFORNIA
PINK CHABLIS**

A SEMI-SWEET PINK TABLE WINE

ALCOHOL 12% BY VOLUME

MADE AND BOTTLED BY GIBSON WINE COMPANY, ELK GROVE, CALIFORNIA

**BROOKSIDE
BURGUNDY**

HARBOR WINERY
1974
**Napa Valley
CHARDONNAY**

Produced and bottled by Harbor Winery
West Sacramento, California

Alcohol 13% by Volume

San Antonio

Famiglia Riboli   EST. 1917

California
French Colombard

MADE AND BOTTLED BY
SAN ANTONIO WINERY, LOS ANGELES, CALIF.
ALCOHOL 12% BY VOLUME

1975

Monteviña

Zinfandel
Amador County

Grown, Produced & Bottled by Monteviña Wines
Shenandoah Valley, Plymouth, California

ALCOHOL 15.5% BY VOLUME

ESTATE BOTTLED

CALLAWAY
Vineyard & Winery

*Estate Bottled
Vintage 1975*

TEMECULA, CALIFORNIA
White Riesling

Grown, Vinified and Bottled by Callaway Vineyard & Winery
Temecula, California   Alcohol 12% by Volume

CENTRAL VALLEY AND SOUTHERN CALIFORNIA WINE LABELS

George Thoukis, Gallo enologist, tours the winery with enophile Burgess Meredith

nisberg Riesling—to be aged in Yugoslavian oak before bottling is a possibility before 1980.

Julio Gallo gives his energies to the vineyards, with the same concern that Ernest devotes to merchandising. Dr. Charles Crawford, chief enologist, oversees Gallo's winemaking in all classifications. Each category of wines is under the direct supervision as well of Dr. George Thoukis, enologist with Gallo for seventeen years. Every afternoon, Julio Gallo tastes wines in the laboratory with Dr. Crawford, Dr. Thoukis, and others. Ernest joins them when time permits.

There are more than forty-eight different Gallo wines, and each of them, along with the ports, sherries, varietals, and generics, is tasted in those laboratory sessions when day is done. Often competitors' products in masked bottles are arranged in a blind tasting for comparison.

Boone's Farm Apple Wine and Strawberry Hill, also apple-based, are among the best-selling wines in the United States. The newest of the carefully engineered products is E. & J. Brandy; smooth, "charcoal-filtered," and easy to sip, it zoomed to the top of all American brandy sales, where it remains.

The translation of art into industry, without the loss of inspiration, is the genius of the whole Gallo organization. It is consistent with the brothers' drive for perfection, their desire to put something better and better into bottled wines, which has made the Gallo winery in Modesto the largest in the world and one of the greatest influences in the world of wine.

SAMPLER SELECTION

Chardonnay (California) Limited Release. Ernest & Julio Gallo proudly present this wine of beguiling drinkability, touched with French oak. Sonoma origins.

Cabernet Sauvignon (California) Limited Release. The first vintage wine from Ernest & Julio Gallo. Aged in French oak, this is the best buy on the market for Cabernet.

Sauvignon Blanc. The driest of the varietals in corked bottles. Clean, smooth, fragrant, and brilliantly finished.

Chablis Blanc. Popular house wine and bar wine, too good to omit from this listing. (Hearty Burgundy is a companion red wine.)

Livingston Cream Sherry. Can compare with the best of Bristol. Rich, mellow, one of America's greatest buys.

GIBSON WINE COMPANY

Grant Line Road at Highway 99, Elk Grove, California 95624

In 1943 wealthy stockbroker Robert Gibson acquired the Elk Grove Winery south of Sacramento, not far from his large cattle ranch in Roseville, where he also raised golden pheasants. The handsome game bird became the trademark for some of his wine labels. He chose to specialize in fruit and berry wines; apricot, raspberry, strawberry, each has its own true fragrance, and the colors are jewel-bright. A perfectionist, Gibson established new standards of excellence in the translation of pure berry nectars into wine.

Gibson died in 1960. The winery is owned today by the Sanger Wine Association of Tulare County, a group of 140 grape growers who also own cellars in Covington, Kentucky, where bulk shipments of their California wines are bottled for Eastern distribution.

The old winery, originally a gas-engine works, still produces the fine fruit and berry wines, plus a prize-winning honey mead. In 1970 an attractive tasting room was opened, in which the Sanger table wines are also presented.

SAMPLER SELECTION

Gibson's Old Fashioned Raspberry Wine. Would you believe fresh raspberries cost more than premium Chardonnay grapes?

Wassail Honey Wine. As classically beautiful as the legendary mead of Lancelot and Guinevere. Bright, golden, sweet.

GIUMARRA VINEYARD CORP.

P.O. Bin 1969, Bakersfield, California 93303

The founder of the winery, Giuseppe ("Joe") Giumarra, came to America from Sicily in 1906. At thirteen he began his new life in the New World with a pushcart, selling bananas in Toronto. Joe Giumarra in his seventies still moves merrily among the grape harvesters "manicuring" some of the most beautiful clusters of table grapes ever grown.

The Giumarra farms include 11,000 acres growing potatoes, apricots, plums, cotton, milo-maize (for chicken feed), table grapes, and wine grapes. The winery operation began in 1946, with younger brother John in charge, and expanded from dessert wines into a program of varietal table wines in 1974. In the first year the Zinfandel came home with a gold medal from the Los Angeles County Fair. Each successive Zinfandel vintage has been another prizewinner. On the wall of the tasting room are gold medals for the '73 Petite Sirah and '73 Cabernet Rouge. The Giumarra Barbera is Piedmontese in style, with a spicy, regional taste that supports the case for an appellation recognizing the individuality of this Central Valley wine region.

SAMPLER SELECTION

French Colombard. A very fruity vintage wine, flowery-fresh bouquet, interesting melon taste. Splendid white wine.

Chenin Blanc. Pleasing balance of fruit acidity with 2.2 percent residual sweetness for popular appeal.

Barbera. Full-bodied, with hints of *amarone* taste in the complex middle-body. Regional distinction.

Cabernet Rouge. Completely proving the merits of the hybrid Ruby Cabernet × Carignane. Soft, fragrant wine.

GUILD WINERIES AND DISTILLERIES

One Winemasters' Way, Lodi, California 95240

Guild is the nation's largest grower-owned cooperative producer of wine and brandy products. Its membership of nearly 1,000 grape growers owns seven wineries throughout the state, with central blending, bottling, and warehouse facilities in Lodi. In 1971, Guild acquired the Roma Winery in Fresno, with the famous Cresta Blanca label; it is operated today as a separate entity, its vineyards and winery in Mendocino, its marketing administration apart, in San Francisco.

Under Robert M. Ivie's leadership, Guild moved into a strong third-place position in the industry, after Gallo and United Vintners. As a result of Ivie's discriminating business sense, the marketing was simplified and the list of wines cut down to known and demonstrated winners like Vino da Tavola and Famiglia Cribari. Today's Board Chairman, Kenneth B. Seibert now continues the Ivie policies.

Guild's prestige label, aside from Cresta Blanca, is Winemasters' Guild. The wine took more than half a dozen years to perfect, but now has a winning hands-across-the-sea tie to winemaking guilds of Europe. French, German, and Italian cooperatives have associated themselves with the California growers. All the middlemen have been passed over so that good basic titles of well-known European wines can be brought into this market at competitive pricing. In June 1977 I visited the co-op that sends Bordeaux wines from St. Émilion. They are pleased with the arrangement, and the wines are excellent.

SAMPLER SELECTION

French Colombard. Winemasters' Guild makes a stylish wine of this new popular "mid-varietal"—sweet-edged, soft.

Cabernet Sauvignon. Winemasters' Guild deepens this popular variety with some Mendocino grapes from its membership.

Zinfandel. Under the same label, this is a winner in price and dependable quality.

Burgundy (Famiglia Cribari). Either dry or mellow, it is a competitor of the Hearty one.

HARBOR WINERY

610 Harbor Boulevard, West Sacramento, California 95831

Charles H. Myers, who teaches English at Sacramento City College, is a self-taught winemaker. His romance with the grape began more than twenty years ago, and he has been encouraged by such experts as Sacramento's leading wine merchant, Darrell Corti, André Tchelistcheff, and grape grower Bernard Rhodes. He was among the first to discover the rich depths of Zinfandel grapes from the Deaver Vineyard of Amador County. The modest winery in West Sacramento today produces Zinfandels and Chardonnays from selected vineyards. Darrell Corti snags the lion's share of the wines for his store in Sacramento.

A rare specialty is an Amador County wine made from hundred-year-old Mission grapevines in harvest seasons when the cooler climate brings the grapes to perfect, sugar-laden ripeness. Following an old Roman winemaking method, additional grape concentrate is added to the fermenting wine, with champagne yeasts that raise the alcohol naturally until fermentation stops. Myers calls the wine Mission de Sol—Blanc de Noirs.

SAMPLER SELECTION

Chardonnay (Napa Valley). Fermented in 500-gallon stainless-steel tanks, aged in French oak. Silky, dry, regal.

Zinfandel (Amador County). Neither filtered nor fined; a dry vintage wine from the Deaver Vineyard. Big, noble wine.

Mission de Sol (Blanc de Noirs). From Mission grapes, a luscious, sweet, vintage wine, naturally almost 16 percent alcohol.

228

MONTEVIÑA

Route 2, Box 30A, Plymouth, California 95669

Once more the accent is on Zinfandel here in the Shenandoah Valley of Amador County. The young enterprise, established in 1973 by retired banker W. H. Field, has Jeff Meyers as enologist and Jeff Runquist as winemaker. Monteviña has a whole group of Zinfandel wines, including Zinfandel Nuevo, exhibiting fragrance and complexity. But there's also Cabernet Sauvignon and Sauvignon Blanc and more in store from Monteviña's 165 acres of vines, which include Piedmont's Nebbiolo, certain to make a wine worth looking for.

SAMPLER SELECTION

White Zinfandel. You can have it Dry or Sweet and each is a conversation piece when poured.

Zinfandel Montino. A vintage wine, ruby-red, and deeply complex.

Monteviña Montenero. A Corti-inspired blending of Zinfandel and Barbera grapes. Big, fragrant, bold, complex.

Zinfandel Nuevo (Shenandoah Valley). Produced by the carbonic-maceration method, accenting berryness. Suggests Beaujolais.

Sauvignon Blanc (Amador County). A superb wine of extraordinary dry fruitiness; the complex flavors suggest pineapple.

PAPAGNI VINEYARDS

31754 Avenue 9, Madera, California 93637

Southeast of Madera, set among its own vines, is a bold new winery out to prove that really fine table wines can be produced here. In October 1976, Angelo Papagni and his wife journeyed to Milan to accept gold medals for three wines competing with their European counterparts at the Terzo Concorso Enologico Internazionale: their Madera Rosé, 1973 Madera Barbera, and Moscato d'Angelo. "For our family's first wines to win in Europe is the achievement of a lifetime," Angelo told me.

In 1912, Demetrio Papagni had arrived in the San Joaquin Valley from Puglia, the hot winemaking

Angelo Papagni in his modern new winery at Madera

region in the heel of the Italian boot. From the beginning, Papagni Vineyards shipped tons of wine grapes to the Eastern seaboard (including Canada), mostly for home winemakers. In 1973, Angelo Papagni, the American-born son, decided to make table wines with his own grapes, accepting the challenges of Region IV; he realized that the sandy loam soil, with some calcium but no lime, had potential. His studies in viticulture at Fresno State had readied him with understanding, plus some daring.

The jury is still out about his Chardonnay. There's no argument, however about the Italian delight Moscato d'Angelo, which undergoes the same slow, cool fermentation Louis M. Martini gives the celebrated Moscato Amabile. Another Papagni specialty is an oak-aged Alicante Bouschet, vintage and estate-bottled. That is daring: the most vulgar, misprized grape in the grape growers' ampelography treated with the concern given the noble Pinot and Cabernet! Papagni may not have received a gold medal for it yet—but here among wine buffs recognition has already arrived.

SAMPLER SELECTION

Moscato d'Angelo. As seductive as sweet, cold, fresh grapes juiced right into your mouth; 12 percent residual sugar.

229

Spumante d'Angelo. The same wine in a sparkling edition. Less exciting somehow, despite the honest bubbles.

Barbera (Madera). Vintage wine, aged in wood, with light body and style, complexity in nose and taste.

Alicante Bouschet (Madera). Vintage wine, oak-aged, with an aromatic spicy bouquet; haunting charms.

SAN ANTONIO WINERY

737 Lamar Street, Los Angeles, California 90031

Within sight of the Los Angeles City Hall, the San Antonio Winery is, according to its owners, "the last producing winery in the City of the Angels." It was saved to become Cultural Historical Monument Number 42, honoring Santo Cambianica, the founder, who began winemaking here in 1917 with grapes from nearby San Gabriel. The winery is named after the patron saint of Padua, in northern Italy, where Cambianica came from.

There are now eight "branch winery" retail stores in suburban southern California. San Antonio wines, made in downtown Los Angeles from grapes of several vinegrowing areas, are sampled and sold along with wine-related items—glasses, corkscrews, wine racks, bread, cheese, books.

SAMPLER SELECTION

French Colombard. A sweet-edged, fresh and fruity wine; popular price and popular appeal.

Velvet Chianti. In competition at the Los Angeles County Fair, this mellow blending has won top awards.

Almondoro. A Marsala-type wine, almond-flavored; excellent for zabaglione.

STELLAR WINERIES OF THE 1980s

"We could, in the United States, make as great
a variety of wines as are made in Europe, not
exactly of the same kinds, but doubtless as good."
—Thomas Jefferson

During the past decade, Jefferson's prophecy has had a gratifying measure of fulfillment, owing largely to the achievements of California winemakers. Seven out of every ten bottles of wine consumed in the United States are produced in California, and their varieties are legion, their quality excellent. The widely publicized wine boom of the seventies gave a renewed luster to the name California, not only multiplying the number of wine buyers but inspiring in them a lively desire to visit the source of their enjoyment. This has brought ever-increasing numbers of tourists to the California wine country. For many, it became an inspiration for a new life-style. Hundreds of new wineries were born. The count swelled to a record of more than 120 operating wineries in the Napa Valley, where a quarter century ago there were only about two dozen. The same "wine rush" has occurred in Sonoma and in Mendocino County—indeed wherever the vine might flourish.

The advances in viticulture and enology in the decades following World War II, which were responsible for the justifiable enthusiasm of the wine boom of the seventies, reached their full flowering in the eighties. Guesswork was no longer part of the adventure of winemaking. Pursuers of the aesthetic challenge of fine winemaking could know with certainty, given wisely chosen vines, which soils would best favor them.

In the heart of each of us there is a response to the land: the fields strewn with wildflowers, the carpets of yellow mustard between vine rows, the redwood groves, as serenely quiet as a cathedral, the coastal bays of Monterey and Carmel, and craggy Mendocino. But the adventure of winemaking goes beyond that expansive feeling for the land. It also involves the narrows of finance, architecture and design, construction, and planting, reaching its annual climax in the exciting days and nights of harvest. Allowance must be made for unlimited patience during hours of study to hone viticultural skills, and shrewd thinking about the final goals of marketing.

Each of the new wineries in the listings

that follow has weathered these trials, emerging with the acclaim of winelovers to join the ranks of California's growing family of premium wineries.

The life-style of California winemakers seems idyllic to the visitor. Hillside vineyards often look out over misty mountain peaks and valley vistas, utopian in their green stillness and quiet. The cycles of nature seem gentle and nurturing to a city-weary observer. But there is hard work in field and cellar: the infinite care needed during the growing stages of the vine and the even more demanding tasks involved in bringing new wine from infancy to a healthy maturity, ripe for bottling. Family fortunes ride, as packed with incident as any soap opera, on all this travail. If the pasture seems greener on the winery side of the fence, cautionary words paying due and proper respect to the hard labors of this seemingly serendipitous calling are in order.

The wineries listed on the following pages are bright new stars in the California wineland constellation. Vintage dates on the sampler selections are of interest but not matters of concern. While the quality of vintages certainly differ in California from year to year, none are failures, as happens often in European winelands. Nature is kinder here, though equally capricious.

ACACIA WINERY
2750 Los Amigos Road
Napa, California 94558

Two young men, Los Angeles tax attorney Jerry Goldstein and Mike Richmond, a freewheeling Texan from Port Arthur with teaching credentials and wine-marketing experience, met in 1979 and decided to join the wine fray. They chose the name Acacia not only because it sounded good but also because it would always be near the top of any alphabetical listing. Whimsy ended there. Brawn and brain, heart and soul, combined with intelligence in the selection of the cool Carneros site and the determination to produce Burgundian-style wines from only Chardonnay and Pinot Noir

grapes. Winemaker Larry Brooks, equally young, and eager to make his mark, came aboard to learn and work with consultant Bradford Webb. The rest is happy history —for winelovers and for Acacia's forty-two limited partners as well.

Grapes come from Acacia's own 50-acre vineyard in the Carneros region and from ten-year-old vines of several neighboring growers. Brooks makes five different vineyard-designation Pinot Noirs and almost as many Chardonnays, all excellent. Imported bottles and classic labels complete the Burgundian image.

SAMPLER SELECTION
Chardonnay (Napa Valley) Carneros District. A rich, buttery wine, judiciously aged in French oak. Skin contact and malolactic fermentation assure a long, elegantly soft wine.

Pinot Noir (Napa Valley) Carneros District. Clean, fruity, well-balanced. Stainless-steel fermenters receive whole berries, to enhance varietal character. Any questions about this grape's potential in California are answered positively by its sheer drinkability.

S. ANDERSON VINEYARD
1473 Yountville Crossroad
Napa, California 94558

Pasadena dentist Stanley Anderson, Jr., and his wife, Carol, brought their interest in wine and food to its logical conclusion with a second home, which includes a vineyard and winery just off the Silverado Trail in the Napa Valley. Here they produce an estate-bottled Chardonnay and a sparkling Blanc de Noirs by the classic *méthode champenoise*, with the wine resting on the yeast for at least two years.

The Anderson Chardonnay, from Olmo clone #72, produces a softer, more elegant wine, one that is complex and, in Dr. Anderson's words, "thick on the palate." The 50-acre property limits the production, which has, however, already earned medals and general acclaim.

Blanc de Noirs (Napa Valley). The nose has a yeasty nuance from the long stay *en tirage* (in the barrel). Maximum production of 3,000 cases per year.

Chardonnay (Napa Valley). Highly recommended as an aperitif because of its opulently flowery bouquet and buttery finesse.

AUSTIN CELLARS

1516 Copenhagen Drive
Solvang, California 93463

Tony Austin's first-release wine from his new winery, a 1981 Santa Barbara County Sauvignon Blanc, won a double gold medal at the prestigious San Francisco Fair and Exposition in September 1983. A month later, at the Third Annual Central Coast Wine Judging, his 1981 Sauvignon Blanc–Botrytis, Sierra Madre Vineyard, Santa Barbara County, won a sweepstakes award as Best White Wine.

It took some courage to start out on his own after being the initial winemaker at the Firestone Vineyard, where his work had won recognition for elegance in styling. But when opportunity knocked, he responded, departing amicably, with all good wishes from Brooks Firestone. Of his prize-winning Sauvignon Blanc–Botrytis wine, veteran California wine observer Dan Berger has said: "It is one of the two best wines of its type from California that I have ever tasted." Austin Cellars joins the ranks of California's exciting new wineries.

BALLARD CANYON WINERY

1825 Ballard Canyon Road
Solvang, California 93463

The lovely Santa Ynez Valley, near the picturesque village of Solvang in Santa Barbara County, has proved to be well suited to fine winegrowing. With the help of family and friends, dentist Gene Hallock and his wife, Rosalie, planted their varietal vineyard in 1974, with the first crush in 1977, and the winery completed in 1978. With a double gold medal attesting the excellence of even their first wines, Dr. Hallock has given up

his practice to devote full time to winemaking. Visitors (by appointment) are welcome.

SAMPLER SELECTION

Chardonnay (Estate Bottled). Fermented in stainless steel, with judicious aging in French oak, the wine is a silky, fragrant accompaniment to fine dining.

Fumé Blanc (Estate Bottled). A double gold medal for the 1981 vintage placed this Sauvignon Blanc wine on collectors' lists.

BALVERNE WINERY & VINEYARDS

P.O. Box 70
Windsor, California 95492

There are seven differently planted vineyards on this historic 710-acre wine estate, with planting dating back to the last century's Sotoyome land grant. President Bill Bird acquired ownership in 1973 and immediately set about eliminating old vines and orchards, planting vines appropriate to each separate microclimate, in elevations from 200 to 1,200 feet above sea level. Marine breezes blow here, and red-tailed hawks are gliding guardians against the depredations of starlings when grapes set on (the handsome bird is immortalized on the label). Mass plantings of rhododendrons and azaleas ornament the new winery buildings, where co-winemakers UC–Davis graduates John Kongsgaard and Doug Nalle handcraft morning-gathered fruit during harvest.

The estate-grown wines all have vineyard designations, with a regional appellation for the Chalk Hill locale. The first Balverne wines were released in 1981. Before the wine was in general release the proprietary Healdsburger was chosen by President Reagan to be served at the White House banquet for West German Chancellor Helmut Schmidt.

SAMPLER SELECTION

Healdsburger (Sonoma County). A proprietary blending of 70 percent Gewürztraminer, 22 percent Johannisberg Riesling, 8 percent Scheurebe (the German hybrid-cross of Riesling × Sylvaner,

grown in Balverne's Annaberg Vineyard). A gentle, soft, delightful wine with 1.8 percent residual sugar.

Sauvignon Blanc (Sonoma County) Stonecrest Vineyard. Hand-harvested Sauvignon Blanc (88 percent) and Semillon (12 percent) grapes, in Graves style, with seven months' aging in French oak, make a distinctive, stylish dry wine, melon-like in flavor and aroma.

BOEGER WINERY

1709 Carson Road
Placerville, California 95667

In the 1860s there were more vineyards in the cool Sierra Nevada hills and valleys of El Dorado County than in either Napa or Sonoma. Prohibition and phylloxera brought about the demise of most of the wineries and vineyards. The Boeger Winery took the first step in the modern reinstatement of the historic region's reputation for truly fine wines.

Quality wines are no accident here; Greg Boeger is a graduate of UC–Davis and a direct descendant of the Swiss Nichelini family of the well-known Napa Valley winery of that name.

The vineyards are planted largely at the 2,000–3,000-foot level, cooled by air masses moving up and down the Sierra Nevadas. Premium grapes such as Chardonnay, Merlot, and Cabernet Sauvignon produce wines of intense fruit, big, deep flavor. Zinfandels are superb.

SAMPLER SELECTION

Hangtown Red (California). Greg and Susan Boeger smile when they recommend this exceptionally fragrant table wine, a blend of leftover lots of almost every grape they grow—primarily Zinfandel, plus Petite Sirah, Cabernet, Barbera, and some Gold Medal Ruby Cabernet. The price is always modest. Don't miss it.

Merlot (El Dorado County). This vintage, estate-bottled, oak-aged wine is garnet red, with spicy, berry-like aroma. Thoroughly Californian in its appetizing distinction.

John Buehler, co-owner with his father of a young Napa Valley vineyard

BOUCHAINE VINEYARDS

1075 Buchli Station Road
Napa, California 94558

Established in 1981, this small winery, with 35 acres of choice varietal vines, was off to a brilliant beginning with owner/partner Jerry Luper, known for his splendid, subtle, and stylish wines, as winemaker. Luper's Chateau Bouchaine label is bound to become of signal importance.

SAMPLER SELECTION

Pinot Noir (Napa Valley–Corneros) Winery Lake Vineyard. The first-release wine of the 1981 vintage was a herald of exquisite Burgundian depths of fine complexity. The 1982 edition was served by President Reagan at the formal banquet he hosted in China in April 1984.

BRANDER VINEYARD & WINERY

P.O. Box 92
Los Olivos, California 93441

Young C. Frederic Brander is a thoroughgoing Californian from Santa Barbara, but his education included travel and study in European winelands, and he also spent time as a winemaker for small wineries in the Los Olivos region. His goal with his own winery has been to produce only two wines, a red and a white, in the manner of a Bordeaux château. To augment this modest output, Brander has announced a second

(but not necessarily secondary) St. Carl label for "blush" white wines from estate-grown red grapes: Cabernet Franc, Cabernet Sauvignon, and Merlot, all exuberant, refreshing picnic wines. Until the Cabernet Sauvignon wines in the 40-acre vineyard mature, the principal wine remains Brander Sauvignon Blanc.

SAMPLER SELECTION

Sauvignon Blanc (Santa Ynez Valley). Beginning with the first release in 1979, this wine, from low-yield vines producing less than two tons of grapes per acre, has continued to show remarkable quality. The process includes skin contact after crushing and barrel fermentation in all-new 60-gallon French Nevers oak barrels, plus judicious further aging in the same barrels before bottling.

BUEHLER VINEYARDS

820 Greenfield Road
St. Helena, California 94574

Nestled in the mountains forming the eastern rim of the Napa Valley above St. Helena, the small cluster of winery buildings and the residence overlook the rolling, vine-ribbed hills and Lake Hennessey—truly a Bacchic landscape. The 165-acre estate, with 60 acres planted to vines in 1972, is a wholly family-owned winery, with three generations now in residence. John P. Buehler, Sr., West Pointer, engineer, retired Bechtel Corporation executive, assigned John Jr. the task of developing the vineyard and winery. Before the winery was established, in 1978, grapes were sold to Burgess, Cuvaison, Chateau St. Jean, and Grgich Hills wineries.

The limited 10,000–15,000-case winery goals are being achieved with distinction. The full-time winemaker is vivacious young Heidi Peterson. Daughter of enologist Richard Peterson, who succeeded André Tchelistcheff at Beaulieu Vineyards, Heidi has grown up in the aura of wines and vines. She studied for five years at UC–Davis; her postgraduate years, from 1975 to 1980, were devoted to learning winemaking

through crush and fermentation procedures in Germany and other European winelands.

SAMPLER SELECTION

Pinot Blanc (Napa Valley) Estate Bottled. With cool fermentation in stainless steel, plus the addition of some barrel-fermented wine, the wine arrives for bottling with crisp, clean fruitiness and the subtle intrigue of oak.

Cabernet Sauvignon (Napa Valley) Estate Bottled. A 100 percent Cabernet wine, well-aged in Nevers oak and softened with malolactic fermentation; its intense bouquet reflects its hillside home. Unique, suitable for long aging.

White Zinfandel (Napa Valley) Estate Bottled. With a slight blush of color and crisp acidity balancing 1.5 percent residual sugar, an ideal Sunday luncheon wine.

CAKEBREAD CELLARS

8300 St. Helena Highway
Rutherford, California 94573

Before becoming a winemaker, Jack Cakebread wore several hats, but when, in 1973, his offer on a vineyard in the heart of the Napa Valley was accepted, he doffed all but one. He and his wife, Dolores, immediately went into the field, replanting the old vineyard to new premium varietals. Son Bruce enrolled at UC–Davis, earning his degree in viticulture and enology. Bruce's wife, Rosemary, also holds a degree in enology from UC–Davis. All the Cakebreads have a total dedication to winemaking, enhanced by their appreciation of the new lifestyle for the whole family. Their four wines —Cabernet Sauvignon, Chardonnay, Sauvignon Blanc, and Zinfandel—have gained quick fame by their distinctive styling. The planting of an additional 12-acre block of Cabernet vines assures the 28,000-case winery of a further and dependable estate-grown wine supply. Steady demand for their product dictates the purchase of select grapes from nearby Napa Valley growers.

The Cakebread Cellars winery nestles conveniently among the vines in the center of Napa Valley

All four members of the family are involved in the quality control. Every lot of wine is examined before final blending of separately fermented and aged wines, each with its own yeast culture from the winery's own laboratories.

Jack Cakebread declares that a great wine requires three people to produce it: (1) the grape grower, (2) the winemaker, and (3) the consumer. Why the consumer? Wines are almost always released before peak maturity; the consumer's role is to hold the wine with proper cellarage until it reaches that peak.

SAMPLER SELECTION

Sauvignon Blanc (Napa Valley). Partial barrel fermentation enriches the appetizing, green-olive aperitif appeal.

Cabernet Sauvignon (Napa Valley). Aged in French oak, and classically fined with egg white, this outstanding deep-ruby claret has jewel-like brilliance and full, berry-like breed and bouquet. A fat, supple wine, capable of aging to elegant maturity.

CALERA WINE COMPANY
11300 Cienega Road
Hollister, California 95023

It has taken more than ten years for wine scholar Josh Jensen to achieve his dream of California production of Burgundian wines, especially Pinot Noir. Following his graduation from Yale, Jensen's vacations from postgraduate work at Oxford found him, in 1970 and 1971, harvesting Pinot Noir in Burgundy. Assiduous soil-selection

studies led him to an abandoned limestone quarry in the benchlands of the Gavilan Mountains near Hollister, and he named the winery he established in 1976 Calera (Spanish for "limestone quarry"). While awaiting the maturity of his own vineyards, Jensen made memorable Zinfandels from several regional vineyards, but at last three Estate Pinot Noirs with vineyard designations—Jensen, Selleck, and Reed—are on the horizon, fulfilling the Burgundian dream.

SAMPLER SELECTION

Pinot Noir (California) Jensen Vineyard. A proud Pinot Noir in classic stance. Smoky, toasty undertones of maple-cured bacon. A superb attainment of a goal.

Pinot Noir (California) Selleck Vineyard. Translucent ruby, as becomes an aristocratic Pinot Noir, with a trace of brick red. Restrained bouquet, reminiscent of truffles, earth, and rose hips. Classic balance of the grape and French oak.

Zinfandel (California) Cienega District. Every "Zin" is a masterpiece of taste and style. The Calera Zinfandels are almost always exotic, with aromas of blackberries, toast, vanillin, and, as Jensen says, "even coconut."

CALIFORNIA WINE COMPANY

155 Cherry Creek Road
Cloverdale, California 95425

This entry might well begin, "In numbers there is strength." Emil Bandiera came to California in 1910 from Tuscany. For several years he worked in the lumber industry in and around the North Coast town of Cloverdale, where he bought some land and planted a vineyard. In 1937 he built a winery on his property and sold barrels and jugs of good, hearty wine to his neighbors. Subsequent generations continued the winery operation. Chris Bilbro, the founder's grandson, together with several local grape growers, founded a co-op called the California Wine Company, dedicated to handling all their own grapes. They used the Bandiera Winery as the focal center, to avoid incurring start-up expenses for individual new wineries.

John Merritt arrived on the scene in April 1982, followed by the distinguished French-born vineyard manager Jean-Marie Martin, and the pattern began to take shape. The now well-known Bandiera Winery flower labels of premium varietals —Chardonnay, Cabernet Sauvignon, Sauvignon Blanc, Zinfandel—were well launched when the Zinfandel won a gold medal at the Sonoma County Harvest Fair.

The California Wine Company owns 200 acres in the Napa Valley, 130 acres in Mendocino County, and 32 acres in Sonoma's new appellation of Dry Creek. With the additional labels Sage Creek and John B. Merritt, their wines join the distinguished portfolio of the American Classics Wine Company, established in 1983 as a new, exclusive national and international marketing division of Seagram.

CASSAYRE-FORNI CELLARS

1271 Manley Lane
Rutherford, California 94573

Visitors to this Napa Valley winery usually see three generations at work, side by side, on the bottling line. The winery, established in 1976, was the realization of an ambition shared by Jim and Paul Cassayre, along with winemaker Mike Forni—all third-generation Napa Valley inhabitants. Members of their families who were originally engineers designed many of the premium wineries here. Encouraged by the quality of their homemade wines, the trio embarked upon their own winery, building it at Mike's homesite. The rest is a history of award-winning wines.

SAMPLER SELECTION

Chardonnay (Napa Valley). The grapes were selected from Napa River and Silverado Trail vineyards, from vines of mature bearing age. Skin contact after crushing, cool stainless-steel fermentation with champagne yeasts, and malolactic fermentation during storage in French oak assure a noble, rich, long, buttery wine of classic style.

Cabernet Sauvignon (Napa Valley). Rich in varietal aromas and generous herb and cedar tones. Capable of long life.

Chenin Blanc (Napa Valley). Simultaneously dry and slightly honied, the always fruity versions of this grape produce a wine that is clean, sprightly, charming.

CHAMISAL VINEYARD

7525 Orcutt Road
San Luis Obispo, California 93401

Norman Goss's career in music and as owner of the several Stuft Shirt restaurants made him a beloved Southern Californian before he moved to San Luis Obispo and dedicated his talents to winegrowing.

There are 53 acres of Chardonnay growing here from a fine old Montrachet clone from the Côte d'Or. Tom Goss, Norman's son, with a degree in viticulture from California Polytechnic State University, San Luis Obispo, tends the Cabernet Sauvignon with a gardener's precision. The family named the vineyard Chamisal, after a native shrub that thrives on the property. All the wines from this haven, currently distributed in twenty-two states, are well worth seeking.

SAMPLER SELECTION

Chardonnay (Edna Valley) Estate Bottled. Ripe grapes travel only yards to reach the fermenters, with skin contact assuring fullness of flavors; clear juice is fermented in stainless steel, then stored in French oak in classic styling. A rich, knockout wine.

CLOS DU BOIS

5 Fitch Street
Healdsburg, California 95448

"At Clos du Bois, we think of ourselves as *winegrowers*," says owner Frank M. Woods. It is a word correctly applied: 100 percent of the Clos du Bois wines come from their own 1,300 acres of vineyards in the Alexander Valley and Dry Creek appellations of Sonoma County. Grapes not needed for their annual production of 20,000–40,000 cases are sold to other wineries.

The first vineyards were set out in 1964, and the first vintage wines were sold from mature vines in 1974. Subsequently, with dozens of awards for their wines, and with the 1981 Early Harvest Gewürztraminer served at the Southern California banquet for Queen Elizabeth in 1983, Clos du Bois wines have become well established, with distribution in forty-seven states.

SAMPLER SELECTION

Chardonnay (Sonoma County) Calcaire. An estate-grown, 100 percent Chardonnay wine, from low-yield vines; given sufficient aging in Limousin oak barrels, it has pleasing elegance and long, long finish.

Gewürztraminer (Sonoma County) Early Harvest. Always a medal winner for its full, rich, spicy, grapefruit/lychee-nut aromas. Textbook perfection of this fruity varietal.

Marlstone (Alexander Valley). A vintage blending of 54 percent Cabernet Sauvignon and 46 percent Merlot gives an intriguing, complex wine of peppery, herbaceous nose and long, well-rounded Cabernet finish. Labels should but do not emphasize the Cabernet character—an example of how legal restrictions on varietal percentages can be crippling to the creative winemaker.

CRESTON MANOR VINEYARDS & WINERY

17 Mile Post Highway 58
Creston, California 93432

The Central Coast region in the vicinity of San Luis Obispo is the newest of California's flourishing vinifera plantings. A limestone soil provides a proper environment for the vine, with southwest exposure for ripening and long summers and cold winters to ensure the successful pioneering of the grape.

Christina Crawford and her husband, David Koontz, with old friends Stephanie and Lawrence Rosenbloom, chose this Indian Creek site for a vineyard and winery, planting Sauvignon Blanc, Chardonnay, Cabernet Sauvignon, and Zinfandel. The first release, a Sauvignon Blanc, blended with Semillon in French Graves style, from grapes purchased in the region, showed evidence of sophisticated skills in winemaking. A second wine, barrel-fermented Chardonnay from their own grapes, gave evidence of the rich potentials in this new area for vinifera cultivation and fine winemaking. Dimitri Tchelistcheff is consultant, and the first extensions of the small winery are already under way to accommodate wines from this 159-acre wine estate.

SAMPLER SELECTION

Sauvignon Blanc (San Luis Obispo). Clean, crisp, long on the palate, unfolding in gentle complexity, the wine indisputably resembles its Graves inspiration.

Chardonnay (San Luis Obispo) Estate Bottled. Tasted prior to release, the wine

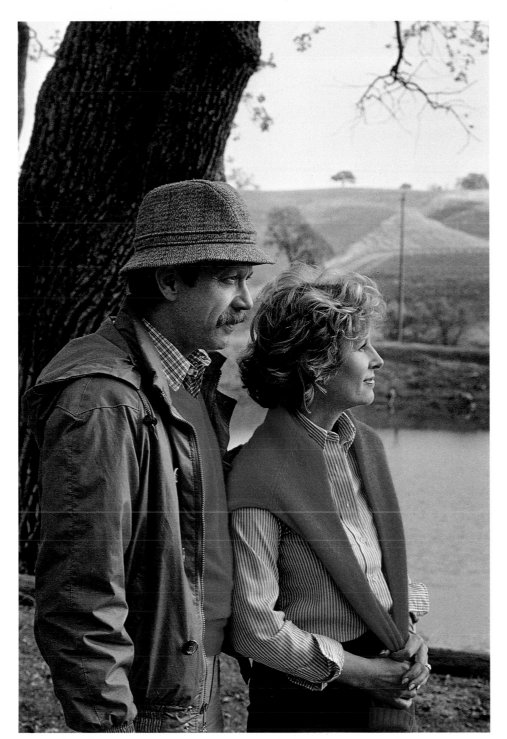

Creston Manor's owners, David and Christina Crawford Koontz, near one of the vineyard's three lakes

shows the richness of the grapes, proving the soil's contribution, plus classic elegance in style from judicious aging in Limousin oak.

JOHN CULBERTSON WINERY
2608 Via Rancheros
Fallbrook, California 92038

Owners John and Martha Culbertson took up the challenge of producing *méthode champenoise* sparkling wines and came home from California's leading competitions with gold and double gold medals. Alas, the *en tirage* Chardonnay and Pinot Noir *cuvée* of their second wine met with disaster when the cooling system for temporary storage, obeying Murphy's Law, failed without warning on a weekend. But the third harvest was on the way, and lovers of sparkling wine may be sure the Culbertson sparklers will continue to be signal contributions.

DOMAINE LAURIER
8075 Martinelli Road
Forestville, California 95436

Agronomist Jacob Shilo and his artist wife, Barbara, made an easy segue into the wine business in 1977 when they found a lovely hillside where the vines were grown long ago—a cool microclimate hidden in the hills of the Russian River Valley, the ocean but ten miles away. With young Stephen Test, a Stanford University graduate (in biology) who holds postgraduate degrees in enology from UC–Davis, and Mary Ann Graf, former winemaker at Simi, as consultant, a handcrafting winery was under way. Small wooden open fermenters are used for estate-grown Pinot Noir, with hand punching of the caps rather than the forceful "pumping over" techniques in general use. Extensive aging in French-oak barrels completes the cycle of old-style Burgundian winemaking.

SAMPLER SELECTION
Chardonnay (Sonoma County). This cool-region wine has inviting citrus and melon hints; a splendid companion for fish and shellfish.

Pinot Noir (Sonoma County). A sometimes testy varietal is made into a showpiece for this small winery; a rich, almost chocolaty wine results from the dedicated handcrafting.

DUCKHORN VINEYARDS
3027 Silverado Trail
St. Helena, California 94574

With the release of its first wine in 1980 under the Duckhorn Vineyards label, the St. Helena Wine Company of Dan and Margaret Duckhorn was off to a distinguished beginning. Everyone applauded their Napa Valley Merlot, made from well-selected mature vines, blended with a significant percentage of equally fine Cabernet Sauvignon. Winemaker Tom Rinaldi has continued this pattern with signal success. The small acreage at the winery is now planted, but the Duckhorns will continue to buy grapes from neighboring growers, with continued focus on Merlot, blending it with Cabernet Sauvignon and Cabernet Franc.

DURNEY VINEYARD
P.O. Box 222016–Carmel Valley
Carmel, California 93922

International acclaim came to Durney Vineyard's 1979 Carmel Valley Cabernet Sauvignon when, in the Second Annual Kapalua Bay Club Wine seminar on the island of Maui, it was judged the finest Cabernet by a stellar jury of twenty-one tasters that included André Tchelistcheff, Robert Mondavi, Mike Grgich, Rodney Strong, Bill Jekel, Jack Cakebread, Len Evans of Australia, and Hubert Trimback from Alsace—all under the supervision of Hawaii's well-known winemaster Eric Hansen.

This victory is particularly significant because it focuses attention not only on the Durney Vineyard but also on one of California's newest viticultural regions, the Carmel Valley. "Prospecting," as Robert Louis Stevenson called our state's trial plantings in new areas for the vine, has made this remote "viticultural outpost" a magnet for other growers. It is a cool microclimate, protected by the coastal mountains of Big Sur, at an elevation of 1,200 feet. William and Dorothy Kingsley Durney acquired this former cattle ranch about thirty years ago and began planting some of its 1,200 acres to the vine in 1968. Son-in-law David Armanasco is the general manager of the winery. Rich soil, fed by underground springs, now supports 140 acres of fine varietals, currently producing 12,000 cases of wine each year.

SAMPLER SELECTION
Cabernet Sauvignon (Carmel Valley) Estate Bottled. World-class claret of noble breed and splendid finesse.
Chenin Blanc (Carmel Valley) Estate Bottled. The cool microclimate and well-drained soil bring in a fruity, rather than grassy, wine. Crisp, clean, refreshing, suggesting Vouvray.

EDNA VALLEY VINEYARD
Biddle Ranch Road
San Luis Obispo, California 93401

The wines and labels of this small, newly emerging winery of the Central Coast region show the unmistakable hallmark of one of California's most talented winegrowers, Dick Graff of Chalone Vineyards in Monterey County. The production is limited, deluxe, with top-quality wines—labels to watch for, especially the Burgundian varieties.

SAMPLER SELECTION
Pinot Noir (San Luis Obispo) Estate Bottled. Ample evidence that Pinot Noir, in the hands of a competent grape grower and winemaker, can produce a translucent wine of great merit and complexity. Well-aged in new and old Limousin oak, softened with early malolactic fermentation, the wine has subtle nuances suggesting black cherries and toasted walnuts. Added bottle age increases the majesty of such wines.

ESTRELLA RIVER WINERY
P.O. Box 96, Highway 46
Paso Robles, California 93446

The double-towered Estrella Winery sits proudly amid the 700 acres of premium va-

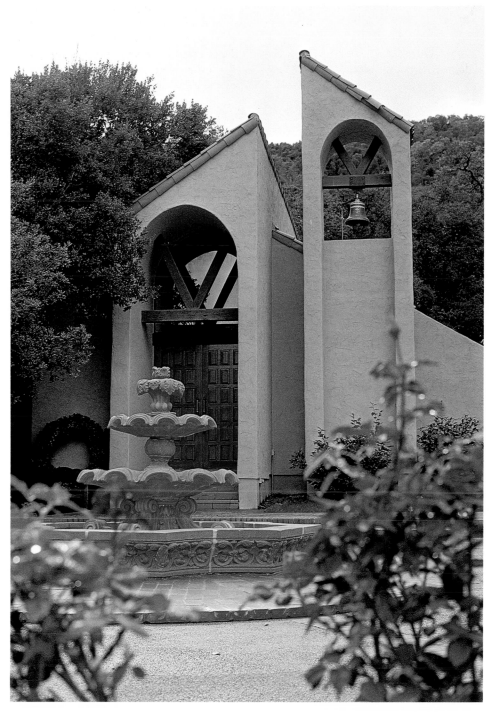

An old Portuguese bell in the wedding chapel belfry rings out good news at Durney Vineyard

rietals planted on this rapidly growing 1,000-acre estate. Directed by the inaugural team of Cliff Giacobine as owner/president, Gary Eberle (his half-brother) as enologist, and Tom Myers as winemaker, a program of dedicated production and rapid expansion brought Estrella more than fifty-five medals in five years. The ultra-modern facility, designed to minimize the handling of wines, has all-stainless-steel-jacketed fermenters, a centrifuge for the must, ensuring fresh, clean tastes, and a bottling room with a flow of sterile air. These are but highlights of the equipment, which reflects Eberle's medical-school education (in cellular genetics) preceding his enological training at UC –Davis. (He has turned over all winemaking responsibilities at Estrella to Myers in order to devote himself to a program of a few wines in his own new Eberle Winery.)

Annual production of 100,000 cases of nationally distributed wines includes a full roster of Chardonnay, Sauvignon Blanc, Chenin Blanc, Johannisberg Riesling, Muscat Canelli, Zinfandel, Cabernet Sauvignon, Barbera, and Syrah.

SAMPLER SELECTION

Cabernet Sauvignon (San Luis Obispo) Estate Bottled. The 1979 edition took the Sweepstakes Award as Best Red Wine in a Central Coast Wine Judging. Rich, chocolaty wine, mingling true varietal character with hints of oak.

Muscat Canelli (San Luis Obispo) Late Harvest. Always a medal winner. Estate-grown wine, low in alcohol, high (17.8 percent) in residual sugar, with a balancing total acidity. A show-stopping, exotic wine for superbly punctuating a dinner.

FAR NIENTE WINERY
P.O. Box 327
Oakville, California 94562

The name given to this historic Napa Valley winery in 1882 is from the Italian phrase *dolce far niente,* ("sweet doing nothing"). Abandoned with the advent of Prohibition, the old winery required three full years of almost total restoration by new owner/proprietor/winemaker Gil Nickel before

Far Niente's nineteenth-century winery, now fully restored

the state-of-the-art, high-technology winery could become fully operative. New caves, carved into the hillside, with wrought-iron gates bearing the winery's crest, silently proclaim this one of America's finest wine estates.

Grape growing and winemaking follow equally luxurious high standards of excellence. Chardonnay and Cabernet Sauvignon come from Far Niente's own vineyard and from the neighboring famed Stelling Vineyard of the late Martin Stelling, whose son Doug is a partner in the enterprise.

Oklahoma-born Nickel was a guided-missile physicist until he chose to become a California winemaker at Far Niente. An ardent winelover, he had started winemaking in his Nob Hill home in San Francisco. This led to enrollment at UC–Davis for professional training in viticulture and enology. "I may have learned more about winemaking in my cellar than attending the University," Nickel observes. The first wine he made in his cellar, a Napa Valley Chardonnay, was entered in the Napa County Fair and won third place.

Nectar of the Chardonnay vines goes by gravity flow from the second-floor grape-reception area into stainless steel for fermentation. It is racked into French oak barrels for the balance of fermentation required to achieve a completely dry wine. There, constantly observed, it remains on the lees for two months, a procedure that captures its subtle and elegant bouquet. Six months of further barrel aging leads to bottling.

UC–Davis graduate Dirk Hampson of Portland, Oregon, became winemaker in 1983, bringing to his California winemaking role experience gained in winery operations at Schloss Vollrads of the Rheingau and Château Mouton-Rothschild of Bordeaux. The first Far Niente Napa Valley Cabernet Sauvignon made by Hampson is scheduled for release in 1985, the winery's "centennial" year.

Far Niente postscript: In January 1984, Gil Nickel and partners purchased Chateau Chevalier, assuming the American Classics Wine Company distribution contract. John Nickel, Gil's brother, took over management duties on March 1.

SAMPLER SELECTION
Chardonnay (Napa Valley) Estate Grown.
   A superb wine, one of California's finest.

FISHER VINEYARDS
6200 St. Helena Road
Santa Rosa, California 95404

   Juelle and Fred Fisher, proprietors and winemakers, as they title themselves, began their Mayacamas Mountain vineyard in 1973, planting only Chardonnay and Cabernet Sauvignon vines on the well-drained, forest-cleared hillsides. These 70 acres basically provide all the grapes for their operation, deliberately kept small so that the cellar master, Fred, can single-handedly provide the care that the wines require. The winery, constructed in 1979 of the Fishers' own Douglas fir and redwood trees, cut and milled on the hillside, was selected by the American Institute of Architects as the best design by California architects since 1975.

   The mountain elevation, with its shallow, rocky soil, proves the adage that "Bacchus loves the hillsides." The Fisher wines have an intensity, against a light background of oak, that sets them uniquely apart among wines outstanding for breed and finesse. With the 1981 Chardonnay the Fishers drew in some aromatic grapes from a valley vineyard and instituted partial fermentation in small French oak barrels, prior to blending and bottling, to make "another fine dinner wine from Fisher Vineyards."

SAMPLER SELECTION
Chardonnay (Sonoma County). Each vintage is a big, complex wine of 100 percent varietal composition with added richness from new French oak.

GRGICH HILLS CELLAR
1829 St. Helena Highway
Rutherford, California 94573

   To many, the Croatian-born winemaster Miljenko Grgich, more familiarly called Mike, is Mister Chardonnay. The route to this complimentary sobriquet has been long and arduous.

   Mike studied enology and viticulture at the University of Zagreb before emigrating

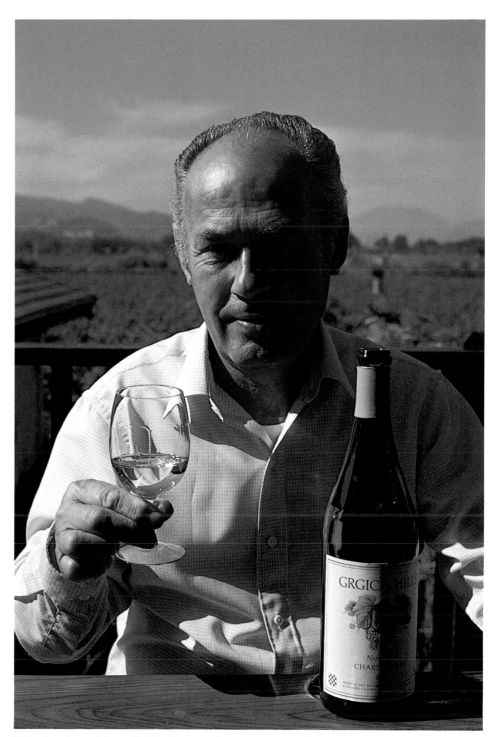

"Mr. Chardonnay" himself, Mike Grgich, about to taste one of his prized wines

to the United States in 1958. His first job in winemaking in America was with Lee Stewart at the young Souverain winery. Next, he spent nine years under André Tchelistcheff at Beaulieu, learning the scientific and academic side of winemaking. Then followed four years of experimental work with Robert Mondavi. In 1972 he became the winemaker at Chateau Montelena. The Chardonnay he made there in 1973 triumphed over five other California Chardonnays and four of France's most famous white Burgundies in the celebrated Steven Spurrier tasting in Paris, with an all-French jury of experienced professionals (May 24, 1976). That news rocked both sides of the Atlantic when it became a lead story in *Time* magazine.

In 1977, with coffee heir Austin Hills, Mike Grgich embarked upon his own winery in the Napa Valley, and his success has been singular and international. In November 1980, in the "Great Chicago Chardonnay Showdown" staged by wine columnist Craig Goldwyn, with 221 wines made from Chardonnay grapes grown all over the world, the Grgich Hills 1977 Sonoma Chardonnay, a then pricey $18.00 wine, was the clear victor, announced as "the best Chardonnay in the world." Perhaps even more gratifying was the selection of his 1980 Napa Valley Chardonnay as the number one choice in the *Los Angeles Times Home Magazine* of October 1983 by juror André Tchelistcheff. Grgich Hills 1978 Chardonnay was served to Queen Elizabeth at Stanford University during her California visit in 1983. President Reagan took the 1979 edition to Paris for the formal banquet in 1982 at the American Embassy honoring President and Mme Mitterand. Need one say more?

Grgich Hills buys only 20 percent of their grapes, growing the rest on their own 160 acres for the 20,000-case annual production.

SAMPLER SELECTION

Chardonnay (Napa Valley). The wine is still pricey, but crowds line up in the Grgich Hills tasting room not only to buy current vintages but also to ask for some of the older, celebrated wines.

Zinfandel (Napa Valley). This once very popular variety, currently in sales decline, if made in Grgich style would zoom again because of its rich, zesty berryness.

GUENOC WINERY
21000 Butts Canyon Road
Middletown, California 95461

In 1888, Lily Langtry, the toast of Edwardian London, hired a Bordeaux winemaker to oversee the vineyards in the Lake County property she had acquired in California. Standing on the second-story balcony of the restored home of "the Jersey Lily," one looks across vine rows to golden hills dotted with live oak trees and to the misty blue hills in the far distance.

The wines made from the choice varietals planted by present owners Orville and Eaton Magoon in the early 1970s are nothing short of wonderful—and no wonder! They are made by Walter Raymond, with viticulturist Roy Raymond, Jr., bringing Napa Valley skills to bear. "Guenoc Valley" is the first single vineyard/single proprietor appellation granted in America. It has its own alluvial soil and special microclimate in its two-mile length at an elevation of almost 1,000 feet. The ultra-modern winery, the last word in technology, is designed for an ultimate production of 100,000 cases annually.

SAMPLER SELECTION

Chardonnay (Guenoc Valley). A golden wine of insistent varietal fragrance, with tantalizing oak finish; certain to delight Chardonnay lovers.

Cabernet Sauvignon (Guenoc Valley). Lake County Cabernet vines, after long, slow ripening, present the perfume of this berry with exquisite directness. A classically made claret, in the Bordeaux tradition of oak finish.

WILLIAM HILL WINERY
P.O. Box 3989
Napa, California 94558

William Hill, an artist/winemaker, is also a thorough pragmatist. The Oklahoman holds an MBA from Stanford University, as well as sound beliefs about what makes great wines great.

In the 1970s, with several groups of partners, Hill set out to prove the soundness of his beliefs, acquiring mountain vineyard lands on both the western and the eastern rim of the Napa Valley. He pioneered vines on the Diamond Mountain Ranch, later sold to Sterling Vineyards (which considers it to be one of its prime resources). But it is the land on the eastern side, at the 1,800-foot level of Atlas Peak, where he has staked his hopes for the future with Cabernets and Chardonnays that can rival the world's finest. In 1983, in a blind tasting that he staged in San Francisco, with 200 wine-lovers selected by lottery, and in another in Beverly Hills, pitting his Cabernets against the First Growths of the Médoc, both his '79s and his '80s were hands-down first-place winners.

While Hill's operation is still small, it is growing. His 1,200-acre mountain-top domain, with initial capacity of 20,000 cases a year, can expand to an eventual 100,000 cases. Quality wines are the single goal.

SAMPLER SELECTION

Chardonnay (Napa Valley) Estate Bottled. A golden wine, softened to buttery richness by malolactic fermentation in the barrel; a prime example of Californian elegance of style.

Cabernet Sauvignon (Napa Valley) Estate Bottled. Grapes from nonirrigated, rocky soils give varietal intensity, nurtured through patient aging in oak to high peaks of finesse.

IRON HORSE VINEYARDS
9786 Ross Station Road
Sebastopol, California 95472

The trim, handsome labels of Iron Horse wines picture a schematic vista of rolling hills ribbed with vineyards, a winery, and a

At Iron Horse Vineyards, Audrey Sterling's Victorian house is set amid the vines and flowers

Victorian house set among trees, and the actual walk from the winery to the residence enchants the visitor's eyes. This is a cool microclimate for Chardonnay and Pinot Noir, first planted in 1970. When partners Barry and Audrey Sterling and winemaker Forrest Tancer redeveloped the property in 1976, their dream—now realized—was skillfully plotted. Tancer brought Cabernet Sauvignon, Sauvignon Blanc, and Zinfandel from his Alexander Valley ranch to round out the offerings. The partners share a common belief: that great wines grow in low-yield vineyards with lean soil, where climate is matched to grape variety. The 150-acre estate is a California *grand cru.*

The cool environment dictated the production of *méthode champenoise* sparkling wines; the classic grapes for the *cuvée,* Chardonnay and Pinot Noir, were already in mature bearing. In 1983, Iron Horse Blanc de Noirs (100 percent Pinot Noir), Brut (70 percent Pinot Noir and 30 percent Chardonnay), and Blanc de Blancs (100 percent Chardonnay) made auspicious debuts in San Francisco.

SAMPLER SELECTION

Blanc de Noirs (Sonoma County) Estate Grown Sparkling Wine. A typical "sparkler," this presents creamy rich, pale pink-gold bubbles in an endless mousse —dry, appetizing, and regal. Each *cuvée* spends 2½ years on the yeasts.

Zinfandel (Alexander Valley) Estate Grown. The virtues of this uniquely Californian variety are demonstrated here: berryness, character, and drinkability.

Tin Pony Chardonnay (Green Valley) Estate Bottled. A secondary label for an outstanding, yet affordable, table wine for daily service. (There is also a Red Table Wine from Iron Horse Vineyards.)

JEKEL VINEYARD
40155 Walnut Avenue
Greenfield, California 93927

Over and over again, the concept of estate-grown wine demonstrates that growing one's own grapes makes possible the

Rick Jekel watches over the stainless-steel fermenters at his winery

achievement of quality wines not otherwise obtainable.

Twins Bill and Gus Jekel chose to develop their own wine estate in the Arroyo Seco district of cool Monterey County. They planted their 140 acres to five varieties: Johannisberg Riesling, Pinot Noir, Pinot Blanc, Cabernet Sauvignon, and Chardonnay. Selected grape stocks were planted on their own roots to maximize the varietal character of the fruit. Vines are irrigated by solid-set, overhead "rainbird" sprinkler systems so that controlled "rainfall" can be delivered to each variety.

The modern winery was built in turn-of-the-century Salinas barn style in 1978 and enlarged to 50,000-case capacity in 1983. International recognition made the expansion imperative. In the fall of 1983 a Jekel Vineyard Monterey County Cabernet Sauvignon took an easy win in London: an English tasting jury chose it over all the French top-growth clarets. The rich, late-harvest Rieslings can rival the finest German *Trockenbeerenausleses*.

SAMPLER SELECTION

Chardonnay (Monterey County–Arroyo Seco) Estate Bottled. Select clusters of fully ripe grapes, given an oak finish, make a wine of the most luscious complexity.

Cabernet Sauvignon (Monterey County–Arroyo Seco) Estate Bottled. Each vintage has individual distinction, varietal breed, and the promise of higher peaks of perfection with longer cellar aging. Classic in style.

ROBERT KEENAN WINERY
3660 Spring Mountain Road
St. Helena, California 94574

When, in 1974, Robert Keenan of San Francisco purchased the old Conradi Winery, 1,700 feet up the east slope of Spring Mountain, most of the vineyards had reverted to forest and scrub manzanita. The commanding view of Mount St. Helena, plus the prospects of fine mountain-grown grapes, inspired the Keenans' enthusiastic drive. With the winery ready by autumn of

1977, the first release was made, a Chardonnay in classic style, from purchased Napa Valley grapes. The last of the 45 acres was replanted to Chardonnay and Cabernet vines in 1980.

Under the Keenan label, both Chardonnay and Cabernet Sauvignon reflect deluxe handcrafting for this limited 7,000-case production. Chosen by the highly selective American Classics Wine Company of Seagram for exclusive marketing rights, Keenan joins Carneros Creek, Chateau Chevalier (also on Spring Mountain), Bandiera, John B. Merritt, and Lambert Bridge in a portfolio of excellence.

THE KONOCTI WINERY
4350 Thomas Drive
Kelseyville, California 95451

In December 1983, John and George Parducci of the famed Mendocino winery became half owners of this remarkable Lake County winery. The twenty-five grower families who established the co-op winery in 1979 own the other half.

A goal of 100,000-case production from Konocti's 500 acres seems well-assured. When samples of Konocti Cabernet and Zinfandel first came my way, I was amazed at their fresh fragrance and utter charm and lost no time in alerting my readers in the *Los Angeles Times*. Put Konocti wines on your shopping list right now.

SAMPLER SELECTION

Cabernet Sauvignon Blanc (Lake County). Unlike most other white Cabernets, this one, of very gentle pressing, is a wine that is truly white. A gold-medal winner of dry delicacy.

Zinfandel (Lake County). Soft and briary, plum-color, rich and berrylike; an extraordinary and irresistible table wine of amazing finesse at a modest price.

LAMBERT BRIDGE
4085 W. Dry Creek Road
Healdsburg, California 95448

When Seagram's American Classics Wine Company, under the discriminating

direction of Ken Onish, included Lambert Bridge in their marketing portfolio, connoisseurs made a closer examination of this Sonoma wine estate.

The name of the 119-acre property, now owned by Gerard and Margaret Lambert, who purchased it in 1969, dates back to an unrelated Lambert who owned a large portion of Dry Creek Valley in the last century and after whom a bridge built across Dry Creek was named.

Seventy-eight acres are now in bearing from vines planted since 1970, with emphasis on Cabernet Sauvignon and Merlot varieties and Chardonnay, with wine from the last made in truly classic Burgundian style.

SAMPLER SELECTION

Chardonnay (Sonoma County). The Lambert Bridge style uses wine from fully ripe grapes for luscious taste, softened with malolactic fermentation and judiciously aged in French oak.

Cabernet Sauvignon (Sonoma County). Vinification follows the Bordeaux style, but regional hints of sage and herbs make this a real California wine. Dry Creek grapes in this cool microclimate do not yield heavy tannin or color, so that emphasis is on balance and silky elegance.

LAUREL GLEN VINEYARD
6611 Sonoma Mountain Road
Santa Rosa, California 95404

Patrick Campbell is sole owner, general manager, vineyardist, and winemaker of this small but remarkable winery devoted exclusively to Cabernet Sauvignon and its clonal cousin, Merlot. He carefully tends his 13 acres of Sonoma Mountain vines, gathers in the harvest, ferments and bottles the wine, and takes it on the road himself. Campbell established his Cabernet vineyard in 1968, bonding the winery in 1980.

SAMPLER SELECTION

Cabernet Sauvignon (Sonoma Mountain). Rich, velvet-textured wine, fragrant of the grape in direct, textbook perfection.

Merlot (Sonoma Mountain). Produced in a limited amount, but worthy of a trek to the vineyard to acquire. (Visits by appointment only.)

LONG VINEYARDS
P.O. Box 50
St. Helena, California 94574

In 1966, Robert Long's family bought this vineyard property on the eastern rim of the Napa Valley, facing north across Lake Hennessey. Long Vineyards is tiny, composed of 7½ acres of Riesling and 7½ acres of Chardonnay. The winery is in the enviable position of selling every bottle of wine it makes, with a waiting list of customers clamoring for larger allocations. "We have more acreage," Zelma Long admits, "but I have no desire to grow. I like a tiny place so that I can touch everything."

Zelma is one of the best winemakers in America—which, given the ascendancy of American wines today, makes her status international. A part-time job at the Robert Mondavi Winery led to eight years there as chief enologist before she moved on to a full-time assignment at Simi. As head winemaker (since 1979) at Simi, she designed the total layout for that winery's $5 million expansion program. When Simi was acquired in 1981 by Moët-Hennessy, Zelma's world took on international dimensions. Nevertheless, to everyone's delight, Long Vineyards' 1,500-case production continues.

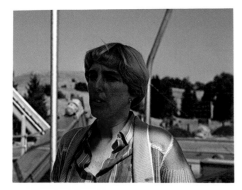

Zelma Long, the talented winemaker at Simi (in background), also produces her own sought-after wines at Long Vineyards

SAMPLER SELECTION
Chardonnay (Napa Valley). The Longs monitor the grapes to assure full ripeness; thus the wine achieves silky texture via the inherent flavonoid compounds. Ages to incomparable elegance.
Johannisberg Riesling (Napa Valley). Whether it is a regular or a late-harvest, botrytis-affected wine, if you see a Long Vineyard Riesling, buy it. It is California's answer to the best of the Rhineland.

MATANZAS CREEK WINERY
6097 Bennett Valley Road
Santa Rosa, California 95404

To taste a bottle of Matanzas Creek wine is to become a devotee, but with production limited to 5,000 cases annually, acquiring that bottle may not be easy. Supplementing their own 50 acres, the Matanzas Creek Winery owners, Sandra and Bill MacIver, and winemaker Merry Edwards grow or seek out only the finest clones, located in proper microclimates. Maximum varietal character is achieved by minimum handling of the wine: fermenting caps are punched down by hand and wines are clarified by letting them settle rather than by multiple filtrations. Cooperage in small oak barrels, with special attention paid to preserving the balance between fruit and oak, enhances flavors and viscosity. Wines are aged from a minimum of nine months up to two years before release, in order to develop bottle bouquet and maturity.

SAMPLER SELECTION
Chardonnay (Sonoma Valley). Mellow-rich wine that unfolds with buttery nuances and a long, lingering finish.
Pinot Noir (Sonoma Valley) Valle Vista Vineyards. The winery staff calls this the "moon mountain Pinot." A gently oak-touched wine, already mellow with subtle flavors, it points to an even finer level of finesse with aging.

MCDOWELL VALLEY VINEYARDS & CELLARS
3811 Highway 175
Hopland, California 95449

The McDowell Valley, one of California's newest vineyard appellations, nestles in the southeast corner of Mendocino County. It is named for Paxton McDowell, who came to California in the gold rush and stayed to plant vines "where summer's sun is robbed of its fierceness by a gently bracing breeze which always finds its way from the ocean, making the days very mild and even in temperature."

This ideal vineland was acquired in 1970 by Karen and Richard Keehn, who embarked upon a program of planting noble varietals suitable to the climate. When their grapes, sold to other wineries, earned medals, they knew it was time to build their own winery.

Seventy percent of their production emphasizes four varieties: Cabernet Sauvignon, Syrah, Chardonnay, and Fumé Blanc. Additionally, what is perhaps the state's most outstanding French Colombard will continue to be made, along with Grenache from old vines, Chenin Blanc, and, of course, a Zinfandel.

SAMPLER SELECTION
Fumé Blanc (McDowell Valley) Estate Bottled. An elegantly dry wine, enriched with eight hours of skin contact prior to cool fermentation and touched with French oak in finish. A small percentage of Semillon graces the blend.
Syrah (McDowell Valley) Estate Bottled. This Rhône Valley varietal is at home here in the rocky soil; the wine made from these 40–60-year-old vines has rich intensity of flavor.

NEWTON VINEYARD
2555 Madrona Avenue
St. Helena, California 94574

Following the sale of Sterling Vineyards, of which he was president/founder, Peter Newton and his wife, Dr. Su Hua Newton, acquired 560 acres of rugged, untamed land, ranging from 500 to 1,300 feet in elevation, in the western hills above St. Helena. Land clearing and vineyard terracing began in 1979. From the outset this site, with its volcanic soil, was conceived as a wine estate to be planted to produce three wines: a Sauvignon Blanc, which would include Semillon, a Merlot to blend with Cabernet Franc, and a Cabernet Sauvignon to be blended with Franc and Merlot— each vintage varied, as is the tradition in Bordeaux. Ric Forman, the inaugural winemaker, has been succeeded by John Kongsgaard, who has a master's degree in enology from UC–Davis. All white wines are barrel-fermented; red wines are fermented in the pagoda-like structure designed by Su Hua Newton. Annual production is 13,000 cases.

OBESTER WINERY

12341 San Mateo Road (Highway 92)
Half Moon Bay, California 94019

Sandy and Paul Obester learned the ways of translating the grape into wine from Sandy's grandfather, John Gemello, who established the highly regarded Gemello Winery in the Santa Clara Valley. They began winemaking as a hobby, which led to the establishment in 1977 of the Obester Winery at Half Moon Bay on the coast below San Francisco.

The Obesters' Sauvignon Blanc, from Mendocino County grapes, Johannisberg Riesling, of Monterey heritage, and Cabernet Sauvignon, from Sonoma County grapes, reveal the scope of their wines. All the grapes are hand-picked in the cool morning hours and crushed within moments by their own vineyard crushing unit. This links today's modern methods to traditions as old as those Grandfather Gemello brought with him from Tuscany.

PAT PAULSEN VINEYARDS

25510 River Road
Cloverdale, California 95425

The famed television comedian Pat Paulsen and his wife, Jane, have seriously entered the California wine game. Since 1970, when they bought their 550-acre ranch near Cloverdale, in Sonoma County, the first 10 acres of Cabernet Sauvignon have been joined by 28 additional acres of bearing vines: Cabernet Sauvignon, Sauvignon Blanc, Chardonnay, Muscat Catelli.

The last-named species won the Paulsens a double gold medal from the 1982 San Francisco Exposition, a silver medal from Orange County, and another silver medal from the highly discriminating jury of the Sonoma County Harvest Fair that year. This 1981 edition, like the ones to follow, is made dry, in Alsatian style. With its exotic perfumey and spicy aromas, it's a real knockout, a wow of a wine.

The Paulsens built their winery in 1979, engaging Mary Ann Graf as consultant; she brought in Jamie Meves from UC–Davis as winemaker. Every one of the Estate Bottled Pat Paulsen wines belongs in the connoisseur's corner of your wine cellar.

ROBERT PECOTA WINERY

3299 Bennett Lane
Calistoga, California 94515

In 1978, Robert Pecota left Beringer Vineyards, where he had long been employed as a wine, grape, and vineyard buyer, to devote himself to his own small acreage, a low-yielding 40-acre plot, planted to Sauvignon Blanc, Cabernet Sauvignon, Muscat Blanc, and Gamay Beaujolais. From day one his wines, addressed to the true connoisseur, had a ready audience.

Introducing his initial release, a 1978 Gamay Beaujolais, made with whole grape clusters in the carbonic maceration technique, plus a secondary malolactic fermentation, he said: "Each label expresses our wine and our winery. By featuring California art and delicate French scripts we are saying, 'We appreciate both tradition and creativity.'" From California to Singapore, Robert Pecota Wines are all collectors' choices. Annual case production is 12,000.

SAMPLER SELECTION

Muscato di Andrea (Monterey County–Arroyo Seco). Pecota has a way with the Muscat vinifera, giving exceptional finesse to a variety not noted for subtlety. Some wines are dry, some are late-harvest examples with low alcohol, high residual sugar, and a balancing total acidity. Not to be missed.

QUADY WINERY

13181 Road 24
Madera, California 93637

When, in 1977, Andrew Quady left a career as a chemist and he and his wife, Laurel, became winemakers, they did not follow an easy pattern governed by practicality. They decided to produce dessert wines and vintage ports in the Central San Joaquin Valley at Madera. After seven years, the demand for Quady California Port wines has risen above 17,000 cases a year, with steady growth despite a receding market and descending sales of dessert wines nationally.

After some success with port wines made from rich Amador County Zinfandel vines from the Shenandoah School Road Vineyard in Sierra gold rush country, Quady turned to a rare Muscat variant called "Orange Muscat" from the San Joaquin Valley. Known in France as Fleur d'Oranger and in Italy as Moscato Fior d'Orancio, it has an aroma reminiscent of orange blossoms. Quady's first edition, a delicate wine of 15 percent alcohol by volume, was, at $9.00, an overnight sellout. Quady has more than doubled production each year, but 4,500 cases annually still do not meet the demand.

Released in mid-1984 was another exotic dessert wine, Elysium. It recalls Constantia, a legendary red muscat wine made in South Africa that was popular in Europe in the eighteenth century. Its roselike aroma came from careful vinification of the Black Muscat, known in Italy as Rose Muscat. Quady recreated this legendary wine with some Black Muscat grapes from a Manteca grower. As the new wine drained from the fermenter, he recalls, "the winery was filled with a most provocative perfume: roses!"

QUAIL RIDGE

1055 Atlas Peak Road
Napa, California 94558

Love of the grape led Elaine Wellesley and her late husband, motion-picture producer Jesse Corallo, to acquire a vineyard perched at an almost inaccessible height on Mt. Veeder in the Mayacamas Range. While

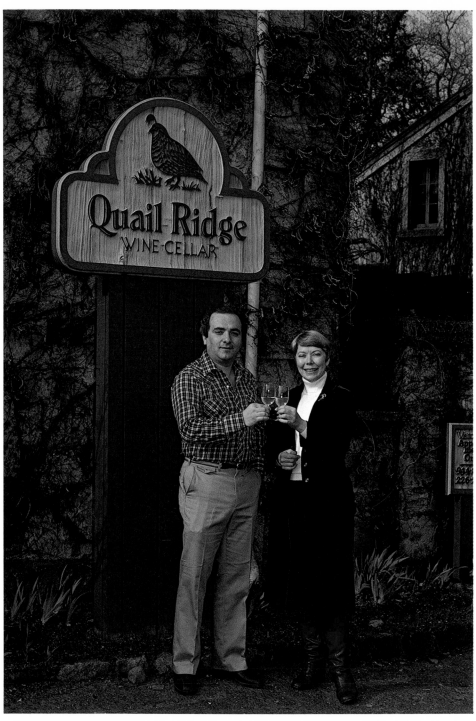

Leon Santoro and Elaine Wellesley, winemakers at Quail Ridge, drink a toast before the nineteenth-century aging cellars

the young vines grew, Elaine earned masters' degrees in both English and Fermentation Sciences at UC–Davis. Their first barrel-fermented Chardonnays were rich elixirs of the grape, noble Napa wines.

Since Jesse's tragic accidental death in a vineyard brushfire, Elaine has bravely pursued their common goals. With Leon Santoro as co-winemaker, she has taken over as storage cellar and sales location the two-story granite Hedgeside Caves, built in 1883, with the longest tunnels in the Napa Valley, dug by Chinese laborers in the boom time of the last century.

Winelovers rank Quail Ridge Chardonnays from the Mt. Veeder vineyard and from Sonoma grapes high in the world roster of wines. The Pinot Noir from Elaine's tiny mountain plot, aged in French oak, fined with egg white, has joined the repertory of splendid wines.

SAMPLER SELECTION

French Colombard (Napa Valley) Cyril Saviez Vineyard. Altogether unique. Barrel fermentation in French oak gives this silky, dry subvarietal almost noble stance —at a bargain price.

RAYMOND VINEYARD & CELLAR
849 Zinfandel Lane
St. Helena, California 94574

In 1978, Roy Raymond, his wife (granddaughter of Jacob Beringer), and their two sons completed construction of a chateau winery on 90 acres of prime vineyards near St. Helena. Since 1974, when the Nestlé Corporation of Switzerland had acquired the Beringer Vineyard and Winery, the Raymonds had been making their award-winning wines in temporary quarters; their new estate winery makes possible a maximum production of 20,000 cases per year and national distribution of their increasingly sought-after wines.

Of the two sons, both trained in viticulture and enology, Walter is winemaker, Roy Jr. vineyard manager. In the classic European tradition, all Raymond wines are made from their own estate-grown grapes:

Cabernet Sauvignon, Zinfandel, Pinot Noir, Gamay, Merlot, Chardonnay, Johannisberg Riesling, and Chenin Blanc.

SAMPLER SELECTION

Chardonnay (Napa Valley) Estate Bottled. Classic wine, with judicious oak. Clean, crisp in style; ages to mellow buttery qualities, since it is always made from ripe, luscious grapes. Lyric, poetic concentration of the vine's true nectar.

RUTHERFORD VINTNERS
1673 St. Helena Highway
Rutherford, California 94573

This small winery in a grove of shade trees, off Highway 29, is a family endeavor of remarkable credentials. Bernard L. Skoda, owner and winemaker, came to California from Alsace-Lorraine, where he had spent his youth in vineyards and cellars, in 1954. In 1961 he joined the Louis M. Martini Winery in St. Helena, retiring as vice-president in 1976.

During their residence in the valley, he and his wife found a 25-acre plot of land at Rutherford, famous for Cabernet Sauvignon. An initial planting of 25 acres was begun in 1968; in 1977 the winery was in operation with fully mature vines, including additional adjacent acreage planted to the Riesling vines so well remembered from Skoda's youth in Alsace.

SAMPLER SELECTION

Johannisberg Riesling (Napa Valley). Exceptionally fragrant and flowery wine; dry finish in Alsatian style.

Chardonnay (Napa Valley). Cold-fermented, with aging in Limousin oak barrels. Dry but with a lingering mellow and buttery richness and complexity.

Chateau Rutherford (Napa Valley) Special Reserve Cabernet Sauvignon. An estate-bottled, selected wine, blended with 10 percent Merlot, released after four years of aging. A world-class claret.

ST. CLEMENT VINEYARDS
2867 St. Helena Highway
St. Helena, California 94574

Dr. William J. Casey, a San Francisco eye surgeon, and his wife, Alexandra, bought this Victorian dollhouse of a winery on Highway 29 from Mike Robbins in 1975. Built in 1876, it had been lovingly restored by Robbins, who began his career as a winemaker in the stone cellar under the house.

In the beginning, Dr. Casey held to a modest program consistent with the demands of his medical practice. As the good wines from Napa Valley grapes grown by local friends have gained a following, his multiple jobs as winemaker, grape producer, and eye surgeon have become part-time.

Dennis Johns, who came from Sterling Vineyards, is full-time winemaker for the enlarged new winery carved into the hills behind the house. Three varieties are made: Cabernet Sauvignon, Chardonnay, and Sauvignon Blanc. All wines are fermented in stainless steel and aged in small French oak cooperage.

SANFORD & BENEDICT WINERY
2000 Santa Rosa Road
Lompoc, California 93436

I first met Richard Sanford and Michael Benedict at their new winery in an old barn among young vines in Lompoc.

Dick Graff, of Chalone, had extolled the wines of these two dedicated friends from the academic halls of UC–Santa Barbara. Benedict's fields were biology, botany, and mathematics, and Sanford's geography and geology—all sciences readily applicable to an adventure in winemaking.

Researching the new field thoroughly, Sanford and Benedict followed temperature records through centuries of winemaking in Burgundy, knowing that Lompoc, unlike other parts of California, has a cool climate comparable to that of the Côte d'Or and favorable for the production of the Burgundian varietals Pinot Noir and Chardonnay. The mountains and valleys, running transverse to the Pacific here, are regularly cooled by on- and off-shore breezes. They planted their vines, took the old, lichen-covered wooden barn apart timber by timber, reconstructed it with insulation, and had their winery. With French oak cooperage and good initial cropping in 1976, they were on their way. Since those first days, the vineyards have expanded to 110 acres. The offerings are: Chardonnay, Pinot Noir, Merlot, Riesling, Cabernet Sauvignon—all intense, splendid vinifications.

SAMPLER SELECTION

Pinot Noir (California). Grown, produced,

The Sanford & Benedict Winery in Lompoc is picturesquely situated on an old sheep ranch and bottled with unparalleled care, each vintage is an echo of fine Burgundian-style wine. Translucent, aristocratic; a wine for the serious collector and the restaurateur.

SANFORD WINERY
7250 Santa Rosa Road
Buellton, California 93427

In 1981, Richard Sanford sold his interest in the Sanford & Benedict Winery to devote himself to his own winery on a splendid 738-acre ranch in the Santa Ynez Valley. The fascination of the property lies in its many different microclimates, some as warm as Bordeaux, others as cool as Burgundy, with comparable differences in the composition of the soil, all of it new to the vine.

While the vineyards are being established and the winery built, Sanford buys grapes from select vineyards of the Edna Valley, Santa Ynez, and San Luis Obispo, still exciting pioneering regions for vinifera, and makes his wines in leased facilities. His first released vintages, 1981 and 1982, of Chardonnay, Sauvignon Blanc, and Pinot Noir –Vin Gris, established the rich, elegant, handcrafting style of winemaking that will ultimately be applied to his own estate-grown grapes.

SCHARFFENBERGER CELLARS
3001 South State Street
Ukiah, California 94582

Young John Scharffenberger has been a grape grower in Mendocino County for ten years. Now, with Robert Porter, a biochemist, and Paul Dolan, winemaker at Fetzer Vineyards, Scharffenberger Cellars is off and running, in pursuit of the declared ambition of its staff "to produce the finest sparkling wine in America in the *méthode champenoise* style." With Chardonnay and Pinot Noir from cool Northern California vineyards, they believe they have the potentials at hand.

Under the Eaglepoint label, Scharffenberger Cellars also offer two still table wines—Blanc de Noir and Chardonnay. Both are touched with French oak, possess crisp acidity, and are made to complement food. All indications point to early achievement of the stated goals.

SHAFER VINEYARDS
6154 Silverado Trail
Napa, California 94558

Like many of California's new breed of wine dynasties, this one was born of a mature urge toward a new life-style. In 1972, John Shafer, after a successful career in publishing, made the definitive move from Chicago to California with his wife, Bett, and their four grown children. They ripped out and replanted 40 acres of old vines in their chosen location, the northern tip of the Stag's Leap palisades. The fame of the fat, rich quality of Cabernet wines from this rugged terrain dictated their decision to emphasize this popular varietal, to which they added Chardonnay and Zinfandel for a limited ultimate production of 12,000 cases annually. Their first release, a 1978 Cabernet Sauvignon, brought solid praise from veteran wine critics. The attractive winery, which may be visited by appointment, is on its way.

SAMPLER SELECTION
Cabernet Sauvignon (Napa Valley) Estate Bottled. The 1980 edition is already rich, dark, briary, and eminently drinkable; it is certain to gain depth and complexity with further aging.
Chardonnay (Napa Valley) Estate Bottled. Made in elegant and restrained style. Pale straw color, crisp, with a lemony aroma and understated presence of oak.

CHARLES F. SHAW VINEYARD & WINERY
1010 Big Tree Road
St. Helena, California 94574

Special project studies of several Northern California wineries while he was getting his MBA at Stanford sparked West Point graduate Charles F. Shaw's interest in the wine industry. Later, a banking assignment in France sent him into several wine-growing regions, where he became fatefully fascinated with the wines and techniques of Beaujolais.

In 1979, Chuck Shaw and his wife, Lucy, formed a partnership following the purchase from the Charles Crocker banking family of San Francisco of a certified vineyard of Napa Gamay and Zinfandel grape stock. While restoring the farmhouse in the center of the vineyard, they completed construction of the adjacent winery, equipped with custom-designed fermenters for the carbonic maceration of wines in an ancient technique perfected in the nineteenth century. Whole clusters of grapes, lowered into the fermenters under a blanketing of carbon dioxide, begin an anaerobic metabolism naturally. In this oxygen-free atmosphere, fermentation takes place within the ripe, juicy sphere of each separate grape. The following phases of free-run juice and press-wine, completing primary fermentation, accommodate malolactic fermentation prior to aging in French oak casks.

Chuck Shaw became a scholar of this type of vinification (with winemaker Ric Forman backing him up on the line), and the resultant wine was his masterpiece. With the announcement of Forman as full-time winemaker, Shaw expanded the output of the winery to include Chardonnay and Fumé Blanc. Prizes from state and local fairs have signaled the success of this splendid California wine estate.

SAMPLER SELECTION
Napa Valley Gamay (Napa Valley) Estate Bottled. Fresh, cherry-like aromas characterize each of the Charles F. Shaw Beaujolais-style wines. A Domaine Elucia wine, with touches of Zinfandel, is a "Reserve" wine to seek out.

SILVERADO VINEYARDS
6121 Silverado Trail
Napa, California 94558

Topping a knoll on the west side of the Silverado Trail is the new winery of Lillian Disney, widow of the famed Walt Disney. A family enterprise, drawing upon 165 acres of vines in the production of Sauvignon Blanc, Chardonnay, and Cabernet Sau-

A graceful presentation of Sanford wines, whose labels by Sebastian Titus celebrate California's wildflowers

vignon, Silverado Vineyards had an enviable beginning. It sold out all the first-release wines of the 1981 vintage, with the second release in 1982 committed before it was bottled. The Cabernet Sauvignon of 1981, released in mid-1984, is described as "intensely fruited, with overtones of cassis and black currants." The 1982 Sauvignon Blanc of winemaker John Stuart was of impeccable finesse, with arresting and intensely concentrated aroma.

SMITH & HOOK WINERY
P.O. Box 1010
Gonzales, California 93926

The founding president of this exciting winery in Monterey County, exclusively dedicated to Cabernet Sauvignon, is Gerald B. McFarland, scion of the pioneer California ranching family for whom the town of McFarland is named. The 642-acre location on the east slope of the Santa Lucia Mountains was acquired by the McFarland and Blake families, with ownership divided among several American and European participants.

The trellised vineyards of Smith & Hook, planted in 1974 with clonal selections made by Dr. Austin Goheen of UC–Davis, are in full, mature bearing. Winemaker Duane DeBoer exercises quality control of wine production from vineyard to cellar. Immediately following hand-picking, grapes arrive from the vineyards in small gondolas. They are then passed over a grading table similar to those used in Bordeaux, prior to going into the crusher-stemmer. Fermentation takes place in open-topped redwood tanks, followed by aging in small oak. The winery plans to maintain a 10,000-case annual production.

I am happy to report, having tasted each vintage, that the Smith & Hook Cabernet wines compare in richness and elegance, cork-to-cork, with any of the classified growths of Bordeaux upon which their production is patterned. They remove irrefutably any doubt about the merits of Cabernet wines in Monterey County—they are superb.

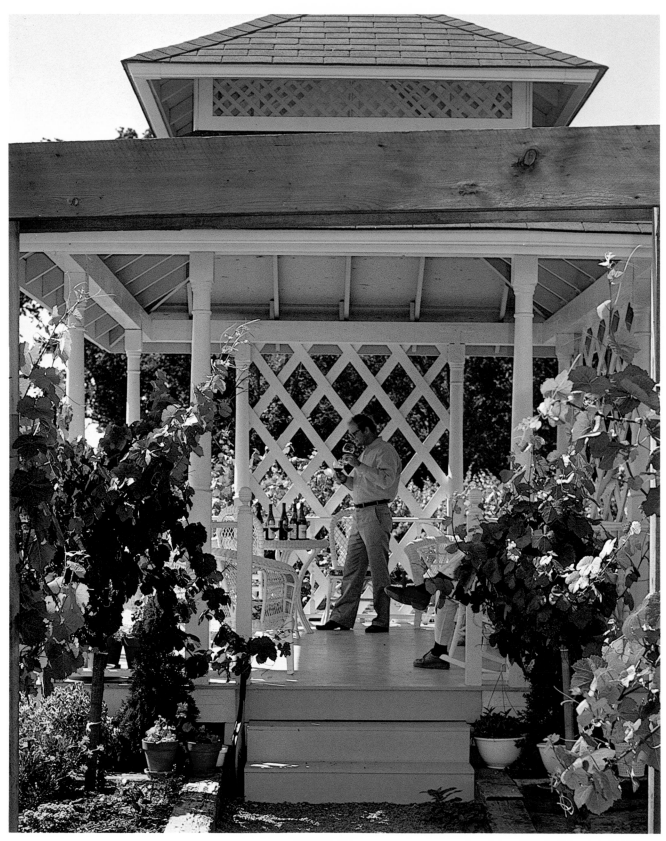

A gazebo set among the vines is the perfect place to taste Charles F. Shaw wines

Gerry McFarland of Smith & Hook, where Cabernet Sauvignon grows high above the Salinas Valley in Monterey County

SONOMA-CUTRER VINEYARDS

4401 Slusser Road

Windsor, California 95492

The reputation of its winemaker, Bill Bonetti, says all that's necessary to the knowing winelover about the future of this small new winery, founded in 1981. Born in Italy, reared among wines and winemaking, Bonetti started his American career at Charles Krug Winery, moving on to become full-time winemaker at Souverain of Alexander Valley. After several years in this multi-million-dollar, multi-million-gallon winery, he yearned to devote himself more simply to handcrafting but one wine, Chardonnay. The first release, Sonoma-Cutrer Chardonnay–Les Pierres, reveals his great talent as an artist/winemaker. It is a luscious, golden triumph.

VENTANA VINEYARD

P.O. Box G

Soledad, California 93960

Aeons ago, when the Santa Lucia coastal mountains rose from the ocean floor, granitic rock debris and calcareous clay were washed to lower areas, filling the deep chasms of the Ventana Wilderness area— and providing the superlative drainage and lean environment, to depths of 45–90 feet, for the slow-ripening vines of Doug Meador's Ventana Vineyard. Meador started vine growing in 1973, originally to supply premium grapes for wineries of limited production. Crop-thinning by hand, positioning the shoots by hand (to protect clusters from too much sun), and handpicking certain varieties, for select clusters —these are some of his labor-intensive routes to better wines from better grapes. He believes that a great grape cannot be grown unless the viticulturist understands the vine and, specifically, the ultimate wine for which that grape will be used. And so he has become a winemaker. His successive vintages of Chardonnay, Pinot Blanc, and Riesling, including several late-harvest botrytis-affected wines, are eloquent proofs of his thesis. However, Meador is deliberately reducing his winery's annual case production so that he can dedicate his energies to his original purpose—grape growing for other wineries' production of prestige wines.

SAMPLER SELECTION

Chardonnay (Monterey County). In a ramshackle old Swiss dairy farm containing a million dollars' worth of the latest equipment, plus French oak barrels, Meador makes landmark white wines of silken perfection; they are becoming collectors' items.

VICHON WINERY

1595 Oakville Grade

Oakville, California 94562

The Vichon Winery, founded in 1980, takes its name from those of its three principal Napa Valley partners, winemaker George Vierra, Peter Brucher, and Douglas Watson. An enthusiastic supporter from the beginning, San Francisco distributor Larry Romano thought the name appropriately French-sounding and consistent with the aims of the founders: to make wines as the French do, to complement food. Most of the other partners are in the restaurant business (technically, the four-star restaurateurs who form the Vichon connection own only the winery building, not the wine).

Vichon produces three wines: Cabernet Sauvignon, Chardonnay, and Chevrier Blanc (a 50/50 blend of Semillon [Chevrier] and Sauvignon Blanc). All are produced from grapes grown exclusively in the Napa Valley in accordance with Vichon requirements, which include checking the grapes in June, constantly monitoring the sugar/ acid health of the vines, and supervising the viticultural practices of the grower.

SAMPLER SELECTION

Chevrier Blanc (Napa Valley). From vine to bottle, this is a handcrafted wine. Fulfilling the founding partners' aim of making wine to go with food, it is a perfect balance of fruit and softly toasted oak, with refreshing, natural, crisp dryness achieved without malolactic fermentation.

Cabernet Sauvignon (Napa Valley) Vineyard Designated. The first two editions were from the Fay Vineyard and the Volker Eisele Vineyard, both big wines bearing the Vichon hallmark of intricacy and elegance. Fine balance and drinkability, with great aging potential.

VINE HILL WINES, INC.
dba SMOTHERS

2317 Vine Hill Road

Santa Cruz, California 95065

Dick and Tom Smothers, of TV's funniest brother act, went innocently and sincerely into grape growing and winemaking, Dick in Santa Cruz and Tom in Sonoma. When the Smothers Vine Hill 1977 Late Harvest Gewürztraminer won a sweepstakes award at the Los Angeles County Fair, Dick's tiny winery was catapulted into fame. Winelovers from coast to coast heard about the big win, but few of them were

At St. Clement Vineyards in St. Helena, Cabernet Sauvignon vines grow in place of a front garden

lucky enough to get a taste of the limited-production wine—a rich, golden essence of the grape. While Dick remains fascinated with late-harvest Rhenish-type white wines, his ventures into red varietals also augur well and show off the talents of his young winemaker, William Arnold.

SAMPLER SELECTION

Pinot Noir (San Luis Obispo). Translucent ruby wine, with a true bouquet extracted from this temperamental Burgundian vine.

Gewürztraminer (Alexander Valley). Sometimes off-dry, sometimes with rich residual sweetness; always refreshing.

Zinfandel (Central Coast). An absolutely stunning red, with raspberry overtones in aroma and bouquet, plus a suggestion of sandalwood from American oak aging. A California masterpiece.

ZACA MESA WINERY

Foxen Canyon Road
Los Olivos, California 93441

The relatively rapid growth of Zaca Mesa in the boom years of the seventies swept away any idea of leisurely retirement that Marsh Ream, executive vice-president of ARCO (Atlantic Richfield Corporation) might have entertained before he and wife Connie moved to California to grow grapes and make wine.

The first step was to find a location. After looking at established properties with no success, Ream made one last sortie to a more remote, wholly undeveloped former cattle ranch on a mesa 1,500 feet above sea level, overlooking the Pacific. "There was something essentially peaceful about it," he told me on my first visit. "*Zaca* is an Indian word meaning 'land of peace and quiet' and also, in the interpretation of another local tribe, 'a gathering place.' I guess we can accommodate both definitions."

254

They also needed to accommodate their daughter's pony. The 1,500 acres of oak-clad mesas and rolling hills, part of an old Spanish land grant, more than satisfied that need.

In 1973 the vineyard planting began in earnest. The winery was built in 1976. By 1982 Zaca Mesa wines had won gold, silver, and bronze medals in competitions throughout California., This led to expansion of the winery in 1983 into an $11 million venture with eighteen shareholders, its potential production growing to the 80,000-case level. Having leaped from 12,000 cases in 1979 to 58,000 cases in 1983—an annual growth of 48.3 percent in a time of serious recession—the winery obviously merits consumer acceptance.

Out of a semiwilderness has grown an orderly garden of vine rows for the production of six premium varietals: Chardonnay, Johannisberg Riesling, Sauvignon Blanc, Pinot Noir, Zinfandel, and Cabernet Sauvignon.

SAMPLER SELECTION

Sauvignon Blanc (Santa Barbara County) American Reserve. This proud, estate-grown wine, integrating Old World ways with the finest American technology, has Semillon to soften the assertive nature of Sauvignon Blanc. A long, crisp, appetizing wine.

Johannisberg Riesling (Santa Barbara County) American Classic. From the winery's Santa Ynez and Santa Maria Valley vineyards, the wine is a complex of both, laced with hints of melon, honey, and spicy green apple. Fresh, fruity, with the well-balanced acidity found in the best *Spaëtleses* of the Mosel.

STEPHEN ZELLERBACH VINEYARD

14350 Chalk Hill Road
Healdsburg, California 95448

Stephen Zellerbach is a fourth-generation Californian, the great-grandson of Anthony Zellerbach, founder of the giant paper company Crown Zellerbach. He is also the nephew of the late Ambassador David Zellerbach, who with his wife, Hannah, established Hanzell Vineyards in Sonoma. Stephen's wife, Cici, is a member of the pioneering Nervo family, who established a winery in Sonoma in 1870. However, it was mutual attraction and not wine connections that brought them together.

Stephen became a full-time winegrower following their marriage in 1975. A 158-acre plot of land acquired in 1969 in the Alexander Valley was planted with Cabernet Sauvignon and Merlot, and he and Cici began home winemaking. The next logical step was building the winery. The Stephen Zellerbach label was launched with the 1978 Alexander Valley estate-grown wine, blended with Merlot in Bordeaux style. John Jaffray was the winemaker. A longtime friend, distributor Henry Vandervoort, who was born at Château Bellegrave in Pauillac, after tasting that first release, called to say, "I wish we could make wine this good in Bordeaux. I'd like to distribute it."

With 14 acres planted to Merlot, and 55 acres to Cabernet for a classic blending, there's been some surplus Merlot, which was extolled by one wine writer as "an American Petrus." But Stephen believes Merlot should be subsidiary to Cabernet, and not vice versa. Nevertheless, in 1979, the winery made its first release of Merlot.

SAMPLER SELECTION

Cabernet Sauvignon (Alexander Valley). A full-bodied wine of intense varietal character; its velvet depths suggest that it will age splendidly. Aging in American and French oak gives a special incense to the bouquet.

Merlot (Alexander Valley). A 100 percent varietal, fermented in stainless steel, aged in Nevers and Kentucky oak barrels. Fine color, ripe fruit aromas. Peak maturity in eight to ten years.

Chardonnay (Alexander Valley) Warnecke Sonoma Vineyard. The grapes come from the John Carl Warnecke Vineyard in the Chalk Hill region of the valley, famed for crisp, clean Chardonnays of exceptional finesse and complexity.

THE WINERIES OF CALIFORNIA

ACACIA WINERY
  Napa
ADELAIDA CELLARS
  Paso Robles
ADLER FELS
  Santa Rosa
AHERN WINERY, LTD.
  San Fernando
AHLGREN VINEYARD
  Boulder Creek
ALATERA VINEYARDS, INC.
  Napa
ALDERBROOK VINEYARDS
  Oakland
ALEXANDER VALLEY
  VINEYARDS
  Healdsburg
ALMADEN VINEYARDS, INC.
  San Jose
ALTA VINEYARD CELLAR
  Calistoga
AMADOR FOOTHILL
  WINERY
  Plymouth
AMADOR WINERY
  Amador City
AMERICAN FOODS
  CORPORATION
  San Francisco
S. ANDERSON VINEYARD
  Pasadena
ANDERSON WINE CELLARS
  Exeter
ARBOR KNOLL WINERY LTD.
  Springville
ARGONAUT WINERY
  Ione
1,2,3,4 ASV WINES
  Delano
AUSTIN CELLARS
  Solvang

BACCALA VINEYARDS
  Ukiah
BALDINELLI/SHENANDOAH
  VALLEY VINEYARDS
  Oakland
BALLARD CANYON
  CORPORATION
  Solvang

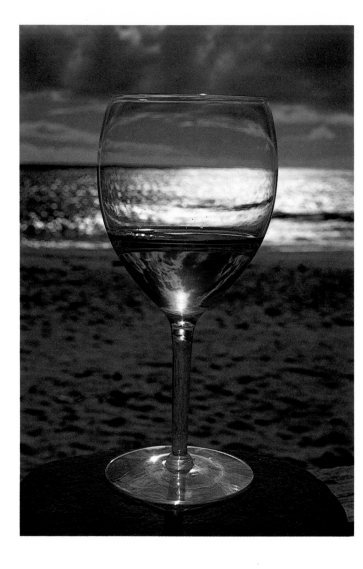

BALVERNE WINERY &
  VINEYARDS
  Windsor
BARGETTO'S SANTA CRUZ
  WINERY
  Soquel
BAY CELLARS
  Berkeley
BEAU VAL WINES
  CORPORATION
  Plymouth
BEAULIEU VINEYARD
  Rutherford

BELLA NAPOLI WINERY
  Manteca
BELLA ROSA WINERY
  Delano
BELLE CREEK RANCH
  Paradise
BELLEROSE VINEYARD
  Healdsburg
BELVEDERE WINE
  COMPANY
  Healdsburg
BERINGER VINEYARDS
  St. Helena

BERNARDO WINERY, INC.
  San Diego
BISCEGLIA BROTHERS WINE
  COMPANY
  Fresno
BLANC VINEYARDS
  Redwood Valley
BLUE HERON WINE CELLAR
  Healdsburg
JULIUS BOCHANTIN
  WINERY
  Pasadena
BOEGER WINERY
  Placerville
BOGLE VINEYARDS, INC.
  Clarksburg
BONNY DOON VINEYARD
  Santa Cruz
CIRIACO BORELLI WINERY
  Stockton
BORRA'S CELLAR
  Lodi
BOUCHAINE VINEYARDS
  Napa
BRANDER WINERY
  Los Olivos
BRAREN PAULI WINERY
  Petaluma
BRONCO WINE COMPANY
  Ceres
BROOKSIDE VINEYARD
  COMPANY
  Guasti
DAVID BRUCE WINERY,
  INC.
  Saratoga
BUEHLER VINEYARDS
  St. Helena
BUENA VISTA WINERY
  Sonoma
BURGESS CELLARS, INC.
  St. Helena
DAVIS BYNUM WINERY
  Healdsburg

CACHE CELLARS
  Davis
CADENASSO WINERY
  Fairfield

CADLOLO WINERY
Escalon
CAIN CELLARS
St. Helena
CAKEBREAD CELLARS
Oakland
CALERA WINE COMPANY
Hollister
CALIFORNIA CELLAR
MASTERS
Lodi
CALIFORNIA GROWERS
WINERY, INC.
Yettem
CALIFORNIA MEADERY
Napa
CALIFORNIA WINE
COMPANY, INC.
Cloverdale
CALLAWAY VINEYARD &
WINERY
Temecula
CAMBIASO WINERY &
VINEYARDS
Healdsburg
CANNERY WINE CELLARS
San Francisco
CAPARONE WINERY
Paso Robles
CARANO CELLARS
Geyserville
J. CAREY CELLARS
Solvang
CARMEL BAY WINERY
Carmel
CARMENET VINEYARD, INC.
San Francisco
CARNEROS CREEK WINERY
Napa
CARROUSEL CELLARS
Gilroy
CASA DE FRUTA
Hollister
CASA NUESTRA
St. Helena
CASSAYRE-FORNI CELLARS
Rutherford
CASWELL VINEYARDS
Sebastopol
CAYMUS VINEYARDS, INC.
Rutherford
CHALONE VINEYARD
Soledad
CHAMISAL VINEYARD
San Luis Obispo

CHAPPELLET VINEYARD
St. Helena
CHATEAU BEL ARBRES
Hopland
CHATEAU BOSWELL
St. Helena
CHATEAU CHEVALIER
WINERY
St. Helena
CHATEAU CHEVRE WINERY
Yountville
CHATEAU DE LEU WINERY, INC.
Green Valley
CHATEAU D'IVRESSE, INC.
Mountain Center
CHATEAU DU LAC,
INCORPORATED
Lakeport
CHATEAU MONTELENA
WINERY
Calistoga
CHATEAU ST. JEAN
Kenwood
CHISPA CELLARS
Murphys
CILURZO VINEYARD &
WINERY
Temecula
CLENDENEN-TOLMACH
VINTNERS
Los Olivos
CLINE CELLARS
Oakley
CLOS DU BOIS
San Rafael
CLOS DU VAL WINE
COMPANY LTD.
Napa
CLOUDSTONE VINEYARDS
Los Altos Hills
COBB MOUNTAIN WINERY
Middletown
CONCANNON VINEYARD
Livermore
CONGRESS SPRINGS
VINEYARDS
Saratoga
CONN CREEK WINERY
St. Helena
A. CONROTTO WINERY, INC.
Gilroy
R. & J. COOK
Clarksburg
COOK-ELLIS WINERY, INC.
Scotts Valley

COPENHAGEN CELLARS
Solvang
CORDTZ BROTHERS
CELLARS
Cloverdale
COSENTINO WINE
COMPANY/CRYSTAL
VALLEY CELLARS
Modesto
COSTELLO VINEYARDS
Napa
H. COTURRI & SONS, INC.
Glen Ellen
CRESCINI WINES
Soquel
CRESTON MANOR
VINEYARDS & WINERY
Los Angeles
CRONIN VINEYARDS
Woodside
CUCAMONGA VINEYARD
COMPANY
Cucamonga
JOHN CULBERTSON
WINERY
Fallbrook
CUVAISON, INC.
Napa
CYGNET CELLARS
Sunnyvale

D'AGOSTINI WINERY
Plymouth
DAUME WINERY
Woodland Hills
DAVAL VINEYARDS
Napa
MICHAEL TRIBAUT DE
ROMERY
San Leandro
De LOACH VINEYARDS
Santa Rosa
DEER PARK WINERY
Deer Park
DEHLINGER WINERY
Sebastopol
DELANO GROWERS
COOPERATIVE WINERY
Delano
DELICATO VINEYARDS
Manteca
DEVLIN WINE CELLARS
Soquel
DIABLO VISTA WINERY
Healdsburg

DIAMOND CREEK
VINEYARDS
Calistoga
DIAMOND OAKS VINEYARD
South San Francisco
J.E. DIGARDI WINERY
Martinez
DOLAN VINEYARDS
Redwood Valley
DOMAINE CHANDON
Yountville
DOMAINE LAURIER
WINERY AND
VINEYARDS
Forestville
DONATONI WINERY
Inglewood
DONNA MARIA VINEYARDS
Healdsburg
DRY CREEK VINEYARD, INC.
Healdsburg
GEORGES DUBOEUF & SON
Healdsburg
DUCKHORN VINEYARDS
St. Helena
DUNN VINEYARDS
Angwin
DURNEY VINEYARD
Carmel
DUXOUP WINE WORKS
Healdsburg

EAST-SIDE WINERY
Lodi
EDMEADES VINEYARDS
Philo
EDNA VALLEY VINEYARDS
San Luis Obispo
EHLERS LANE WINERY
St. Helena
EL DORADO VINEYARDS
Camino
EL PASO DE ROBLES
WINERY & VINEYARDS
Paso Robles
ELLISTON VINEYARDS
Sunol
ENZ VINEYARDS
Hollister
ESTRELLA RIVER WINERY
Paso Robles
EVENSEN VINEYARDS &
WINERY
Oakville

FBF WINERY
Somerset
FAR NIENTE WINERY
Oakville
FARNESI WINERY
Sanger
FELTON-EMPIRE
VINEYARDS
Felton
FENESTRA WINERY
San Jose
FENTON ACRES WINERY
Healdsburg
FERRARA WINE CELLARS
Escondido
FERREIRA WINES
Newcastle
FETZER VINEYARDS
Redwood Valley
FICKLIN VINEYARDS
Madera
FIELD STONE WINERY
Healdsburg
FIELDBROOK VALLEY
WINERY
Arcata
J. FILIPPI VINTAGE
COMPANY
Mira Loma
A. FILIPPI WINERY
Mira Loma
FILSINGER VINEYARD &
WINERY
Placentia
FIRESTONE VINEYARD
Los Olivos
FISHER VINEYARDS
Santa Rosa
FLORA SPRINGS WINE
COMPANY
St. Helena
THOMAS FOGARTY WINERY
Portola Valley
FOLIE A DEUX WINERY
St. Helena
L. FOPPIANO WINE
COMPANY
Healdsburg
FORTINO WINERY
Gilroy
FORTUNA CELLARS
Davis
FRANCISCAN VINEYARDS, INC.
Rutherford
JAS. FRASINETTI & SONS
Sacramento

CHRIS A. FREDSON WINERY
Geyserville
FREEMARK ABBEY WINERY
St. Helena
FRETTER WINE CELLARS, INC.
Berkeley
FREY VINEYARDS, LTD.
Redwood Valley
FRICK WINERY
Santa Cruz
FRITZ CELLARS
Cloverdale
FROG'S LEAP WINERY
St. Helena

GALLEANO WINERY, INC.
Mira Loma
E. & J. GALLO WINERY
Modesto
GEMELLO WINERY
Mountain View
J.H. GENTILI WINES
Redwood City
GEYSER PEAK WINERY
Geyserville
GIBSON WINE COMPANY
Sanger
GIRARD WINERY
Oakville
PETER & HARRY GIRETTI
Gilroy
GIUMARRA VINEYARDS
CORPORATION
Edison
A. GIURLANI & BROS.
Sunnyvale
GLEN ELLEN WINERY
Glen Ellen
GLENOAK HILLS WINERY
HUGO'S CELLAR
Temecula
GOLDEN CREEK VINEYARD
Santa Rosa
GRAND CRU VINEYARDS
Glen Ellen
GRAND PACIFIC VINEYARD
COMPANY INC.
San Anselmo
GRANITE SPRINGS WINERY
Somerset
GRAPE EMPIRE WINE
COMPANY, INC.
San Leandro
GREAT AMERICAN
WINERIES, INC.
dba Chateau Julien, Carmel

GREEN & RED VINEYARD
St. Helena
GREENSTONE WINERY
Ione
GREENWOOD RIDGE
VINEYARDS
Philo
GRGICH HILLS CELLAR
Rutherford
GROTH VINEYARDS &
WINERY
Oakville
GROVER GULCH WINERY
Soquel
GUENOC WINERY
Middletown
EMILIO GUGLIELMO
WINERY
Morgan Hill
GUILD WINERIES &
DISTILLERIES
San Francisco
Bear Creek Winery, Lodi;
Central Cellars, Lodi;
Del Rio Winery, Woodbridge;
Fresno Winery, Fresno;
L.K. Marshall Winery, Delano;
McCall Winery, Sanger;
Cribari Winery, Fresno;
Cresta Blanca Winery, Ukiah
GUNDLACH-BUNDSCHU
WINERY
Vineburg

HMR LIMITED
Redondo Beach
HNW CELLARS
Rutherford
HACIENDA DEL RIO
WINERY
Fulton
HACIENDA WINE CELLARS
Sonoma
HAFNER VINEYARDS
Healdsburg
HANDLEY CELLARS
Philo
HANZELL VINEYARDS
Sonoma
J.J. HARASZTHY & SONS
Sonoma
HARBOR WINERY
West Sacramento
HART WINERY
Temecula

HAYNES VINEYARD
Napa
HAYWOOD WINERY
Sonoma
HEALDSBURG
WINEGROWERS, INC.
Healdsburg
HECKER PASS WINERY
Gilroy
HEITZ WINE CELLARS
St. Helena
HEUBLEIN, INC.
Oxnard
HIDDEN CELLARS
Talmage
WILLIAM HILL WINERY
Napa
HOP KILN WINERY AT
GRIFFIN VINEYARD
Healdsburg
HOPPER CREEK WINERY, INC.
Napa
HORIZON WINERY
Santa Rosa
HOWELL MOUNTAIN
VINEYARD
St. Helena
HULTGREN & SAMPERTON
Healdsburg
HUSCH VINEYARDS
Philo

IRON HORSE VINEYARDS
Sebastopol
ISLAND WINE COOLER
COMPANY
Lodi

JADE MOUNTAIN WINERY
Cloverdale
JEKEL VINEYARDS
Studio City
JIMARK WINERY, INC.
Healdsburg
JOHNSON TURNBULL
VINEYARDS
Oakville
JOHNSON'S ALEXANDER
VALLEY WINES
Healdsburg
JORDAN VINEYARD &
WINERY
Healdsburg

KALIN CELLARS, INC.
Novato

KARLY WINES
Plymouth
ROBERT KEENAN WINERY
St. Helena
KATHRYN KENNEDY
WINERY
Saratoga
KENWOOD VINEYARDS
Kenwood
KENWORTHY VINEYARDS
Plymouth
KIRIGIN CELLARS
Gilroy
KIRKPATRICK CELLAR
WINERY
Eureka
KISTLER VINEYARDS
Glen Ellen
KONOCTI WINERY
Kelseyville
KORBEL CHAMPAGNE
CELLARS
Guerneville
HANNS KORNELL
CHAMPAGNE CELLARS
St. Helena
THOMAS KRUSE WINERY
Gilroy

LSI/BULK TERMINALS
Stockton
LA CREMA VINERA
Petaluma
LA JOTA VINEYARD
COMPANY
Angwin
LA MONT WINERY,
INCORPORATED
Di Giorgio
LA PURISIMA WINERY
Mountain View
LA ZACA VINEYARD
COMPANY
Los Olivos
LAKESPRING WINERY
Napa
RONALD LAMB WINERY
Morgan Hill
LAMBERT BRIDGE
Healdsburg
LANDMARK VINEYARDS
Windsor
LAS MONTANAS
Glen Ellen
LAS TABLAS WINERY
Templeton

LAUREL GLEN VINEYARD
Santa Rosa
LAWRENCE WINERY
San Luis Obispo
LAZY CREEK VINEYARDS
Philo
LEEWARD WINERY
Oxnard
LEOPARD TRADING CO.
Napa
LIBERTY WINERY, INC.
Acampo
LIVE OAKS WINERY
Gilroy
LIVERMORE VALLEY
CELLARS
Livermore
LLORDS & ELWOOD
WINERY
Woodland Hills
LOLONIS WINE CELLARS
Redwood Valley
LONG VINEYARDS
St. Helena
LOS ALAMOS WINERY
Los Alamos
LOS VINEROS WINERY, INC.
Santa Maria
LOWER LAKE WINERY
Lower Lake
LUCAS WINERY
Lodi
LYETH VINEYARD &
WINERY, LIMITED
Geyserville
LYTTON SPRINGS WINERY
Healdsburg

MADRONA VINEYARDS
Camino
MARIETTA CELLARS
Healdsburg
M. MARION & COMPANY
Saratoga
MARK WEST VINEYARD &
WINERY
Forestville
MARKHAM VINEYARDS
St. Helena
MARSTON VINEYARDS
St. Helena
MARTIN BROTHERS WINERY
Paso Robles
MARTIN WINERY, INC.
Culver City

LOUIS M. MARTINI
St. Helena
MARTINI & PRATI WINES, INC.
Santa Rosa
PAUL MASSON VINEYARDS
Saratoga
MASTANTUONO, INC.
Pasa Robles
MATANZAS CREEK WINERY
Santa Rosa
J. MATHEWS/NAPA VALLEY
WINERY
Newport Beach
JOSEPH MATHEWS WINERY/
LISBON WINERY
Napa
MAYACAMAS VINEYARDS
Napa
GIUSEPPE MAZZONI
WINERY
Cloverdale
MC DOWELL VALLEY
VINEYARDS
Hopland
MC HENRY VINEYARDS
Santa Cruz
MC LESTER WINERY
Inglewood
MENGHINI WINERY
Julian
MESA VERDE VINEYARDS &
WINERY
Temecula
LOUIS K. MIHALY
VINEYARD
Napa
MILANO WINERY
Hopland
MILL CREEK VINEYARDS
Healdsburg
F.J. MILLER & COMPANY
Napa
MIRASSOU SALES COMPANY
San Jose
MIRASSOU VINEYARDS
San Jose
C. MONDAVI & SONS
St. Helena
ROBERT MONDAVI WINERY
Oakville
MONT LA SALLE VINEYARDS
Napa
   Fromm & Sichel, Inc.,
      San Francisco
MONT ST. JOHN CELLARS
Napa

R. MONTALI WINERY
Oakland
MONTCLAIR WINERY
Piedmont
MONTEREY PENINSULA
WINERY
Monterey
THE MONTEREY VINEYARD
Gonzales
MONTEVINA WINES
Plymouth
MONTICELLO CELLARS
Yountville
MORGAN WINERY
Salinas
J.W. MORRIS WINERY
Healdsburg
MOUNT EDEN VINEYARDS
Saratoga
MOUNT PALOMAR WINERY
Temecula
MT. VEEDER WINERY &
VINEYARDS
Napa
MOUNTAIN HOUSE WINERY
Cloverdale
MOUNTAIN VIEW WINERY
Mountain View

NAPA CELLARS
Oakville
NAPA CREEK WINERY
St. Helena
NAPA VALLEY
COOPERATIVE WINERY
St. Helena
NAVARRO WINERY
Philo
NEVADA CITY CELLARS
Nevada City
NEWLAN VINEYARDS &
WINERY
Napa
NEWTON VINEYARD
St. Helena
NICASIO VINEYARDS
Soquel
NICHELINI VINEYARD
St. Helena
NIEBAUM-COPPOLA ESTATE
Rutherford
NOBLE CREEK VINEYARDS
Cherry Valley
NOBLE VINEYARDS LTD.
Kerman

A. NONINI WINERY
Fresno
NORDMAN OF CALIFORNIA
Fresno
NOVITIATE WINES
Los Gatos

OAK GLEN WINERY
Yucaipa
OAK VALLEY WINERY
Oakdale
OBESTER WINERY
Half Moon Bay
OLD CASTEEL VINEYARDS
Paso Robles
OLD CREEK RANCH WINERY
Oakview
ED OLIVEIRA WINERY
Arcata
OLSON VINEYARDS
Redwood Valley
OPICI WINERY, INC.
Alta Loma
ORLEANS HILL
VINICULTURAL ASSOC.
Woodland
OZEKI SAN BENITO, INC.
Hollister

PACHECO RANCH WINERY
Ignacio
PAGE MILL WINERY
Los Altos Hills
PALO CEDRO CELLARS
Palo Cedro
PAPAGNI VINEYARDS
Madera
PARADISE VINEYARDS
Paradise
PARDUCCI WINE CELLARS
Ukiah
PARSONS CREEK WINERY
Ukiah
PASTORI WINERY
Cloverdale
PAT PAULSEN VINEYARDS
Cloverdale
ROBERT PECOTA WINERY
Calistoga
PEDRIZZETTI WINERY
Morgan Hill
J. PEDRONCELLI WINERY
Geyserville
PELLEGRINI BROTHERS
WINES, INC.
South San Francisco

PENDLETON WINERY
Santa Clara
ROBERT PEPI WINERY
Oakville
PEPPERWOOD SPRINGS VYDS.
Philo
PESENTI WINERY
Templeton
JOSEPH PHELPS VINEYARDS
St. Helena
PICONI WINERY, LTD.
Temecula
PIEDMONT CELLARS
Piedmont
PINA CELLARS
Rutherford
PINA CELLARS
Napa
PINE FLAT CELLARS
Soquel
PINE RIDGE WINERY
Napa
PIPER SONOMA
Windsor
PIRRONE WINE CELLARS
Salida
L. POCAI & SONS
St. Helena
POINT LOMA WINERY
San Diego
POMMERAIE VINEYARDS
Sebastopol
POPE VALLEY WINERY
Pope Valley
PORTER CREEK VINEYARDS
Healdsburg
PRAGER WINERY & PORT
WORKS
St. Helena
PRESTIGE VINEYARDS
Cabazon
PRESTON VINEYARDS
Healdsburg

QUADY WINERY
Madera
QUAIL RIDGE
Napa

A. RAFANELLI WINERY
Healdsburg
RANCHITA OAKS
WINERY, INC.
San Miguel
RANCHO DE PHILO
Alta Loma

RANCHO SISQUOC WINERY
San Francisco
RAPAZZINI WINERY
Gilroy
RAVENSWOOD
San Francisco
MARTIN RAY VINEYARDS
Palo Alto
RAYMOND VINEYARD &
CELLAR, INC.
St. Helena
RENAISSANCE VINEYARD &
WINERY, INC.
Renaissance
RICHARDSON VINEYARDS
Sonoma
RICHERT CELLARS
Soquel
RIDGE VINEYARDS, INC.
Cupertino
RITCHIE CREEK VINEYARD
St. Helena
RIVER ROAD VINEYARDS
Forestville
RIVER RUN VINTNERS
Watsonville
RODDIS CELLARS
Calistoga
ROLLING HILLS VINEYARDS
Camarillo
ROMBAUER VINEYARDS
St. Helena
ROSENBLUM CELLARS
Emeryville
ROSS-KELLEREI
Nipomo
ROSS WINERY
Napa
ROUDON-SMITH
VINEYARDS, INC.
Santa Cruz
ROUND HILL CELLARS
St. Helena
RUBIDOUX WINERY
Riverside
CHANNING RUDD CELLARS
Middletown
RUTHERFORD HILL WINERY
St. Helena
RUTHERFORD VINTNERS
Rutherford

SAGE CANYON WINERY
Rutherford
ST. ANDREW'S WINERY
Napa

ST. CLEMENT VINEYARDS
St. Helena
ST. FRANCIS WINERY &
VINEYARD
Kenwood
SAINTSBURY
St. Helena
SALTER WINERY
Somerset
SAN ANTONIO WINERY, INC.
Los Angeles
SAN BENITO VINEYARDS, INC.
Hollister
SAN JOAQUIN WAREHOUSE
COMPANY
Lodi
SAN MARTIN WINERY
San Martin
SAN PASQUAL VINEYARDS
Escondido
SAN PIETRO VARA
VINEYARD & WINE
COMPANY
Calistoga
SANFORD & BENEDICT
VINEYARDS
Lompoc
SANFORD WINERY
Buellton
SANTA BARBARA WINERY
Santa Barbara
SANTA CRUZ MOUNTAIN
VINEYARD
Santa Cruz
SANTA YNEZ VALLEY
WINERY
Santa Ynez
SANTE MINERAL
WATERS, INC.
Santa Rosa
SANTEE VALLEY WINERY
Santee
SANTINO WINES
Plymouth
SARAH'S VINEYARD
Gilroy
SATIETY
Davis
V. SATTUI WINERY
St. Helena
SAUCELITO CANYON
VINEYARD &
WINERY
Arroyo Grande
SAUSAL WINERY
Healdsburg

SCHARFFENBERGER
  CELLARS
  Talmage
SCHENLEY DISTILLERS, INC.
  Lawrenceburg
SCHRAMSBERG VINEYARDS
  COMPANY
  Calistoga
SEA RIDGE WINERY
  Cazadero
SEBASTIANI VINEYARDS
  Sonoma
SEGHESIO WINERIES, INC.
  Cloverdale
THOMAS SELLARDS
  WINERY
  Sebastopol
SEQUOIA GROVE
  VINEYARDS
  Napa
SHAFER VINEYARDS
  Napa
CHARLES F. SHAW
  VINEYARD & WINERY
  St. Helena
SHENANDOAH VINEYARDS
  Plymouth
SHERRILL CELLARS
  Woodside
SHOWN & SONS VINEYARDS
  Rutherford
SIERRA VISTA WINERY
  Placerville
SIERRA WINE
  CORPORATION
  Delano
SILVER MOUNTAIN
  VINEYARDS
  Los Gatos
SILVER OAK WINE CELLARS
  Oakville
SILVERADO VINEYARDS
  Napa
SIMI WINERY
  Healdsburg
SKY VINEYARDS
  Glen Ellen
SMITH & HOOK
  Gonzales
SMITH-MADRONE
  VINEYARDS
  St. Helena
SODA ROCK WINERY
  Healdsburg
SOMMELIER WINERY
  Santa Rosa

SONOMA COUNTY CELLARS
  Healdsburg
SONOMA COUNTY
  COOPERATIVE WINERY
  Windsor
SONOMA COUNTY
  VINTNERS COOPERATIVE
  Windsor
SONOMA-CUTRER
  VINEYARDS, INC.
  Fulton
SONOMA HILL WINERY
  Santa Rosa
SONOMA VINEYARDS
  Windsor
SOTOYOME WINERY
  Healdsburg
SOUTH COAST CELLAR
  Gardena
SOUVERAIN CELLARS
  Geyserville
SPOTTSWOODE WINERY, INC.
  St. Helena
SPRING MOUNTAIN
  VINEYARDS
  St. Helena
STAG'S LEAP WINE CELLARS
  Napa
STAG'S LEAP WINERY
  Napa
P&M STAIGER
  Boulder Creek
STELTZNER VINEYARDS
  Napa
ROBERT STEMMLER
  WINERY
  Healdsburg
WM. STEPHEN, INC.
  Coarsegold
STERLING VINEYARDS
  Calistoga
STEVENOT WINERY
  Murphys
STONEGATE WINERY
  Calistoga
STONERIDGE
  Sutter Creek
STONEY CREEK
  VINEYARDS
  Somerset
STONY HILL VINEYARD
  St. Helena
STONY RIDGE
  Pleasanton
STORY VINEYARD
  Plymouth

STORYBOOK MOUNTAIN
  VINTNERS
  Calistoga
SULLIVAN VINEYARDS
  WINERY
  Rutherford
SUMMERHILL VINEYARDS
  Gilroy
SUN-MAID GROWERS OF
  CALIFORNIA
  Fresno
SUNRISE WINERY
  Cupertino
SUISUN CELLARS
  Suisun City
SUTTER HOME WINERY, INC.
  St. Helena
JOSEPH SWAN VINEYARDS
  Forestville
SYCAMORE CREEK VINEYARDS
  Morgan Hill

TKC VINEYARDS
  Ridgecrest
TAFT STREET
  Forestville
TAKARA SAKE USA, INC.
  Berkeley
ROBERT TALBOTT
  VINEYARD & WINERY
  Carmel Valley
TEJON MARKETING COMPANY
  Arvin
TEMP TROL
  St. Helena
THACKREY & COMPANY
  Bolinas
THOMAS VINEYARDS
  Cucamonga
TIJSSELING VINEYARDS
  Ukiah
TOBIAS VINEYARDS
  Paso Robles
TOPOLOS AT RUSSIAN
  RIVER VINEYARDS
  Forestville
R. TORRE & COMPANY, INC.
  San Francisco
TOYON WINERY & VINEYARDS
  Healdsburg
TRADER JOE'S WINERY
  South Pasadena
TRAULSEN VINEYARDS
  Calistoga
TREFETHEN VINEYARDS
  Napa

TREMONT VINEYARDS
  Davis
TRENTADUE WINERY
  Geyserville
TUDAL WINERY
  St. Helena
TULOCAY WINERY
  Oakville
TURGEON & LOHR WINERY
  San Jose
TURNER WINERY
  Woodbridge
TWIN HILLS RANCH
  Paso Robles
TYLAND VINEYARDS
  Ukiah

UNITED VINTNERS, INC.
  San Francisco
  Italian Swiss Colony, Clovis;
  Petri Wineries, Escalon;
  Community Wineries, Lodi;
  Inglenook Vineyard, Oakville;
  Cella Wineries, Reedley

VALLEY OF THE MOON
  WINERY
  Glen Ellen
VEGA VINEYARDS WINERY
  Buellton
VENTANA VINEYARDS
  WINERY, INC.
  Soledad
VERDUGO VINEYARDS, INC.
  Acampo
NICHOLAS G. VERRY, INC.
  Parlier
CONRAD VIANO WINERY
  Martinez
VICHON WINERY
  Oakville
VIE-DEL COMPANY
  Fresno
VILLA ARMANDO WINERY
  Pleasanton
VILLA BIANCHI WINERY
  Kerman
VILLA MT. EDEN WINERY
  Oakville
VILLA PARADISO
  VINEYARDS
  Morgan Hill
VILLINGER WINERY
  Woodbridge
VINA VISTA VINEYARD
  Geyserville

VINE HILL WINES, INC.
Santa Cruz
VINTAGE VINEYARDS
Napa
VOSE VINEYARDS
Napa

WALKER WINES
Palo Alto
WATSON VINEYARDS
Rolling Hills
WEIBEL CHAMPAGNE
VINEYARDS, INC.
Mission San Jose
WEINGARTEN CASTLE
Healdsburg
WENTE BROTHERS
Livermore
WERMUTH WINERY
Calistoga

WESTCOM INDUSTRIES
Pleasant Hill
WHALER VINEYARD
Ukiah
WILLIAM WHEELER WINERY
Healdsburg
WHITE OAK VINEYARDS
Healdsburg
WHITEHALL LANE WINERY
St. Helena
WINE APPRECIATION, INC.
Oakville
WINE CELLARS
Kelseyville
WINE GROUP FRANZIA
WINERY
San Francisco
WINE SERVICE
COOPERATIVE, INC.
St. Helena

WINTERS WINERY
Winters
WITTWER WINERY
Eureka
WOODBRIDGE VINEYARD
ASSN.
Lodi
WOODBURY WINERY
San Rafael
WOODEN VALLEY WINERY
Suisun
CHRISTINE WOODS
WINERY
Philo
WOODSIDE VINEYARDS
Woodside

YANKEE HILL WINERY
Columbia

YERBA BUENA
INDUSTRIES, INC.
San Francisco
YORK MOUNTAIN WINERY
Templeton
YVERDON VINEYARDS
St. Helena

ZD WINES
Napa
ZACA MESA WINERY
Los Olivos
ZAMPATTI'S CELLAR
Carmel
STEPHEN ZELLERBACH
VINEYARD
Healdsburg

INDEX

Numbers in italics denote a page on which an illustration appears.

266